THINGS I'VE
LEARNED FROM
WATCHING THE
BROWNS

OTHER BOOKS BY TERRY PLUTO

ON SPORTS:

Joe Tait: It's Been a Real Ball (with Joe Tait)

LeBron James: The Making of an MVP (with Brian Windhorst)

The Franchise (with Brian Windhorst)

Dealing: The Cleveland Indians' New Ballgame

False Start: How the New Browns Were Set Up to Fail

The View from Pluto

Unguarded (with Lenny Wilkens)

Our Tribe

Browns Town 1964

Burying the Curse

The Curse of Rocky Colavito

Falling from Grace

Tall Tales

Loose Balls

Bull Session (with Johnny Kerr)

Tark (with Jerry Tarkanian)

Forty-Eight Minutes, a Night in the Life of the NBA (with Bob Ryan)

Sixty-One (with Tony Kubek)

You Could Argue But You'd Be Wrong (with Pete Franklin)

Weaver on Strategy (with Earl Weaver)

The Earl of Baltimore

Super Joe (with Joe Charboneau and Burt Graeff)

The Greatest Summer

ON FAITH AND OTHER TOPICS:

Faith and You, Volume 1

Faith and You, Volume 2

Everyday Faith

Champions for Life: The Power of a Father's Blessing (with Bill Glass)

Crime: Our Second Vietnam (with Bill Glass)

TERRY PLUTO

AND HUNDREDS OF BROWNS FANS

THINGS I'VE LEARNED FROM WATCHING THE BROWNS

GRAY & COMPANY, PUBLISHERS
CLEVELAND

Gray & Company, Publishers
www.grayco.com

Library of Congress Cataloging-in-Publication Data
Pluto, Terry
Things I've learned from watching the Browns / Terry Pluto.
p. cm.
ISBN 978-1-59851-065-2
1. Cleveland Browns (Football team : 1999-) 2. Cleveland
Browns (Football team : 1946-1995) 3. Football fans—Ohio—
Cleveland—Anecdotes. I. Title.
GV956.C6P576 2010
796.332'640977132—dc22
2010039233

Printed in the United States
10 9 8 7 6 5

To the Browns fans . . .
Just as the Browns are your team,
this is your book.

Contents

Being a Browns fan is completely, utterly irrational. But you already know that.

If you were born after 1960, you know that being a Browns fan makes no sense. None. Zero. That's because the team's most recent championship was in 1964.

OK, maybe some of you born in 1960 actually believe you remember that stunning 27-0 victory over the heavily favored Baltimore Colts in the 1964 championship game. I'll simply remind you that in 1964, you would have been 4 years old. What else do you remember from the age of 4?

Here's how it works . . .

I remember seeing Paul Brown coach the Browns. I really do remember seeing him coach, only I know I didn't. I was born in 1955. Brown's last season was 1962. I know that my father never took me to a Browns game until the late 1960s. He couldn't get tickets. I know I never saw Paul Brown coach the Browns on television, because at that age, I was not about to spend three hours on a Sunday staring at a black-and-white TV, watching the Browns.

So I know I never saw Paul Brown coach the Browns.

Only I know I did see him, because my father talked about how Paul Brown always wore a hat but seldom a smile. How he and Otto Graham won all those titles, seven in 10 years. How Brown had messenger guards bringing in plays from the sidelines. I know

I saw all that, only I didn't see any of it. I just heard about it from my father. We weren't a football family. Baseball was our game, the Indians our team. But I still remember Paul Brown, thanks to my father.

Just as many of you heard about Otto Graham, Paul Brown, Jim Brown and Gary Collins. Just as many of you insist you remember the 1964 championship game, even though you were born in 1968. It's the football version of the repressed memory syndrome. Do we really remember it, or do we just want to?

I asked fans who read *The Plain Dealer* to send me e-mails for this book, to try to explain why they still follow the team and what it means to them.

Remember, this isn't just a team that never has played in a Super Bowl. It's not just a team that loses more than it wins. It's not just a team that is best known for two games—The Drive and The Fumble. (Both of which make grown men cry . . . 20 years later!)

It's not only that the Browns have won a grand total of one playoff game since 1990. Or that the team has had only three winning seasons between 1990 and 2009.

The dawg-gone team up and moved!

Gone to Baltimore after the 1995 season. Gone for no good reason other than Art Modell was a rotten businessman who could not figure out how to make money in a league where nearly every other owner—and most of these guys will not be confused with Warren Buffett—turns a profit. The point of this is not to rehash the move or to pile on Modell. It's to state the fact that the team MOVED. After the move was announced in the middle of the 1995 season, the Browns still had four more home games. Here are the attendance figures for those games with a lame duck team, an unpopular coach and a hated owner: 57,881 . . . 55,388 . . . 67,269 . . . 55,875. Those were fans in the seats, not tickets sold. The Browns even sold 600 tickets in the first 24 hours after the team announced it was moving.

Does any of this make any sense?

As Gay Snyder e-mailed, Browns fans have "The Drive . . . The Fumble . . . The Move."

And no other NFL fans can (or would want to) claim that terrible trifecta.

*   *   *

Despite being born in Cleveland, spending all but four years of my life in Northeast Ohio and having covered sports here since 1980, not even I can fully understand the power the Browns have over their fans.

This is why I wanted to write a book about what I've learned from watching the Browns. Some of this is history. Some of it is catching up with former Browns such as Bernie Kosar, Earnest Byner, Sam Rutigliano and Brian Sipe. Even Bill Belichick couldn't wait to write an e-mail about the influence Paul Brown had on him and pro football.

But I also wanted to hear from you, the Browns fans. I wanted to know what the team means to you, why you still care about a franchise with the NFL's second-worst record (thank you, Detroit Lions) since the Browns returned as an expansion team in 1999. I asked for input . . . just once . . . in *The Plain Dealer*.

More than 1,000 overwhelmed me with e-mails. Some were short; many went on for thousands of words. Some fans kept sending in more e-mails as they thought of something else to add.

As Kevin Robison e-mailed: "The Browns are in our DNA. . . . They have become family to many of us. The names and faces of the players change, but the orange and brown are always present. They are passed down from generation to generation, like blue eyes and male-pattern baldness. We just can't help our chemical predispositions."

Justin Zawaly took it down to the street when he e-mailed: "Being a Browns fan is much like being an alcoholic or a drug addict. It's an addiction with no cure."

But like many Browns fans who start out angry or frustrated with their favorite team, Zawaly turned sentimental: "My grandfather was a season ticket holder back in the days of Otto Graham. My grandmother won't let him watch the games anymore because he gets too emotional. At 89 years old . . . the Browns can be a health issue! My Mom and Dad were Kardiac Kids. . . . I do think there is something extra when you are born into it. It is in my blood. . . . Now, I have three kids, and they have the Browns addiction as well. You know what they say . . . 'Misery loves company'!"

None of this is rational, and the fans know it.

Jeff Biletnikoff e-mailed: "When the news broke that Art Modell was moving the Browns, no matter where you went in Cleveland, there was silence and disbelief. It's like the whole town froze. I'll never forget how the city felt to me. The *Sports Illustrated* cover that had a cartoon of Art Modell sucker-punching a 'dawg' in the stomach captured that day perfectly."

If ever there were a time for fans to turn their backs on a franchise and a professional league, it was when the NFL brought back the Browns as an expansion team that truly was set up for failure. I wrote an entire book about it, *False Start*. I thought it would be too depressing for most fans. It was extremely grim, but it became a local bestseller.

As Biletnikoff's e-mail continued: "I can't explain it, but the Cleveland Browns are in my DNA. Something about seeing those orange helmets come on to the field is exciting. Some people who aren't Browns fans say Cleveland's helmets are among the ugliest in sports, and *I could not disagree more*. Cleveland has the best helmets in all of football. That helmet (and uniform in general) stands for *Excellence*, even though they are temporarily down. That is such a Browns fan reaction, isn't it? They're 'temporarily down' after 20-plus years! I know it makes no sense . . . ."

*   *   *

It makes no sense, but Browns fans are proud of their team's history, even if they weren't around to see the best of it. As Greg Johnson e-mailed: "No logos on the helmet. No dancing girls (cheerleaders). No climate-controlled dome. . . . Even the name 'Browns' lacks glitz. . . . It's just honest, down-home, Ohio football. There is no better stage than the Super Bowl to showcase our city, and no better team to represent it. The simplest and most humble uniform, the simplest and most humble name."

Greg, did you say . . . Super Bowl?

And did you suggest the Super Bowl be played in Cleveland . . . with the Browns in it?

Greg, great points about no logos, no cheerleaders and orange helmets. But you really kicked the ball between the literary goal posts with the "humble" part. If any franchise has been humbled, it's this one.

Of course, you are not alone in this sports delusion. You have lots of company: millions of Browns fans across the globe.

And the word "globe" inspired Mike Olszewski to turn poetic: "Two words: the helmets. Eleven globes of sunshine breaking through the often bleak and blustery late-fall Cleveland afternoons, melting away the snow for a few brief hours. The jerseys and pants may change from brown to white, solid or striped, but there is nothing like those bright orange icons of Cleveland football. Some say they are ugly and boring. I say they exude power and tradition."

Lindsay Dudas knows being a Browns fan is strange, sort of like being trapped in a dysfunctional family. As Lindsay e-mailed: "Hypothetically, you say that if your child ever went to prison you would not visit them because of that embarrassment and failure. The Browns have been in prison for most of the last 10 years. I have not given up on them and still visit them every fall and winter on the shores of Lake Erie."

Lindsay, it's more like they've been locked into losing for the past 20 years . . . except when they were in solitary confinement for three seasons during The Move.

Then again, as Mike Griffin e-mailed: "We watch games surrounded by people wearing dog masks, throwing dog bones and barking. It's great fun!"

Griffin doesn't mean at the Stadium, he means at a Browns Backers meeting in Denver. And he drives 70 miles each way to meet with other Browns fans in Colorado. As he explained, they are "Pilgrims in an Unholy Land!"

Aaron Funke tried to explain this irrational exuberance about the Browns: "I was born near Cleveland and grew up watching the team during the 1980s. When I was in fourth grade, my family moved to Chicago. It was tough to find the games on TV. So on Sundays, we'd get in our Chevy Astro van after church and just start driving east into Indiana to try and pick up a radio signal. I remember how excited we would get when we could finally hear it come in. Then we would just sit in some gas station parking lot or rest area for the duration of the game."

This guy hasn't lived in Cleveland since the fourth grade but remains hooked on the Browns in Chicago.

"We wised up and found a bowling alley where the Browns Backers of Chicago met, and we started going there to watch the games," explained Funke.

Dale McCombs wrote: "I first became a Browns fan in 1968 at the age of 10. Bill Nelsen with his bad knees, well, he signed a picture of himself that I still have buried in the attic. Back in those days, the signings were for free."

So far, so good.

Bill Nelsen was one of my favorite players, too. He was the Brian Sipe of my youth, although Sipe was a much better player.

McCombs continued: "You should definitely write about old Municipal Stadium and those awful poles that always seemed to block the view. My most memorable game was in the dog pound in 1978 against Houston when the bleachers broke out in a riot where fans were throwing bottles onto the end zone. I was in Row 2, and all the drunks up in row 40 with the weak arms were not getting the bottles onto the field. They were whizzing by me. I was on the front page of *The Plain Dealer* the next day. Stupid me, I never saved the paper, and it still haunts me to this day."

Ah, the memories of drunks throwing bottles! And the old stadium, where parts of it smelled like an animal died years ago, but no one could find the carcass.

*   *   *

"I was raised on Cleveland Browns football," e-mailed John Greg Jr. "My bedroom was plastered, floor to ceiling, in Browns posters and paraphernalia. If I wasn't wearing an article of clothing with the Browns' logo on it, it was only because I was in the bathtub at that moment. I was the only kid in kindergarten who didn't associate *The Wizard of Oz* with Judy Garland and the Wicked Witch of the West. At 7 years of age, the first song I learned the complete lyrics to, beginning to end, was Messenger's *The Kardiac Kids*."

Greg added, "It's impossible to walk away or turn my back from them, although I'd admit to covering my eyes in horror a time or two."

A time or two? How about for a decade or two?

But it is the memories that are the cement. It could be when Bernie Kosar made Browns fans proud. Or when Brian Sipe pulled off another impossible win. Or when Jim Brown kicked off the arms of tacklers with his piston-like legs. Or when it was Graham-to-Lavelli, passes so beautiful they almost made Paul Brown smile.

"I still see Webster Slaughter streaking down the left sideline taking a perfect pass from Kosar for a winning touchdown," e-mailed Tony Vallo. "It was the Sunday before Thanksgiving. I was too hoarse from yelling that I couldn't even talk on Thanksgiving Day."

More memories . . .

Dan Lind e-mailed: "Every Sunday home game from 1989 to 1995 was the same for me. I'd drive down to old Municipal Stadium with my big brother and pour my heart and soul into the Brownies. We'd go early, cruise down Carnegie and stop for ribs at Hot Sauce Williams on the way. We'd listen to WKNR pre-game and chuckle at 'Mike from Brunswick,' who'd always call in and swear this was his FINAL year buying season tickets. . . . My love affair for the franchise started right there and continues to this day. . . . Win or lose, the sights and sounds make the NFL an extraordinary product. Each game was a story, and every play was important. Watching Joshua Cribbs and Phil Dawson today gets my heart pounding just like cheering for Eric Metcalf and Matt Stover in the 1990s. I grew up on the Browns, and despite their lack of success this past decade, I will loyally support that franchise till the day I die."

You have a feeling that Lind really means it.

Consider how McCombs—who lovingly recalls those days of beer bottles whipping by his head—ended his e-mail: "The most important reason to write the book is to show how the Browns and their fans unite together and bond over our misery. . . . My grandfather passed away in 2006 at the age of 96. For nearly 40 years, we commiserated each week over the Browns. I last talked to him three days before his death. He was in and out of consciousness. I said, 'Grandpa, I don't know if you know who I am, but you know how sucky those Cleveland Browns are.' He raised his head in a near-comatose state, looked at me and smiled. . . . It was his last smile."

It is a family thing.

"Some fathers and sons work on cars or go fishing," e-mailed Nicholas Allburn. "We watch, read and wring our hands about the Browns. . . . Most of all, it's strengthened my bond with my father."

Or as Willard Stanley e-mailed: "No matter how often they disappoint us, I'll always love and be grateful to this football team for bringing my family closer together. There aren't many topics that will keep the attention and provide common ground for a computer programming father and his three sons: One a graduate student in Vietnamese history, another a biologist and the last a student of European history."

Mike Lebowitz e-mailed about his military service in Iraq, "where I'd hope the combat mission would end in time so we could return to the base and watch the Browns. . . . I'd wake up at 4 a.m. to catch a Browns game (in Iraq). . . . No matter where I've lived, it finally dawned on me: The Browns, good and bad, equate to home."

And it goes on. That's the reason for this book, and for ending this chapter with this e-mail from Aimee Andrich.

"My best day at Cleveland Browns Stadium was September 16, 2007—the first game my husband and I took our (30-month-old) son Max to see," she explained. "We had discussed for weeks whether he should attend only the game, or if we should give him the full experience by taking him to the Muni Lot to tailgate. We decided that it must be all or nothing.

"We dressed him in all of his Browns gear and painted his hair to match the Browns' helmet. On our walk into the lot, fellow fans were giving him high-fives and cheering for him from the parking garages. He even ended up on the Channel 19 tailgate show holding his "This is my first Browns game" sign. The smile on his face was matched only by the final score of the game: Browns 51, Bengals 45. . . . After the last TD pass, I remember telling Max to never forget this day because the Browns may never put up 51 offensive points again!

"Fast-forward to the 2009 season. After a particularly ugly loss, I was listening to my regular sports talk radio show when frustration over the continued poor performance had gotten the best of me. As embarrassing as it is, I stood in my kitchen and shed a few tears. Max caught me at this low moment. He asked why I was so sad. I told him that I was sick and tired of losing.

"I then proceeded to tell him that he should pick another team to root for because there was still time for him to find a winner. He looked up at me and said, 'Mommy, the Browns are my team because they are your team.' The tears flowed again, but this time it wasn't over the losing."

CHAPTER 2

The Fumble didn't cost the Browns a chance to go to the Super Bowl.

On the flight home from Denver following The Fumble, following the 38-33 loss, following another heartbreaking Browns loss, Earnest Byner found himself crying—again.

He still couldn't believe what had happened, how the ball had been stripped out of his hands only one step from the goal line. Or how what he considers perhaps the best game he ever played for the Browns ended in a loss. Or how he couldn't think anything except, "I let everyone down."

He meant his teammates. His fans. His adopted city of Cleveland.

There were tears on the field after The Fumble. More tears in the clubhouse as he undressed. Even more tears on the jet headed home.

"Then Carl Hairston came up to me," recalled Byner. "I started to apologize, and he put his big hand on my shoulder and said that I had nothing to be sorry for—that I was the reason that we were even in the game until the end."

My favorite Brown was Earnest Byner. He never dogged it. He played every down, and played far above his ability. He is a MAN. In the infamous "Fumble" game, he ran for the tough yards. I knew when the ball was fumbled; it was because he had spent all his energy up to that point. I hurt for Earnest and for myself.

—Thomas G Taylor

Not long after The Fumble, Byner discovered the power of friendship. He mentioned how Bernie Kosar, Brian Brennan, Reggie Langhorne and so many others kept calling to check on him.

"And Marty," said Byner, his voice choking up more than 22 years later. "Marty Schottenheimer was like a father to me. I loved him, and he loved me."

Now a running backs coach with the Jacksonville Jaguars, Byner uses The Fumble as a teaching tool. He insists, "It made me a better player, a better man and now, a better coach. I am more patient with people, more sympathetic when they make mistakes."

That's why it's foolish to reduce Byner's career with the Browns to these words: The Fumble. Listening to some fans, you'd think The Fumble cost the Browns the trip to the Super Bowl. You'd think Byner did nothing in that game but fumble. You'd never know the only reason the Browns were in position to the tie the game—that's right, *tie* the score, not win—is because of Byner.

How many different ways can this be said? Byner's fumble occurred with 1:12 left in the game. Denver was leading 38-31. He was not heading for a game-winning touchdown when the ball was stripped out of his hands on the 2-yard line. If he scored, the touchdown would have put the Browns in a position to tie the game if they made the extra point.

Suppose Byner had scored, and the extra point was good.

What happens next?

Denver would have had the ball with about a minute left. Depending on whether it's a touchback . . . a decent return . . . a squib kick, Denver would have had the ball between the 20- and 35-yard lines.

On their previous possession, the Broncos scored a touchdown in 62 seconds to go ahead 38-31.

John Elway would have had the ball in his hands, at home, needing only a field goal against a defense that hadn't stopped him all day.

The game was in Denver where the air in the mile-high city is thinner, meaning the ball carries farther than a place such as Cleveland.

The Broncos were driving into the closed end of the stadium with the wind at their backs.

Denver already had scored 38 points—six scoring drives—and gained 437 yards.

The Browns defense was hurting. Bob Golic missed the game with an arm injury. His replacement, Dave Puzzuoli, was injured during the game. His replacement, third-stringer Darryl Sims, was in the lineup for most of the game. Defensive back Mark Harper also was hurt during the game.

If the game had gone to overtime, the coin flip probably would have decided it. Let's suppose Cleveland somehow had managed to stop Denver from going 45 yards and the game had gone into overtime. The team that got the ball first probably would have won.

So for the Browns to win this game, they needed Byner to score. The extra point to be good. To stop Denver in the final minute at home. To win the coin flip in overtime. To score in overtime.

The Fumble was not why they lost. The final score was 38-33 because Denver took a safety right near the end of the game.

> Earnest Byner. Hard-nosed. Overachiever. He always is vilified for The Fumble, but no one seems to remember that he played an amazing second half. The Browns were down 21-3 at the half, and then Bernie Kosar and Byner dragged them back into the game.
> **—Mike Ogrodnick**

It's easy to forget that it was almost a football miracle that Earnest Byner made the Cleveland Browns in the first place. He was

a 10th-round pick in the 1984 NFL Draft from East Carolina—279
players selected before him. He wasn't especially fast, nor did he
seem to have the overpowering strength to be a starting NFL running back.

But Byner was relentless. Byner was fearless. Byner believed
in Byner.

"When I came to camp with the Browns, I didn't think that I
was a 10th-round pick (and that) I had no chance," he recalled.
"Instead, I figured they drafted me for a reason. I thought if they'd
just give me a chance, I'd show them I could play."

By midseason, he had beaten out Charles White and Boyce
Green for a spot in the 1984 backfield next to fullback Mike Pruitt.
Byner ran for 426 yards as a rookie, then pushed to 1,002 yards
in 1985. In 1987, the season of The Fumble, guess who was the
Browns' leading receiver? Yes, Byner with 52 catches for a 10.6-
yard average. He also led the team with 10 touchdowns—eight on
the ground, two on receptions.

"I tell young players to control what they can," he said. "It's up
to you to stay on top of all your work. So study the playbook. Pay
attention in meetings. Listen to the coaches. Ask good questions.
It's not where you start the season, it's where you end up. Don't be
starstruck—they brought you to camp for a reason."

Byner told himself those things, over and over. He did all the
right things off the field. And on the field . . .

Byner could run. Byner could block. Byner could catch
passes.

A strong case can be made that in that 38-33 playoff loss at
Denver, Byner was perhaps the game's Most Valuable Player, or at
least the MVP after either quarterback.

Here are the stats:

Rushing

	Team	Att	Yds	TD	Lng
Earnest Byner	CLE	15	67	1	16
Kevin Mack	CLE	12	61	0	14

Receiving

	Team	Att	Yds	TD	Lng
Earnest Byner	CLE	7	120	1	53
Kevin Mack	CLE	4	28	0	9
Webster Slaughter	CLE	4	53	1	24
Reggie Langhorne	CLE	2	48	1	30
Brian Brennan	CLE	4	48	0	19
Ozzie Newsome	CLE	3	35	0	25
Clarence Weathers	CLE	1	19	0	19
Derek Tennell	CLE	1	5	0	5

So, Byner led the team in rushing and receiving. He had the longest rush and the longest reception. He scored two of the Browns' four touchdowns. If you were giving out game balls, maybe Bernie Kosar (26-of-41 for 356 yards and three touchdown passes) would edge out Byner. But since Byner was his leading receiver, it's kind of a coin flip. The more you look back at the game, the more the frustration boils over—but not at Byner.

Byner's fumble was the fourth Browns turnover of the day. On a drive in the first half that ended in a field goal, Byner did drop a pass that could have kept the drive alive and perhaps ended in a touchdown. Who knows?

But we do know this:

On the Browns' first possession, Webster Slaughter had a catchable pass go through his hands. It was picked off by Denver's Freddie Gilbert. It counted as an interception for Kosar, but it was really more of a fumble. It led to Denver's first score.

On the very next possession, Kevin Mack fumbled at Denver's 45. Denver took it in for a touchdown—aided by a holding penalty on Frank Minnifield in the end zone.

Late in the first half, Slaughter was penalized for a personal foul. Immediately after Slaughter's penalty, Brian Brennan fumbled the ball to halt a drive. Jeremiah Castille—the guy who stripped Byner—was one of the guys who stripped Brennan.

Matt Bahr missed a 45-yard field goal on the final play of the first half.

On Denver's 80-yard touchdown pass to Mark Jackson, Browns defensive backs Mark Harper and Felix Wright missed tackles. On another to Sammy Winder that put the Broncos ahead, 38-31, Wright and Minnifield missed tackles.

The two plays before Byner's fumble were incompletions by Kosar; he overthrew Byner on a post pattern in the end zone. On a play where Denver jumped offside—meaning it was a free play—Kosar and Reggie Langhorne missed a connection.

On the play where the fumble occurred, Jeremiah Castille was covering Slaughter. Slaughter was supposed to run a corner route to draw Castille away from the play. If Castille tried to move up, he was supposed to block him. Slaughter took a couple of steps forward and stopped. He didn't even touch Castille.

On January 17, 1988, I was 12 years old. I had been collecting Cleveland Browns posters from Convenient Food Mart stores in Lorain, Ohio. My entire bedroom was decorated with all types of Browns gear including Convenient posters: Webster Slaughter, Kevin Mack, Earnest Byner, Reggie Langhorne, Bernie Kosar, etc. It was another typical Sunday at my home in Lorain where all the neighbors were over watching the Browns vs. Broncos game. I was dressed in my jersey, Browns pants, and strap-on "dawg nose."

I was as excited as I had ever been in my young life as Byner ran into the end zone for what appeared to be the game tying score. As we all did, I soon realized the horrific truth . . . Byner fumbled the ball. I immediately broke down into tears, ran into my bedroom, and ripped down all my Convenient Browns posters.

—Andrew Branham

The Browns were trailing 38-31. They started their final drive at their own 25-yard line. Byner was a monster, ripping off a 16-yard run. Then he ran for two more yards. Kosar hit Brennan with two passes—14 and 19 yards. Then Byner ran for six more yards. Kosar overthrew Byner in the end zone. Then Byner ran for eight yards, fumbling near the end zone. After Denver recovered, Byner sat on his helmet, not far from the bench—staring at the field, seemingly embarrassed to be with his teammates.

"I was dog-tired by the end of that game," he said. "I just ran that pass pattern in the end zone. But I was not coming out. It came down to this—I had to hang on to the ball. That was my responsibility. They can say that this guy missed a block, or someone else should have made a play—but The Fumble was on me."

> After commercial break, the cameras were panning the Browns sideline. Earnest was on a knee with his head down, completely alone on the sidelines. Bernie walked over. My dad and I were the only ones left in the room when I heard him say—"George, look over there, look what Bernie's doing."
>
> I saw Bernie on the screen, walk over to Earnest, who was on a knee, completely alone. Bernie bent over to put his hand on his shoulder and said something quickly. My dad said, "There's a champ. That's how you play football, George."
>
> My dad, the biggest non-jock around, wanted me to appreciate that sports is so much more than the scoreboard. I learned from my favorite player and my favorite team (still trying to get in the Super Bowl) that a show of loyalty, gratitude and respect for a teammate, when it hurts the most, means the most. Bernie showed us in that moment what it is to be a true champion.
>
> In a strange way, "The Fumble" is my Super Bowl. It has a completely different meaning and memory for me—one way more important, I think, than I ever would have learned at that age from a winning headline.
> **—George L. Cimballa III, Esq.**

Anyone who blames Byner really needs to think again. In fact, the negativity around The Fumble haunted Byner in 1988, despite still leading the team with 576 yards rushing and 59 catches. He

had some personal fouls in a playoff loss to Houston, and criticism piled up. They thought he needed a fresh start elsewhere,
shipping him to Washington for the nondescript Mike Oliphant.

In Washington, Byner played for coach Joe Gibbs, who loved
the running back's tenacity. From 1990 to 1992, Byner rushed for
1,219, 1,048 and 998 yards. He made the only two Pro Bowls of his
career. He played on a Super Bowl winner. He retired with 8,261
yards rushing, 512 catches and 14 years in the NFL. In Washington and elsewhere, he was appreciated as a man of character who
overcame the adversity of The Fumble.

Coach Marty Schottenheimer said more than once: "If you
lose by a touchdown or less, it means literally one play made the
difference. When a game turns on one play, every player on the
team could have made the difference in the game."

Byner is amazed that The Fumble has become such a huge
part of the history of Cleveland sports.

"I wish I had a nickel for every time they show it on TV," he said.
"I also see how they try to force it into situations to make a point.
I saw it during the Cavs' playoff games. Nothing that happened to
the Cavs in the playoffs had anything to do with The Fumble. It's
crazy."

Byner has "never run away" from The Fumble, to use his own
words. He talks about how it led to him being traded to Washington, where he had a better career than with the Browns. He said
that when he returned to the Browns in 1994, "the fans treated me
like a hero. Even some of the guys in the media who were on me
the first time around were nice to me."

Byner said Browns Backers clubs "are super. We talk about
The Fumble. It's part of our shared legacy. I think we can learn
how not to be stuck in anger or bitterness, and how we can move
forward. I said before that it has helped me be a better person,
but it has done the same for a lot of the fans—at least based on
how they have treated me. Whenever I run into a Browns fan, I
get nothing but love."

And that's how it should be.

CHAPTER 3

The Browns do have a rivalry with the Steelers, but not the kind you think.

I live in Pittsburgh, and I'm surrounded by Steelers fans. My friends all know my allegiance is with the Browns and that I won't change, no matter how bad the Browns are compared to the Steelers. Everyone was amazed that I was such a rabid football fan but that I'd never been to a pro football game. . . . I jokingly said my ideal game would be a Browns-Steelers game. . . . On December 10, 2009, my goal came true. My brother sent me a text message and asked if I wanted to go to the Browns-Steelers game as a friend of his got tickets but couldn't go.

I was 36 years old but was bouncing around like a teen at a Jonas Brothers concert. Once we got to the stadium, my brother negotiated with a scalper to trade our tickets for seats in the Dawg Pound. I didn't care that it was minus-10 with the wind chill, I was at a Browns-Steelers game! Sitting in the Dawg Pound! I yelled and screamed and barked like I'd never done before.

Then the unthinkable happened. The Browns beat the Steelers. The same team that had won two Super Bowls in the past four years and were supposed to go on to the playoffs that year. My Browns, my team that was only doing slightly better than the Detroit Lions, beat the seemingly unstoppable

Steelers. . . . I may never get to another Browns-Steelers game, or even another game at Cleveland Browns Stadium, but I will never forget December 10, 2009.

—Heidi Patterson-Orlando

I'm 56 years old, and I've been a Browns fan ever since I could walk. My first words were, "Beat Pittsburgh!"

—Gay Snyder

I wrote Coach Eric Mangini early in the 2009 season explaining how important it was to beat that team "East" of us (Pittsburgh) so that my kids might see us as a winner. . . . He responded in writing and responded with a victory!

—Ron Stenger

When Eric Mangini was hired as the Browns' coach in 2009, he knew what it meant to beat the Pittsburgh Steelers. He had been with the Browns as an intern under Bill Belichick in 1994-95, watching the team lose FIVE times in two years to Pittsburgh. He knew the Browns were 3-18 against the Steelers since the Browns returned as an expansion team in 1999. In fact, Chris Palmer was 2-2 vs. Pittsburgh in 1999-2000. In the eight years after Palmer, the Browns were 1-16. They hadn't won a Steelers game since 2003. Mangini lost his first game in 2009 to the Steelers 27-14 in Pittsburgh. That made it 12 losses in a row to the Steelers.

Before the final Steelers-Browns game of the 2009 season, Mangini brought his 1-11 team together. Yes, the Browns were 1-11, the Steelers were 6-6 and in the playoff race. It was a wild, windy, almost snow-blind Thursday night. Wind chills were below zero. Mangini seemed destined to be fired as the coach by the end of the season. Many of the Browns players wondered where they'd be the following season. Mangini then talked to his team about how his father died suddenly of a heart attack when he was 16. He talked about how life was short, that he had no idea his father would die at the age of 56. Or that his father would never see him coach a game.

"Nothing in life is guaranteed," he said. "Some of you have lost people, and you know that."

Mangini then talked about how no one expected him to ever coach in the NFL. He played Division III college football. He had no NFL connections.

"Like many of you, I was labeled," he said. "I'm not supposed to be here."

"Some of you are supposed to be too small," he said. "Some, too slow. Some, not smart enough or tough enough."

Mangini was becoming emotional, his soft voice even quieter than normal.

"We all get labeled at some point," he said, implying that this Browns team was labeled as losers, one that would never have a chance against Pittsburgh.

"Every day, you get a chance to write your own label," he said. "You can write what you want on that label tonight."

He paused.

"Never give anyone that pen to write that label for you," he said. "Write it yourself."

The Browns did that night, beating the Steelers 13-6 in a game where Ben Roethlisberger was sacked eight times, and the Browns won the game with defense, grit and determination. They began to write their own labels, stating they were not about to quit as they won the final four games of that season.

> The Browns always reminded me of my dad . . . a hard-working, blue-collar, "God, country, family"-first kind of mentality. My dad was in a serious vehicle accident in November of 2008. He has lost most of his mental faculties. He still remembers two things very clearly: He loves his Browns and hates the Steelers. . . . The Browns have always symbolized, to me at least, what the city of Cleveland, and my dad, were all about: giving it your best, fighting to the end with your nose to the grindstone.
> **—Matthew Klinkovsky**

Once upon a time, the Pittsburgh Steelers were terrible. They were similar to the Indians from 1960 to 1993—dismal decade after dismal decade. The Steelers were founded in 1933 as the Pittsburgh Pirates. (They were renamed the Steelers in 1940.) In 1972, coach Chuck Noll's rebuilding program finally blossomed, and they went 11-3. In the 37 seasons before Noll:

• Their first winning season was in 1942, their 10th season in the league.

• They had only seven winning seasons.

• They made the playoffs only once (1947).

• Even in the 1960s, the Steelers were 46-85-7 (.358). Browns fans talk about not winning a championship since 1964. In those first 37 seasons, the only playoff game for Pittsburgh was a 21-0 spanking by the Philadelphia Eagles in 1947.

There were a lot of bad things about the Steelers in the old days. Here's an example. In 1941, they lost their first two games. Mike Basrak, the Steelers' first All-Pro, had played for Duquesne, a private college in Pittsburgh. When Bert Bell stepped down as coach two games into the season, the Steelers replaced him with Aldo Donelli, who was the coach of the Duquesne Dukes. Not "former" coach of the Dukes, the current coach. The Steelers began practicing on the Duquesne campus. Donelli would hold practices for the Steelers in the morning while his college players were in class. Then he'd coach the Dukes in the afternoon. He coached the Dukes' game on Saturday, the Steelers' game on Sunday. Duquesne had an undefeated season and was nationally ranked in 1941. But he lost his first five games with the Steelers and then resigned, claiming that he couldn't do both jobs.

Even in their worst moments, the Browns were never this bad—or bizarre.

In 1943, the Steelers combined rosters with the Philadelphia Eagles (who had gone 2-9 in 1942). They played a joint schedule, with co-coaches. They justified this by saying that the war was on and it was an economic move to save gas. Since it was a temporary move, the team had two coaches. But Walt Kiesling and Greasy Neale had a longstanding grudge dating back to Kiesling's days as a player. They allegedly refused to speak to each other. So Neale coached the players on offense. Kiesling coached the defense. The players were so poorly paid that they all had fulltime jobs. The team was christened "The Steagles" and went 5-4-1.

In 1944, the Eagles decided they didn't need the Steelers and played their own schedule. The Steelers combined with a team from Chicago, and finished 0-10. There's more craziness in the 1940s and 1950s in Pittsburgh, where the Rooney family of that era acted a lot more like Ted Stepien than the beloved and revered Rooneys of modern football. It began to change in 1965 when Art Rooney allowed his son Dan to run the team as general manager.

As a 49-year-old, third-generation Browns fan, it's very disturbing to have a 9-year-old son (Michael) who is a Steelers fan. But there's hope. Lately, he has been collecting football cards and ran across some old Browns players. We went to the Hall of Fame, and he surprised me by naming some early Browns that he wanted to see—especially videos of Jim Brown and Otto Graham. He has come to realize the Browns had some very good teams.

—Ben Williams

Meanwhile, back in Cleveland, they showed the world that this should be the capital of football, especially when Paul Brown took over the new Cleveland Browns in the brand-new All-American Football Conference. Starting in 1946, the Browns won four consecutive league titles. When the AAFC and NFL merged in 1950, the Browns won the NFL championship in their very first year. After losing the NFL Championship Game in 1951, 1952 and 1953, the Browns won championships in 1954 and 1955. If you were a Steelers fan in 1956 (and you would've had to have been a world-class masochist to follow that team), you were having a good year if your team finished at .500. But Cleveland fans had watched their team play for the championship for 10 consecutive seasons.

When the Browns entered the NFL, they naturally had no trouble with Pittsburgh.

1950: Cleveland won both games: 30-17 and 45-7.

1951: Pittsburgh was shut out—twice. The final scores were 17-0 and 28-0.

1952: It was closer, but the Browns won again by scores of 21-20 and 29-28.

1953: Two more Browns wins, 34-16 and 20-16.

1954: Pittsburgh finally won, 55-27 on October 17, 1954. The Browns fumbled six times (losing two) and threw six interceptions. Paul Brown must have been the most miserable man in the galaxy after that game. The Browns did hammer the Steelers, 42-7, two months later.

The Browns were 16-4 vs. the Steelers in the 1950s. In that decade, they had nine winning seasons, the exception being 5-7 in 1956 when Otto Graham retired. They went to the championship game eight times.

As for the Steelers, they didn't even make the playoffs in the 1950s. They did have two winning records—in 1958 and 1959. After 25 seasons, it was the first time Pittsburgh finally had consecutive winning records. Since they also finished .500 three times (1950, 1953 and 1957), it was by far their best decade. If you want to feel even better as Browns fan, consider that Dan Rooney claims he scouted and signed Johnny Unitas for the Steelers. But the coaches cut Unitas over his objections. The future Hall of Fame quarterback sent letters to every team in the NFL asking for a try-out after he was cut by the Steelers in training camp in 1956. Paul Brown sent this letter back: "We've already set our roster for this year, but I've heard good things about you and I'll be happy to try you out next summer."

Unitas started playing semi-pro football, figuring he would go to Cleveland in 1957. But the Baltimore Colts had some injuries, needed a player, pulled out his letter and told him to come. Unitas won a job and began a Hall of Fame career. Otto Graham had retired after the 1956 season. It's pure speculation, but if Brown had sent a letter saying "come right now," he might have had one of the greatest quarterbacks of all time, and the Browns might have won several more titles.

> My best/worst days as a Browns fan were both Steelers games. The best was Oct. 24, 1993. It was my first game with my dad, Steve Krajnak. Eric Metcalf returned two punts for touchdowns into the teeth of the Dawg Pound. The worst was 2005 on Christmas Eve when the Steelers killed our Browns, 41-0. What a letdown, especially with the thousands of black-and-gold blankets in the stands in OUR HOUSE! I took my wife to this game, and it was her first Browns game. I couldn't stand to leave even though we were embarrassed—those Steelers fans weren't going to kick me out of my own house.
> **—Keven Krajnak**

It all changed when Pittsburgh hired Chuck Noll. Chuck Noll of Cleveland Benedictine High School. Chuck Noll, who played for the Browns from 1953 to 1959. Chuck Noll, who played for Paul Brown, serving as one of the two "messenger guards" who brought the plays to the quarterback. Chuck Noll, who at that time was the defensive coordinator of Don Shula's Baltimore Colts. And, yes, that's the same Don Shula who played for John Carroll and also for Paul Brown with the Browns in 1951-52.

Noll was hired by the Steelers in 1969 and was 1-13 as a rookie head coach. He was determined to build a winner with defense, and in 1969, they drafted future Hall of Fame defensive tackle Joe Greene. They also took eventual six-time Pro Bowl defensive end L.C. Greenwood and Jon Kolb, a tackle who played 13 years.

In 1970, they drafted two future Hall of Famers. In the first round, it was quarterback Terry Bradshaw. In the third round, cornerback Mel Blount. The 1970 season also was when they moved to Three Rivers Stadium. The Steelers had played their home games in either Forbes Field (the home of the baseball Pirates) or the University of Pittsburgh's Pitt Stadium. They practiced in the county-owned fields used to host the Allegheny County Fair.

But the Steelers had never had a stadium that was new. They'd moved into Forbes Field when it was 27 years old. Three Rivers had a practice facility that was modern and clean. The stadium had luxury boxes. The restrooms worked, and there was parking.

In 1971, Pittsburgh drafted yet another future Hall of Famer—linebacker Jack Ham. That draft also produced five other starters.

In 1972, Pittsburgh drafted future Hall of Fame running back Franco Harris. In four consecutive drafts, the Steelers picked at least one Hall of Famer. The 1972 Steelers were 11-3 and went to the playoffs for only the second time in franchise history—the first was 1947.

Suddenly, the Steelers had their own Paul Brown.

In 1974, the Steelers picked four future Hall of Famers in the first five rounds. Think about that, four Hall of Famers in five rounds!

Round 1: Receiver Lynn Swann.

Round 2: Linebacker Jack Lambert.

Round 4: Receiver John Stallworth.

Round 5: Center Mike Webster.

The Steelers won four AFC titles in the 1970s and four Super Bowls.

My Dad was a local truck driver, and my mom was an elementary school teacher. One of the few guilty pleasures our family had was Browns season tickets. My Dad traded four games to his friend, who had seats right beside him for the four other games in return. My mother went with my dad to three of the four games. I have a birthday in November. My present every year was to go with the old man to the other game. We had average seats in the upper deck of the old stadium, at about the 30-yard line.

Growing up in the Bernie Kosar years, the Dawg Pound had a magical pull on me. I'd sit in our seats with my binoculars and watch what looked like a party. I wanted to be a part of it more than anything. One year, Dad traded in his comfortable two seats and scored us a pair in the Pound. I was 13 years old.

It was December. We were dressed in our orange sneakers, Starter jackets, and Browns stocking caps. You could feel the energy crackling in the air as we walked from the RTA station to the gate. As we neared the Pound, the beers were flowing, guys were woofing. I was home! It was time to sit back and enjoy the game.

Five minutes before kickoff, a Steelers fan . . . Yes, a *Steelers* fan . . . walked into the Pound. He was immediately assaulted with boos and worse. And where do you think he sat? Right next to me.

Not more than 30 seconds after he was in his seat, a mob of shirtless Dawg Pounders converged on him. They ripped off his black-and-gold Steelers stocking cap. They threw it in the aisle and relieved themselves on it. They put the soaking, steaming hat back on his head! He didn't dare say a word. He sat in his seat with that hat on his head and didn't move until the end of the first quarter! Then he left and never came back!

Oh, did I mention we were playing the Houston Oilers?
—Lonny J. Levenson

Meanwhile, in Cleveland, the 1970s became a lost decade. They had won the 1964 NFL Championship. They made it to the championship game again in 1965, 1968 and 1969—but lost all three times. Consider that Ernie Davis had died without playing a game for the Browns. He had cost the team future Hall of Famer Bobby Mitchell in a trade. Jim Brown retired after the 1965 season at age 30. He probably could have played three more years. They were 15-5 vs. the Steelers in the 1960s.

But in 1970, the Browns traded future Hall of Famer Paul War-field for the third pick in the draft—quarterback Mike Phipps. The Browns also traded Ron Johnson (who would run for more than 1,000 yards in 1970 and 1972 for terrible Giants teams) for receiver Homer Jones, who proved he was no Paul Warfield.

The Browns toppled from 10-3-1 in 1969 to 7-7 in 1970. That was Blanton Collier's final season as coach. A warning of what was to come, the Browns lost 28-9 at Pittsburgh in that 1970 season, Noll's second year when the Steelers were only 5-9.

Nick Skorich was hired to replace Collier. He was 9-5 and made the playoffs in 1971, followed by a 10-4 record in 1972. Those play-off appearances in 1971 and 1972 were the last for the Browns in that decade.

While the Steelers were drafting future Hall of Famers in the 1970s, the Browns' first-round picks that decade were: Phipps, Bob McKay, Clarence Scott, Thom Darden, Steve Holden, Pete Adams, Mack Mitchell, Mike Pruitt, Robert L. Jackson, Clay Matthews, Ozzie Newsome and Willis Adams.

Obviously, they grabbed a future Hall of Famer in Newsome, a great player in Matthews, some good ones in Pruitt, Darden and Jackson. But this hardly compared to what was happening in Pittsburgh. The Browns did things such as a 1973 trade of their 1974 first-round pick and a second-rounder in 1975 to San Diego for linebacker Bob Babich and a 1975 fourth-rounder. Babich was a former first-rounder who never realized his great expectations. Also, the Browns' second-round pick in 1974, Billy Corbett, never played a down in the NFL.

There are a several more draft and trade blunders, but Browns fans are miserable enough when it comes to the subject of the Steelers. Pittsburgh swept the season series in 1975, 1977, 1978, 1979 and 1981. Cleveland did not win at Three Rivers Stadium until 1986.

For the 1970s, the Browns went 5-15 against Pittsburgh, all five wins at home.

Sam Rutigliano gave fans some fun moments in his six-plus seasons as the Browns' coach (1978-84), but he was 4-9 vs. Pittsburgh.

As time passes, Marty Schottenheimer has to be considered even a greater coach for the Browns than fans realized. In four seasons, he made the playoffs each year. He never believed in "The Three Rivers Jinx" or anything that would stop the Browns from beating Pittsburgh. Critics charge Marty with not winning the big games. But they always forget to mention that he swept the season series in 1986, 1987 and 1988 from the Steelers. He record was 7-2, both losses very close and in Three Rivers—23-20 in 1984 and 10-9 in 1985.

My best day at Browns Stadium is probably pretty high on people's worst day lists: the 41-0 loss on Christmas Eve to the Steelers in 2005. One of the first things we saw after we got to the Muni lot at 8:00 a.m. was an old, rusty black van pulling in with a faded yellow stripe through the center and a hand-spray-painted white Steelers logo on the side. It was just what you'd expect on a Steelers fan's daily driver. Sensing something special was about to happen, I pulled my wife aside and had her watch as a group of 15-20 Browns fans blocked the path and yelled colorful, maybe even a few off-color, remarks to the van full of people.

My wife, having never seen a confrontation like that, worried that a fight might break out, but after a few minutes of harassing, the fans parted, waved to the van and let it through. They even moved a grill so the van could park.

"That," I told her, "is what makes this special."

The stadium was packed full during the first quarter only to empty out by halftime. Even after seemingly all the Browns fans had gone home in disgust, leaving only Steelers fans chanting at the game, my wife and I stayed. We're not gluttons for punishment or anything, it's just that I was finally able to share something with my wife that has been a part of me.

—Gabe Knuth

The teams didn't like each other, and they played hard. There were a lot of vicious hits and dirty plays—on both sides. There was the 1976 game in Cleveland where Joe "Turkey" Jones grabbed Steelers quarterback Terry Bradshaw and plunged him helmet-first into the turf. Jones received a personal foul penalty and was fined $3,000. Bradshaw suffered a concussion. Browns fans still talk about that play.

In the 1990s, the Browns were 4-9 vs. the Steelers, including a 29-9 playoff loss in the 1994 season. Then Art Modell moved the Browns to Baltimore after the 1995 season. The Rooney family and Buffalo's Ralph Wilson were the only owners to vote against the move.

I stopped hating the Pittsburgh Steelers on Nov 13th, 1995.

I had grown up in the '70s era where Cleveland kids had to endure the great Steelers teams. The prime teams to root against were the Yankees and Steelers. I inherited these dislikes like I inherited my name. This was who I was as a sports fan as much as the Browns and Indians were my teams. But in 1995 my world was turned upside down.

I went to the Browns-Steelers game in Pittsburgh armed with banners ("Go to Hell Art Modell"), my soon-to-be-burned Browns gear and a bad attitude. What I discovered inside was unimagined. Instead of the normal taunts and comments from the Pittsburgh fans, I got sympathy and shared anger. What I did not expect was the loss that the Steelers fans felt as well. They saw the injustice to the Cleveland fans and supported us. My loss was larger than myself.

—Paul Willson

I grew up when the Steelers were the biggest, most emotional rivalry a man could have in Cleveland. We hated them and talked horribly about them. I know more than one guy that kicked in or threw something through the TV screen when we lost close ones.

Then came the move. Our last "Monday Night Football" game was against the team from the dark side, the Steelers in Pittsburgh. The Steelers fans wore orange armbands as a sad farewell to us. I still get choked up thinking about it. After that season, I became a Steelers fan, and while I am a Browns fan, I am still a Steelers fan unless they are playing the Browns. Thanks, Pittsburgh, that was classy!

—Joseph Palmer

How I Fell in Love with the Browns

In 1983, I was born in the backseat of my biological parents' car on the way to the hospital in Erie, Pa. Three months later, I was adopted by my family and have lived an incredible life with them. As I grew up, I researched my biological family and discovered an interesting tale. My biological father had gone to Clemson and cheered for Kevin Mack and the Tigers. When Mack was drafted by the Browns the spring before I was born, he had Mack's jersey. I was wrapped up in it when I was born that September in their car.

I was literally born a Browns fan and have watched the team passionately since. . . . I finally had a chance to meet Kevin at the Akron Browns Backers banquet in 2008. I shared my story with him, and we took a picture together. It truly was one of the greatest moments of my life and one I will never forget.

—*Patrick D. Althof*

I was 5 years old when my father took me to my first game in Cleveland Municipal Stadium. My dad had given me the ticket along with a brand-new football as my birthday present. Five years old and being a girl, I thought to myself, "What kind of a present is this???" To my amazement, I had a great time. What kind of kid wouldn't like an endless supply of hot dogs, hot chocolate and cotton candy for three straight hours? Being a season-ticket holder, my dad knew every person who sat around him, and they loaded me up with anything I wanted. It became a yearly event for me to attend a game with my dad on my birthday. While I still got whatever I wanted from three rows of Browns fans, somewhere along the line I began to learn the game.

I turned 14 years old the October it was announced the Browns were moving. Nine straight years of going to games once a year with my Dad had become a tradition, and now it was going to come to an end. Being a die-hard, my Dad decided the entire family would attend the last game with him. As we walked into the stadium that day, I noticed things had changed. There were no signs anywhere. We weren't allowed to buy a thing at the stadium. No way was my Dad going to support a man who would strip this city of their great team.

As the clock started to wind down, I looked at my dad and asked, "What is that noise?" All you could hear was some odd creaking and cracking, only to see benches from the Dawg Pound being heaved onto the field. I turned to my Dad only to see tears in his eyes. I knew it was time to keep my mouth shut. As we walked up West 3rd Street to get on the Rapid, I could see many people had tears in their eyes. It made me stop, and as I turned back to look at the stadium, I finally got it. I finally understood what this place was about. It's about tradition and loyalty. It is about the "family" you come to see every Sunday.

I have had my own season tickets since 1999 when the Browns came back to Cleveland. Every home game, I sit in the parking lot with my Dad, uncle and cousin. We walk up that hill and enter those gates together as a family to continue our tradition. I will turn 30 this year, and one thing I know for certain: win or lose, we will be in that parking lot celebrating as we have done for the past 25 years and will for many more to come.

—*Kat Warnke*

I became a fan shortly after my Dad was killed in a plane crash in France. He was a career man in the Air Force, and the day after the crash, we were whisked away to a small community in the northeastern corner of Ohio. I knew nothing of Cleveland, or the sports teams for that matter, when we arrived. My introduction to the Cleveland Browns was a pick-up basketball game when one of my opponents exclaimed that Lou Groza was retired. . . . Who in the world is Lou Groza? Of course, in due time it was cleared up, and then my thoughts drifted to why this would be an important subject of conversation in the middle of a serious game of b-ball. Once the worm is in, it burrows deep. Richie and the rest in the gang had the worm. I would get it shortly. Forty years later and still burrowing.

—Mike Conway

When I was 10 in 1980, my fifth-grade teacher gave us students an assignment to write to one of the Ohio professional sports teams. I chose the Cleveland Browns. When the Browns responded to my letter, I received a couple of orange helmet stickers, a couple of football cards and an 8X10 glossy team photo. That was it for me. I have watched every single snap from that point on. I have been there from Red Right 88 to the trade of Brady Quinn. I watch no other team. I watch no other sport. I love the Browns. I am afraid that if I quit watching them, that will be the year the Browns win it all. I have invested way too much time to chance missing it when they finally do reach the Super Bowl.

—Aaron Chochard

My first interaction with the team came when I stumbled across a box of videotapes at my grandparents' house. Those tapes introduced me to guys like Bernie Kosar, Hanford Dixon, and Marty Schottenheimer. I was forever hooked. Most of the tapes ended in heartbreak for the brown and orange, so I was acclimated early on to what would come. Over a decade later, I am preparing to go to college and am still waiting for a team resembling those in the videotapes to appear. Every Sunday, I pull on a jersey, throw on a hat and settle in for three hours of fun. Often times, the end result isn't fun, but I'm still there every week. . . . I don't fully know why I watch every week, and I might never know. It may be because of the stories my dad and grandfather have told me about the glory days. It may be because a part of me wants to be able to share stories with my kids like they do with me. But what I do know is, when the Browns are in the middle of the field hoisting the Lombardi Trophy one day, it all will have been worth it.

—Dale Armbruster

I'm 30 years old, the oldest of three girls. While my dad had to buy us many Cabbage Patch Dolls and My Little Ponies, he also raised three die-hard Browns fans. My dad has had season tickets since 1984. I grew up going to the games with my dad. That means the old Dawg Pound. . . . I remember going to the game with my dad when I was a little girl. We would get all bundled up, take the Rapid downtown. I'm still a season-ticket holder in the Dawg Pound.

My dad's basement has just about every imaginable thing one can own for the Browns . . . pop cans . . . bags of chips . . . glasses . . . blankets . . . even our bleacher seats from municipal stadium. Today we host a tailgate before the home games. . . . I get asked a lot how I can possibly love the Browns so much. I just do.

I have a pair of orange knee-high boots that I wear to show my team colors. I have decided to take them on the road to every NFL stadium. Last year, I took them to Denver. They have also been to Paul Brown Stadium. I am single. My friends ask, "How can you possibly be single—having a connection to Dawg Pound seats and loving the Browns so much?"

Not sure how I am, but one of these days, I'll find a guy who appreciates my love for the Browns, just like my dad.

—Tabitha J. Kunsman

I do not blame John Elway.
I do not blame Earnest Byner.
I do not blame Art Modell.
I do not blame Mark Jackson.

I do not blame Rich Karlis (even though that was a miss in my young eyes).

I blame my ancestors.

Two hundred years ago, when they came to America from Ireland, they could have chosen anywhere to drop anchor, grow some roots and start their new lives. They chose Cleveland. Now it has been passed down to me. Sure, I could move, but it is already in my blood. I blame them. How many rebuilding eras can I go through? I know the answer already—as many it takes.

—*John F. David*

CHAPTER 4

Fans know the draft is important, which is why it often makes them scream.

I'm a 42-year-old lifelong Clevelander. I am married, live in Hudson with my wife and two boys, 11 and 5. I am a longtime season-ticket holder, having missed only one home game since the Browns returned in 1999. That was in 2009, due to the swine flu! I also host a large tailgate every home game out of the back of a bus that I have remodeled and painted orange. . . . NFL draft day is like those baptisms down by the river. I'm not an overly religious guy, but the way I feel in the days after draft day is how I imagine the person being dunked in the river in the name of God must feel, reborn, new life, new chances.

—Terry Waye

As I began to write this, I thought about fans such as Terry Waye, a guy who has attended every home game (but one) from 1999 to 2009. And he missed the one game because of the swine flu. Too bad the men doing the draft for his favorite team couldn't have called in sick a few of those years when they were picking players. When I want a headache, I simply open the Browns media guide and stare at the draft picks since 1999. In my book, *False Start*, I explained all the reasons the NFL set up the Browns to fail in their first few seasons—the key being the Browns were given the shortest start-up time of any expansion team since 1970. But the NFL didn't force Carmen Policy to hire Dwight Clark and put the former 49ers receiver in charge of two of the most important drafts in team history. That's because those first two drafts—1999 and 2000—meant double picks for the Browns. It was one of their few rewards for being an expansion team. When I really want to get sick, I think about how if Art Modell had simply sold the Browns to Al Lerner, then it would have been Ozzie Newsome and his staff handling the draft—not the five different regimes between 1999 and 2010.

For those counting at home, here's the breakdown:

1999-2000: Carmen Policy, Dwight Clark
2001-2004: Butch Davis, Pete Garcia
2005-2008: Phil Savage
2009: Eric Mangini, with a little help from George Kokinis
2010: Mike Holmgren and Tom Heckert

Holmgren and Heckert are excused from this discussion because they've had only one draft at this writing. Mangini is only a year away from his draft, but at least he found Alex Mack in the first round. The starting center for all 16 games as a rookie, I'd rate Mack as the fourth-best player picked by the Browns since they returned in 1999. That's a nice tribute to Mack and Mangini, but when a rookie center ranks that high, boy is there something wrong with the drafts. In fact, I don't even know how to rank the 1999-2009 drafts in terms of the top-10 players, because there is only one true star—Joe Thomas. Think about that, all those picks for all those years and only one player (Thomas) has made multiple Pro Bowls for the Browns. OK, a long snapper did, too. As did an undrafted return man. More about them later.

Just keep in mind that the Browns had the No. 1 overall pick in 1999 and 2000.

And the No. 3 overall pick in 2001, 2005 and 2007.

Those are the selections in the top three of five different drafts, the picks made by three different people.

I'll rank the elite picks first with the name of the man who selected him.

1. Joe Thomas, 2007 (Savage)
2. Braylon Edwards, 2005 (Savage)
3. Tim Couch, 1999 (Clark)
4. Courtney Brown, 2000 (Clark)
5. Gerard Warren, 2001 (Davis)

Kellen Winslow II and Edwards made Pro Bowls (once) for the Browns. Both had attitude issues. Both were traded by Mangini. Over the long haul, I doubt the Browns will miss either. Here's my top 10 from all Browns selections in drafts from 1999 to 2009. No doubt, you will disagree with some of the rankings, but the problem is the players. Hey, a long snapper is No. 10! Then again, Ryan Pontbriand made the Pro Bowl in 2007 and 2008, and his snapping ability allowed Butch Davis "to sleep at night," as the former coach said after picking Pontbriand.

1. Joe Thomas, 1st round (2007)
2. Kevin Johnson, 2nd round (1999)
3. Kellen Winslow II, 1st round (2004)
4. Alex Mack, 1st round (2009)
5. Braylon Edwards, 1st round (2005)
6. Jeff Faine, 1st round (2003)
7. Kamerion Wimbley, 1st round (2006)
8. Tim Couch, 1st round (1999)
9. Andra Davis, 5th round (2002)
10. Ryan Pontbriand, 5th round (2005)

If you'd like to argue about players such as Dennis Northcutt, D'Qwell Jackson, Sean Jones, Anthony Henry, Lawrence Vickers, Chris Crocker or Daylon McCutcheon should be on the list, rather than some of those other names—fine with me. I needed two Advils just to make this list. After a couple of key players, I don't know who belongs on this list! So much mediocrity from which to choose! I do know the best player after Thomas acquired by the Browns out of college is . . . Joshua Cribbs! The undrafted free agent from Kent State was signed for $2,500 by Savage. Also, another undrafted free agent was Leigh Bodden, signed in 2003 during the Butch Davis Era.

> NFL draft day is like the first real day of spring, not the official day in March when the last bit of snow and ice has melted and you can step firmly and safely on solid ground. Draft day is the renewal of spring—the crisp air, the blue sky, the ability to run down the driveway, cut left and onto the sidewalk, then race up the block. Draft day is a fresh start, with the hope in the air so thick that you can take a bite out of it.
> **—Barry Grey**

From reading Barry's e-mail, he sounds as if he runs more precise patterns than the receivers drafted by the Browns. How about this? The Browns took receivers in the second round in each of the first FOUR seasons after they returned. It was receiver after receiver after receiver: from Kevin Johnson (1999) to Dennis Northcutt (2000) to Quincy Morgan (2001) to Andre Davis (2002). Eric Mangini even caught the fever, drafting TWO of them in the second round of 2009—Brian Robiskie and Mohamed Massaquoi.

But I digress . . .

Drafting in the NFL is the difference between winning and losing. It's more important than the drafts in baseball and basketball.

Baseball excludes players who live in other countries from the draft. It has a minor-league system—where you can acquire prospects. You can build a team simply by scouting good foreign players and acquiring other teams' talent, as the Indians actually did in 2005 and 2007. Poor drafting does catch up with you eventually, as it did for the Tribe of late. But it's not always fatal. In football, it's always fatal. And with a harsh salary cap, NFL teams simply can't endlessly buy young stars who become free agents as teams such as the Yankees have done in baseball.

You can't build an NFL team by signing free agents or trading for veteran players. Teams such as Washington keep trying, but it doesn't work for long, if at all. It's the scouting and drafting of college players (and the undrafted free agents) that build NFL teams.

Unlike basketball, any team can legitimately hope to do well in the draft.

In the NBA, unless you are in the lottery—and high up, in some years—it is almost impossible to draft a consistent All-Star. Most of the young, great NBA players were all high lottery picks—LeBron James, Dwyane Wade, Carmelo Anthony, Chris Paul, etc.

A big difference is you won't see an NFL franchise deliberately try to lose a ton of games to grab a high pick, the way NBA teams do. In fact, many NFL teams will "trade down" to get more selections. It would be unheard of for an NBA team to do that. The NFL has 22 positions (and that's not even counting kickers, punters and other special teams players), while the NBA has five. That means an NFL team has so many more holes to fill and so many more players needed to win.

Which brings us to the Browns, especially the Browns of 1999 and 2000, when they had the No. 1 overall picks in both drafts.

Here's a list of the No. 1 overall picks between 1990 and 2009:

Year	Name	Pos.	Team	Pro Bowls
2009	Matthew Stafford	QB	Detroit	0
2008	Jake Long	OT	Miami	2
2007	JaMarcus Russell	QB	Oakland	0
2006	Mario Williams	DE	Houston	2
2005	Alex Smith	QB	San Francisco	0
2004	Eli Manning	QB	San Diego	1
			(Traded to N.Y. Giants)	
2003	Carson Palmer	QB	Cincinnati	2
2002	David Carr	QB	Cleveland	0
2001	Michael Vick	QB	Atlanta	3
2000	Courtney Brown	DE	Cleveland	0
1999	Tim Couch	QB	Cleveland	0

1998	Peyton Manning	QB	Indianapolis	10
1997	Orlando Pace	OT	St. Louis	7
1996	Keyshawn Johnson	WR	N.Y. Jets	3
1995	Ki-Jana Carter	RB	Cincinnati	0
1994	Dan Wilkinson	DT	Cincinnati	0
1993	Drew Bledsoe	QB	New England	4
1992	Steve Emtman	DT	Indianapolis	0
1991	Russell Maryland	DT	Dallas	1
1990	Jeff George	QB	Indianapolis	0

Here are some quick conclusions:

1. Ten of the 20 picks made the Pro Bowl at some point during their career. Nine of them (Mario Williams of Houston being the exception) improved the team enough to get them into the playoffs within two years. Only one team that blew the pick—chose a player who didn't make the Pro Bowl (Cleveland, who took Courtney Brown)—got into the playoffs within the next two years.

2. The 20 picks had a combined total of 35 Pro Bowl selections.

3. Eleven of the 20 picks were quarterbacks. Five of the 11 made Pro Bowls: Eli Manning, Peyton Manning, Drew Bledsoe, Michael Vick and Carson Palmer.

4. Rather than see the dangers in drafting quarterbacks so high, teams are doing it now more than ever. Between 1990 and 1999, only four QBs were picked: Tim Couch, Peyton Manning, Drew Bledsoe and Jeff George. From 2001 to 2009, there were seven QBs selected. Only Eli Manning and Carson Palmer would be considered successes.

5. The Browns tried it both ways, with a QB in 1999 (Couch) and a defensive lineman in 2000 (Brown). Neither worked out for a variety of reasons, and both players sustained major injuries.

6. Six of the No. 1 failures were picked by three teams: Cleveland, Cincinnati and Indianapolis. In all three cases, the same GM picked both busts. It's not all bad luck. Before letting Bill Polian do the drafting, the Colts missed with Jeff George (1990) and Steve Emtman (1992). Before letting Marvin Lewis and his staff makes

the picks, the Bengals' Mike Brown and his people struck out with Ki-Jana Carter (1995) and Dan "Big Daddy" Wilkinson (1994).

7. In 1998, Bill Polian picked Peyton Manning, and the Colts went from awful to excellent.

8. In 2003, Lewis selected Carson Palmer, and the Bengals went from terrible to competitive.

I love draft day. I love following the mock drafts starting in January . . . who moves up, who moves down. There's the complete silliness of the NFL combine. . . . You have three years of film on a guy, and his 40 time or cone drill time has an impact on where he gets drafted? Really? Really? On draft day, the rubber hits the road. Who makes the bold moves? Who gets left behind compared to their divisional foes? Who comes away from the draft with a solid package of players to help their team compared to what draftniks say they should do? Love it.
—**Michael Filice**

Which brings us to the Browns in 1999 and 2000.

The 1999 draft was supposed to be terrific. Well, 14 of the players taken in the first round made the Pro Bowl. There were four in the second round, four in the third round. But the striking thing about the draft was that eight of the first 11 players taken made the Pro Bowl.

In order:

QB Donovan McNabb (pick 2)

RB Edgerrin James (4)

RB Ricky Williams (5)

WR Torry Holt (6)

CB Champ Bailey (7)

WR David Boston (8)

CB Chris McAlister (10)

QB Daunte Culpepper (11)

The three players in the top 11 who missed the Pro Bowl? Quarterback Akili Smith (No. 3, Bengals), linebacker Chris Claiborne (No. 9 Detroit) and Couch at No. 1 by the Browns. To make Browns fans feel worse, consider this was the year that New Orleans coach Mike Ditka wanted Ricky Williams. He was offering the No. 14 pick and six other picks—one of them a future first-rounder, that became the No. 2 selection in the 2000 draft. The Browns passed. Washington took the offer and made some other deals in conjunction with that.

It's not worth going into how Washington ended up with Champ Bailey, a good move. But it is revealing to see how an expansion team had a chance to add precious picks at a time when it really had NO players. You can be sure that Bill Belichick or Eric Mangini or anyone else who believes in the Mr. Big Volume approach to drafting would not have allowed Ditka off the phone until a trade was made.

There were some warning signals about Couch. One is that the track record of college quarterbacks with fewer than 35 starts and completing fewer than 60 percent of their passes is questionable. This is called the Lewin Theory of quarterbacks, and it applies only to those from major schools who are being considered in the top two rounds of the draft. Couch started only two seasons at Kentucky. He also played in a unique spread offense for a coordinator named Mike Leach. Yes, that's the same Mike Leach who was sort of an eccentric genius when he later coached at Texas Tech and put together incredible offenses that hid the weaknesses of quarterbacks. As for another miss, Smith played only two years at Oregon before he was picked by the Bengals.

The patterns of Tim Couch and David Carr (the top pick in 2002) are the same. Both were the top picks of expansion teams. Both were rushed into starting jobs. Both were under Chris Palmer, who called the plays. Palmer believed that if you have a young quarterback, and he's your eventual starter . . . and you have a bad team . . . start him now and let him get the experience. He often mentioned how Hall of Famer Troy Aikman was 0-11 as a rookie. Or how Peyton Manning took a beating as a rookie. I am a huge fan of Chris Palmer. As a quarterback coach, he helped develop Tony Romo and Eli Manning in their breakout seasons after

Palmer left the Browns and Houston. But his theory about throwing a rookie quarterback on an expansion team into the teeth of various defenses just seems too risky. Carr and Couch had their careers stunted by injury, but some would argue that some of the injuries were their fault. Both had a bad habit of hanging on to the ball too long, taking sacks instead of throwing the ball away. Both players took a staggering number of sacks (and had very high fumble numbers as a result), which indicates some issues with decision-making.

Couch was sacked 117 times (on 1,068 attempts) in his first three years. In the 2002 season, when the Browns made the playoffs, he posted a 76.8 passer rating with 18 touchdowns compared to 18 interceptions. It was a decent season, and he did lead the team to the playoffs.

In Carr's five years in Houston, he led the league in getting sacked three times. He went down 249 times in 2,070 attempts and fumbled 68 times. His career lasted longer than that of Couch, who played his last regular-season game in 2003 at the age of 26. But Carr seemed shell-shocked by his early years. The more he played, the more his confidence and effectiveness faded. Would either quarterback have been better if he had sat for a year or so? Who knows? But it's hard to imagine it being any worse.

Yet, I rated Couch as the eighth-best player drafted by the Browns since they returned in 1999. Why? Because he has started more games at quarterback for the Browns than anyone since that time. Heading into 2010, he is the only Browns quarterback to get his team into the playoffs—although he was hurt for that playoff game, as Kelly Holcomb started. Couch even had three victories in his career against Pittsburgh. I'm not saying he was great, but at least he did something!

In 1999, the Browns did get some mileage of out Couch, Kevin Johnson and Daylon McCutcheon, picked in the first three rounds. You'd think the drafting would have been better in 2000, as Clark had more time to prepare, more time to bring in scouts. He had more time for everything.

But the 2000 draft was even worse!

I start with a confession: I thought Courtney Brown was absolutely, positively the best pick at No. 1 for the Browns. The defensive end from Penn State was a regular All-American, an academic honors student, a super guy, a relentless worker. He never missed a practice—much less a game—in either high school or college. With the Browns? He played a full season as a rookie, but then missed 11, five, three and 14 games over the next four years. After one season in Denver, where he looked like a shell of his former self, coach Mike Shanahan cut him and told him to retire before he permanently injured himself. He blew out a knee, tore up a biceps, just fell apart physically.

After Brown at No. 1, six of nine picks made the Pro Bowl: linebacker LaVar Arrington, tackle Chris Samuels, running back Jamal Lewis, defensive tackle Corey Simon, running back Thomas Jones and linebacker Brian Urlacher. One of three misses (at No. 8) was Plaxico Burress, who was an impact wide receiver and caught a Super Bowl-winning pass.

There were 13 picks in the first round who made the Pro Bowl, five more in the second round. The Browns' second-rounder was Dennis Northcutt, a so-so receiver and above-average return man. After Northcutt come names such as Travis Prentice, Lewis Sanders, JaJuan Dawson and Lamar Chapman. The only other useful player was Aaron Shea, a fourth-rounder. You can play the "What if?" game, as in the Browns picked quarterback Spergon Wynn (No. 183) ahead of future Hall of Famer Tom Brady, who was netted by New England at No. 199.

But the real story is that for all their picks—25 picks, plus three players added through trading picks—not a single Pro Bowl player was drafted. None of these players have had long careers. They just wasted tons of picks.

> On draft day, each Browns fan is permitted out of his cell for 15 minutes of hope.
> **—Gerard Zuber**

> Draft day . . . in a word . . . means befuddlement. . . . If
> that's not really a word, it should be because it applies to SOOO
> many draft day blunders by the Browns management.
> **—Jim Jarrell**

Then came the Butch Davis years. In 2001, it was Gerard Warren instead of LaDainian Tomlinson (Palmer's last recommendation before being fired) or Richard Seymour (the choice of the Browns scouts). William Green, who had personal problems in school, was his first-rounder in 2002. The personal troubles continued, and there were some injuries. He started two years and was out of the NFL after four seasons. In 2003, Davis selected a solid center in the first round—Jeff Faine, and long-snapper Ryan Pontbriand in the fifth round. In 2004, Davis was outsmarted by . . . the Detroit Lions, of all teams. He was faked into dealing a second-rounder to move up a single slot in the draft and grab Kellen Winslow II at No. 6. Yes, that was ahead of Ben Roethlisberger. But even more damaging, the Lions had no intention of picking Winslow. Had the Browns stayed put, they could have kept a second-round choice.

I'm not going to run through each pick. At least Phil Savage (hired as general manager in 2005), did a few things right. He ignored the noise and glitz, and he grabbed Joe Thomas in the first round of 2007. Some of his own coaches wanted him to take Brady Quinn at No. 3. Savage did trade a second- and a future first-rounder to Dallas for Quinn, which did not work out.

Savage and nearly everyone drafting for the Browns has been horrible in the third round, where you still can find some value. That is especially true on good teams. The Browns haven't used a third-rounder well since 2002, when Butch Davis drafted a center named Melvin Fowler. He was a sometime starter/viable backup for Buffalo for years. The best third-rounders before that were Anthony Pleasant in 1990 and Reggie Camp in 1983. Savage's third-rounders were Charlie Frye and Travis Wilson. He traded his other two picks in the third round. At least three of Savage's four picks in the first round are NFL starters: Braylon Edwards, Kamerion Wimbley and Thomas. Quinn is the only big miss.

In 2008, Savage went against every beat of his heart and drop of drafting blood in his veins by dealing a second-round pick for Corey Williams and a third-rounder (and Leigh Bodden) for Shaun Rogers. After being 10-6 and missing the playoffs by a game in 2007, Savage went into "win now" overdrive with the blessing of his owner. Goodbye, draft picks. Hello, trades. Right now, all the Browns have to show for the 2008 draft is Rogers, Ahtyba Rubin and a few low-round future picks from other trades . . . along with Peyton Hillis, acquired in the Brady Quinn deal with Denver.

Since I've been in a list-making mood, here's how I rank the Browns' first-rounders since the return. Keep in mind the only ones remaining with the team are Alex Mack and Thomas.

1. Joe Thomas, 2007 (Savage)
2. Kellen Winslow II, 2004 (Davis)
3. Alex Mack, 2009 (Mangini)
4. Braylon Edwards, 2005 (Savage)
5. Jeff Faine, 2003 (Davis)
6. Kamerion Wimbley, 2006 (Savage)
7. Tim Couch, 1999 (Clark)
8. Gerard Warren, 2001 (Davis)
9. Courtney Brown, 2000 (Clark)
10. William Green, 2002 (Davis)
11. Brady Quinn, 2007 (Savage)

I don't even know what to tell fans about this . . .

The NFL draft is a day of hope, sometimes like Christmas in April as you anticipate what your present might be. Unfortunately, there have been too many times when instead of the cool gift you had hoped for . . . Aunt Clara gave you a tie or cuff links that will never be used.
—Stan Stefanoff

Maybe Aunt Clara should have been brought in as a special assistant for some of these drafts.

> Draft day is like Christmas and Easter Mass. You leave with a feeling of hope that all is good . . . things will change. . . . It renews the spirit in me that someday it will happen in Cleveland . . . someday.
> **—Dom Dipuccio**

The Browns now have Mike Holmgren and Tom Heckert running the draft. They seem to be sane, serious and experienced men. It's far too early to judge them, but it's never too early to start praying for them as they head into the next draft!

CHAPTER 5

Brian Sipe is still young in the hearts of most Browns fans.

Brian Sipe was the skinny kid from Southern California who seemed loose and likable. He was the smallish, confident leader who made Cleveland proud. It always startled me that Braylon Edwards was allowed to have his number. I loved that Sipe had the desire to become an architect, then went on to become one. He was a fascinating, intelligent man. . . . I was always proud that he belonged to Cleveland.
—**Bill Beck**

I fell in love with Brian Sipe. There was nothing better in orange pants than that man . . . My boyfriend at the time bought me my own binoculars because he was tired of getting his back with the lenses steamed up.
—**Debra Harwood**

Brian Sipe answered his phone in the football office at San Diego State University with a hint of amazement in his voice.

"I never thought I'd be doing this," said the former Browns quarterback.

"This" being the quarterback coach at his alma mater. "This" being a guy who was a rookie college assistant at the age of 59. And for Browns fans, this is Sipe being 60 years old in 2010. It was back in 1980 when he was the ultimate Kardiac Kid and named the NFL's Most Valuable Player.

"I remember when the Browns drafted me," he said. "It was the 13th round in 1972. I figured I'd never last. I already had another job lined up when I went to training camp."

Another job?

"I was going to move to Steamboat Springs (Colorado) and be a waiter," he said. "Really, I was moving there to ski all day with some friends, who also were working at restaurants."

Most Browns fans don't know the early Browns history of Brian Sipe.

"I was a beach kid from southern California," he said. "When I came to the Browns, no one was anxious for me to play. For the first two years, I was on the taxi squad. I wore a baseball cap, a sweat suit and held a clipboard on the sidelines."

Sipe played for San Diego State, which was known in the late 1960s and early 1970s as the "cradle of quarterbacks." The Aztecs were a Division II school (known as the "Small College" division at the time), but they sent two starting quarterbacks to the NFL: Buffalo's Dennis Shaw and Denver's Don Horn. The Aztecs won or tied for Small College national titles three times in the late 1960s. They had a streak of 66 victories in 67 games, and went undefeated in 1966, 1968 and 1969. Their offense was creative and wide open, with the nickname of "Air Coryell." That was for coach Don Coryell, who popularized the "I" formation, split the tight end away from the line, and sometimes used two tight ends. He also created the "H-back" and started using multiple defensive substitutions—including the "nickel" and "dime" packages.

All of this is common to modern football, but Coryell either came up with it or is credited with being the first coach to use most of these formations. Coryell also coached Isaac Curtis, Fred Dryer, Haven Moses, Willie Buchanon, Gary Garrison and Sipe. His offensive line coach was Joe Gibbs, who became a Super Bowl coach with the Washington Redskins. His defensive coordinator was John Madden, another Super Bowl coach and, later, star television NFL analyst.

The reason for this background is to explain why a 13th-rounder from what was a Small College Division school who was physically underwhelming (Sipe was barely 6-foot-1 with average arm strength) actually was more prepared for the pros than big-name quarterbacks from the major football powers. But few people knew it at the time.

"My college coaching was as good or better than most of what you'd get in the NFL back then," he said. "I had Rod Dowhower as my quarterback coach (later another successful NFL assistant), and he helped prepare me."

A few years ago, a friend and I went to the Little League World Series in Williamsport, Pa. During the pregame ceremonies, there was a familiar face that they were honoring for being part of the 1961 Little League Word Series championship team. It was Brian Sipe. After the ceremony, he went up and took his seat roughly 20 feet away from me. There is literally nobody else in the world that I would go out of my way to meet other than Brian Sipe. When he went down to grab a hot dog, I followed him. Standing in line behind him, I struck up a conversation. I mentioned that he was my all-time favorite quarterback. He then said, "And you just happened to be standing behind me in line?" Actually, he was a nice guy, he wanted to know more about me than tell me about himself.

—Marshall Siegel

Sipe liked to talk about being small and slow, but he did admit, "I was a pretty good athlete."

Good enough to be the youngest member (11 years old) of the El Cajon team that won the Little League World Series. He was a part-time catcher, a sometimes center fielder. At Grossmont High in the San Diego area, he was one of the state's best quarterbacks. Then he won several honors at San Diego State, playing in the Shrine Bowl and the East-West College All-Star game.

Brian Sipe was drafted 330th as the Browns' last pick. ("Too small, but we might as well take him.") He was the Most

Valuable Player in the NCCA Small College Division that year. In
the first couple of practice sessions, he made the team. Then
every year after, I would ask former *Plain Dealer* football writer
Chuck Heaton, "How's Brian Sipe?"

"He won't make the cut—too small," Chuck told me.

I listened to that for about three years. When he was in
for short bursts, he moved the team. That is why they kept
him around. . . . When Mike Phipps got hurt, Sipe kept the
job behind a very mediocre line. If the Steelers had him, they
wouldn't have lost that game with super offensive teams loaded
with Pro Football Hall of Famers.

—Bill Wynne

Ah, yes, Mike Phipps.

This is not to blame Phipps, any more than it is to blame Danny
Ferry for the Cavaliers trading Ron Harper. But that 1970 deal cost
them Hall of Fame receiver Paul Warfield. It also meant Sipe had
to sit for several years as the Browns tried to make a quarterback
out of Phipps. By 1974, Sipe had been on the team for two years
without taking a snap in a game.

"I hardly even played in practice," he said. "It seems when they
did put me in, it was near the end—and I usually fumbled."

He had one supporter—former Browns coach Blanton Collier,
who was a team consultant by this point. Sipe said Collier's kind
words kept him working and helped him wait for a break.

Sipe's first coach was Nick Skorich, who didn't know a lot about
quarterbacks, nor did he like to use young players. In his mind,
it was bad enough that he was stuck with Phipps. He certainly
didn't want to replace the phenom with this scrub of a kid from
San Diego whose arm seemed too weak to succeed. Sipe never
started until the Browns were 1-6 in 1974. With the Browns losing
21-9 and Phipps having another dismal game, Sipe came in and
led the team to two scores and a win. Even then, Skorich didn't
trust Sipe. In 1974, the Browns were 4-10. In 1975, the Browns fell
to 3-11. It was mostly Phipps. It wasn't until 1976 when the Browns
finally gave the job to Sipe.

In July of 1977, the Cleveland Browns organization sponsored a Family Day at Dix Stadium in Kent, Ohio. The weather was beautiful, and all the players were on the field. The fans were allowed to take pictures of or with each player. I waited in one of the longest lines to have my picture taken with Brian Sipe. To this day, I treasure that photo with his arm around my shoulder.
—Loretta Caruso

I was about 11 when the Browns came to Denver for a preseason game. My Dad took me down to the game early so we could watch the team coming into the stadium. I almost couldn't breathe as I saw my idols marching toward the locker room. I was decked out in my Brian Sipe jersey, just waiting for him to appear. Then my boyhood hero walked off the bus. Suddenly, my Dad pointed down at me and yelled, "Hey, Sipe, do you have a second to sign an autograph for a big fan?"

Sipe grinned and walked right over. He said hello and that he was surprised to find a fan of his way out in Colorado. I was so nervous that I couldn't hold my pen up for him because I was shaking so badly. He was polite, patient. I'll never forget his graciousness in walking out of his way to sign that piece of paper for me instead of just waving and moving along.
—David E. Settje

Sipe said it took awhile for him to grasp what football meant to Browns fans.

"Once I did, I felt this enormous responsibility," he said. "The Browns are like family to so many people. And they love to tell you about going to Browns games in terrible weather."

Sipe said he missed the beach when he was in Cleveland. "When I was drafted by the Browns, I actually pulled out a map to see if Cleveland was near any kind of beach. I tried Lake Erie, but after surfing in the ocean . . . "

Well, he discovered Cleveland is all about football, and lousy weather is part of it.

"It takes awhile, but you make the cold and the wind your asset," said Sipe. "You learn to play in it by practicing in it. Then when the other teams come to the Lakefront, they aren't ready for it."

Sipe paused.

"You should embrace the cold," he said. "It helps you as a quarterback because it slows the game down. You can see things better. We didn't have a fieldhouse back then; we practiced outside every day. That makes sense. If you don't practice in it, you can't play well in it. Playing in that weather is part of what made us a tough team mentally," he said.

He said he grew to love Cleveland and the fans, adding, "It's a pure football town."

That was especially true in 1980, when the Browns were 11-5 but lost to Oakland in the playoffs, 14-12, in the infamous Red Right 88 game.

Sipe will always be my favorite Browns player because there was almost something magical going on during that 1980-81 season. The magic seemed to emanate from that right arm of Number 17 that season. It was as if you never felt as a fan that the Browns were out of any game no matter how deep it was in that game. Sipe just had ice water in his veins and would calmly, almost routinely that season, lead the Browns down the field for last-minute drives time and time again. The man himself looked no more the part of a star football player than many regular guys off the street, but he sure had a heart every bit as big as Municipal Stadium itself. I was at the stadium on October 19 and witnessed the magic act in person as Sipe connected with Dave Logan on a long touchdown to beat the Green Bay Packers with about 25 seconds left. To add to that memory, my first child, my daughter, was born the next day. If she had been a boy, we may have considered naming him Brian.

—Bill Beasley

As a child, my favorite player was Brian Sipe. I told my babysitter and kindergarten teacher that I WAS Brian Sipe. About 25 years later, I had the chance to meet him. I had a jersey made at the NFL shop to have him sign it. As the night went on and it appeared that I would not get my chance to get in line to meet him, my wife (a non-sports fan) became livid, yelling and finding someone in charge (very out of character) for me to get this autograph.

I ended up getting the autograph (Brian couldn't have been nicer). On the way home I jokingly remarked something about her being pregnant because the way she acted was so not like her. When we got home, she secretly went upstairs and took a home pregnancy test. She came running down the stairs screaming that indeed she was pregnant. That's how I found out I was going to be a father for the first time!

—Curtis Fisher

Sipe is in his second season as quarterbacks coach of his alma mater. Before that, he spent eight years at Santa Fe Christian in San Diego, winning four state titles.

"I never thought I'd be a football coach," he said. Sipe studied architecture in college and worked in that field for a while. Then he helped out at the small high school as an assistant, moving up to be head coach.

"When San Diego State asked me to be quarterback coach, it was meaningful because it's my school," he said. "I feel like I'm on a mission."

Sipe still is amazed when he returns to Cleveland or runs into Browns fans elsewhere. "After all these years, they treat us like royalty," he said. "Not just me, but all the guys from that (1980) team. They are fantastic people."

CHAPTER 6

The greatest Brown ever is a Brown, but his first name is not Jim.

The Browns have a great history, and that history all began with Paul Brown. When he started the team, he built them into one of the true dynasties of all time. He revolutionized the game; the success of his teams here in Cleveland was legendary. I have always felt he was cheated out of his true legacy here because of the ego of one man, Art Modell. Paul Brown Stadium should have happened here, not in Cincinnati. Now that Modell is gone, I would like to see Brown's legacy honored in a way more befitting of what he did for this team and city. I think a statue of him erected outside Cleveland Browns Stadium would be fantastic. Much like the Bob Feller statue. After all, the rich history of this team and its accomplishments and what it means to the people here was all because of Paul Brown.

—Jim Moravcik

The greatest Brown ever is Paul Brown.

Greater than Jim Brown. Greater than Otto Graham. Greater than anyone.

Paul Brown was more than a Hall of Fame coach, more than a man who started and built pro franchises in Cleveland and Cincinnati. A strong case can be made that he invented pro football, at least as we know it today. Brown didn't concoct the actual sport, but he had a huge hand in how the game is still played today.

Even hardcore Browns fans may not appreciate what Paul Brown has meant to the franchise or to the NFL. As time passes, the more his memory seems forgotten—yet, the more we can see how his coaching fingerprints are all over the modern NFL.

And this is a man who hasn't coached a game for the Browns since 1962. The Browns have won only one title since—in 1964—with a roster primarily built by Paul Brown. But this book also will make the case in a different chapter that the 1964 Browns needed a coaching change to win that title. None of that diminishes what Paul Brown means to Cleveland football fans—or to the NFL.

I'll go into greater detail later, but think about having the coach of your team being the man who first put assistants in the press box to watch the game and relay information to the field. And the first to make extensive use of game films to prepare for games. And the first to call plays from the sidelines. And the first to hand detailed playbooks to his athletes, and then give them tests to make sure they learned the material. He even invented the practice squad to develop players.

He was like the first pitcher to throw a curveball, the first basketball coach to conceive a zone defense or a pick-and-roll play. He was the first pro football coach to use a lot of black players, and the first to have full-time assistant coaches.

In his first 10 years as Browns coach, he won seven titles. The other three years? He lost in the title game.

"He was like Red Auerbach to the NBA, or Branch Rickey to baseball," said former Browns coach Sam Rutigliano. "He was a giant."

I e-mailed Bill Belichick about Brown, and he came back quickly with this reply:

"He was the father of professional football, 90% of everything coaches do today, PB did when he was the head coach of the Browns. This is based on many conversations with Jim Brown when we talked about the way PB did things when Jim played.

It's also based on my long friendship with Rick Forzano, who coached with Paul in Cincinnati.

"My dad had a relationship with PB through Bill Edwards, who was my godfather. Bill and Paul were together at Ohio State, and my father played for Bill at (Western) Reserve and with the Lions in 1941. Our family visited the Browns training camp every summer that I can remember when they trained at Hiram, and then we visited the Bengals when PB took over there in Wilmington for camp. Paul respected my father as a player, and drafted my dad after the war, but already had Marion Motley on his roster.

"There will never be another Paul Brown, who was ahead of his time in organization, personnel evaluation, schemes, and development of players and future coaches. Paul's offense later became well-known as the West Coast offense under Bill Walsh. Walsh took Paul's offense with him from his days as an assistant with the Bengals.

"Paul's tree of coaches, such as Bill Walsh and Don Shula, have left their mark on the NFL, but many of their philosophies and methods came from Paul Brown. Paul Brown's coaching branch extended through Rick Forzano. Rick has been a lifelong friend, and I worked for him with the Detroit Lions. Many of Rick's methods came from Paul and I observed them in Detroit, and later put them into my coaching style: Discipline, preparation, practice schedules, situation football, and projects for assistant coaches."

When Brown died, former Dallas coach Tom Landry told *The Plain Dealer*'s Chuck Heaton that Brown "pretty much shaped my coaching philosophy. No one had more influence on me than he had. He was the first IBM coach. He used the briefcase and the hat. He brought organization into pro football. We thought we had to perfect our defense to the point they perfected their offense."

Hall of Fame coach Don Shula insisted Brown had more influence on him than any other coach.

Older Browns fans know this, but many younger fans really don't understand his full impact—especially since most Browns fans have now been born after 1962, the last season Brown coached in Cleveland. They'll tell you that Marty Schottenheimer or even Rutigliano was the best Browns coach. No disrespect to those men, but they'd be the first to admit they're no Paul Brown.

That's because no one was, nor will anyone ever be like Paul Brown.

Both sets of my grandparents loved telling me stories of the old Browns teams from the 1940s, stories of Otto Graham, Dante Lavelli, and even Paul Brown became a part of these conversations and made me a Browns fan at a very young age. My one grandfather even admitted to running onto the field after the Browns won a championship game and helped tear down the goalpost. When I was old enough to read, I got my hand on every Browns book I could find and enjoyed reading about the history of the team.

From a very early age, I understood how important the team was to not only my family but several other fans as well. My first ever Browns game was at the old Municipal Stadium against the Jets when I was in third grade. It was the game in which Tommy Vardell blew out his knee, but I recall how passionate and excited the fans were walking into the stadium and giving high fives to everyone when the team scored. It was from that point on I knew I was going to be a Browns fan for a long time. It might be a mess watching the team, but I'm willing to wait for a winner like my grandparents saw growing up.

—**Jeff Sabo**

Ohio football fans have been talking about Paul Brown since the 1920s. Think about that. Today, many never saw Paul Brown coach. They never heard his voice. Never saw him on TV, except in some old news clip. But Paul Brown is the Godfather of Ohio football. Most fans, at least those in Northeast Ohio, believe high school football was born in Massillon, which is right near Canton and the Pro Football Hall of Fame. Paul Brown was Massillon's starting quarterback in 1925 and 1926. The school (known as

Washington High) was a combined 15-3 in those seasons. He attended Ohio State and wanted to play football but was considered too small. Some say he weighed 145, others 120. Either way, he was skinny enough so that it seemed a good sneeze could knock him over. He transferred to Miami of Ohio, where he was a second-team Small College All-American.

Remember this, Paul Brown was smart. Real smart. Real smart as in he qualified for a Rhodes Scholarship smart. That was in 1930, during the Great Depression. He didn't have the money to travel to England to continue his studies. So he coached prep football at Severn Academy in Maryland for two years, the only time he ever coached outside of Ohio.

Talk about a local legend.

His next stop was his high school alma mater, where he had an 80-8-2 record at Massillon. The season before he was named coach, the Tigers' record was 2-6-2.

Under Brown:

1932: 5-4-1

1933: 8-2

1934: 9-1

From 1935-40, Massillon won six consecutive state titles. This was before the Ohio high school playoffs, and champions were picked by a vote of the Ohio media conducted by the Associated Press. In 1937, Massillon was 8-1-1. In the other five seasons, they were undefeated.

In 1940, Massillon outscored the opposition 477-6!

Yes, this is the same Massillon High that was 2-6-2 before Brown arrived.

Then they lost a total of only eight games in the next nine years. Only four games in his final eight years. In four seasons, they didn't lose any games!

High school football never had seen anything quite like it, and Brown ruined Massillon for every other coach to follow him at that school.

In 1940, Ohio State was 4-4. Brown was hired and immediately raised the Buckeyes to 6-1-1, ranked No. 12 in the country in 1941.

Here's the breakdown of the rest of his college coaching career:

1942: Brown was 9-1, winning the Big Ten. Depending on the poll, the Buckeyes either won the national championship or shared it with Georgia. The one loss came in a game where the players traveled by train and caught dysentery by drinking water from the fountains. Brown, predictably, felt it was his fault for choosing second-class arrangements.

1944-45: Brown was drafted into the military at the age of 36 and assigned to Great Lakes Naval Station. He was put in charge of one of the regional football teams. Facing other service teams and whatever colleges would play his team, Brown was 15-5-2. One of the five losses was to Ohio State (26-6) in 1944. But his team also defeated Notre Dame, 39-7, in 1945. It was at Great Lakes where Brown met a man named Blanton Collier, and both would change the future of Cleveland professional football.

> My first recollection of a game was the Browns' championship win over the Rams. Family vacations consisted of trips to Hiram College to watch Otto Graham, Dante Lavelli, Lou Groza in training camp. The highlight was shaking Paul Brown's hand.
>
> During the middle '50s we started attending games with my father, sitting in the bleachers for my 50-cent student rate and his $1.50 ticket. It cost 25 cents to park in the Muni lot. We got to games about an hour early to watch the pregame warm-ups, munch sandwiches my mother made and just talk—about a lot of things.
>
> In 1977, my father had a massive heart attack. After the Monday night Browns game, I decided to call him even though he was ill. He answered the late night call and said, "I knew you would call." We had a great chat, and it was the last one, as he died the next day.
> **—Robert D. Giammar**

For so many older Browns fans, Paul Brown is the Browns. That's because he started the franchise.

In January 1945, Brown signed a contract to run the Cleveland

Browns in the new All-American Football Conference. The team was scheduled to start play after World War II ended—perhaps 1946 or 1947, the league wasn't sure. But it was the invention of Arch Ward, the sports editor of the *Chicago Tribune*. Ward loved to come up with new ideas and then promote them. Noticing that July 6 was an off-day for every Major League Baseball team in 1933 and that fell during the World's Fair in Chicago, Ward proposed an exhibition game to raise money for charity.

It's now called the All-Star Game.

In 1934, Ward proposed that the top graduating seniors from college football play an exhibition against the NFL champion. That idea caught on, too, and was played from 1934 to 1976.

In 1935, Ward decided that the *Tribune* (which sponsored a local amateur boxing tournament) should invite other newspapers to have a competition in their cities—then host a competition of each city's champions. We call that idea the Golden Gloves.

After turning down a chance to be commissioner of the new NFL in 1941, Ward thought about starting his own pro football league. In 1944, he met with a bunch of millionaires to form a second league. The idea was to create a first-class football league, then schedule a championship game with the NFL.

The Cleveland franchise was owned by Mickey McBride, a former newspaperman. He also owned cab companies in Cleveland, real estate in Chicago, Cleveland and Florida. Oh, yes, he also owned radio stations, a racing wire (which provided race update from tracks by telegraph to betting parlors) and printing companies. Like a lot of rich men, he wanted to be famous. He'd tried to buy the NFL Rams, but the owners wouldn't sell.

McBride barely knew that the football was fatter and a different shape than a baseball, but he was smart enough to know he needed a great coach. He first approached Frank Leahy, but the Notre Dame coach rejected the offer. His next stop was Paul Brown, who initially had little interest in a new pro league.

Then McBride began to talk money. Big money. Compare this list below to the $10,000 offer (one-year contract) that awaited Brown at Ohio State after the war:

- A 5 percent ownership interest in the team
- A five-year guaranteed contract at $25,000 per year (about $312,500 a year in today's dollars), which would begin when the war ended and Brown left the Navy
- A $1,500-per-month salary to be paid when Brown was in the Navy as he plotted to put together a team for after the war
- According to some accounts, 15 percent of the profits in any season. That didn't seem like a big deal, because the Cleveland Rams of the NFL lost about $20,000 in 1945.
- McBride appealed to Brown's ego and pride. The coach could run the team any way that he wanted. He could make a huge impact on a struggling pro sport in his home state. This was a natural progression, from Massillon (the best high school in the state) to OSU (the best university) to Cleveland, the largest city, a pro city.

Brown signed up.

When I was a kid, my Dad always took me to the Browns' summer camp at Hiram College. After practice, we were hanging around looking for autographs. Up the hill from the practice field emerged two gentlemen, not really athletic in appearance. My Dad said one was Paul Brown. So I rushed up to him with my autograph book, and he graciously signed it. When I turned and offered the book to the other guy, Brown says, "This guy isn't a star. Forget about it." With that I immediately turned and ran back to my Dad, leaving the second guy open-mouthed. Dad identified the non-star as *Plain Dealer* Browns beat writer Chuck Heaton.
 —**Dr. Joe Wasdovich**

In his prime, no one could upstage Paul Brown. Not a future Hall of Fame writer such as Chuck Heaton or a future Hall of Fame quarterback named Otto Graham.

"When Paul Brown started in pro football, the image of players was that of fat bellies, big cigars, foul mouths and hard drinking," said Graham. "Paul would tell us that we were the New York Yankees of pro football. No drinking. No smoking. No swearing. Wear sports coats and ties in public. He really did trade players who were drunks and chased women. He'd tell us, 'One bad apple in a basket of apples will rot all the apples.' He really tried to run the team that way."

Paul Brown scared his players. There's no other way to say it. He seemed to have more power than any coach, more power than any general manager. More power than anyone in the NFL.

When doing interviews for my book *Browns Town 1964*, player after player told me how Brown frightened them.

Defensive back Bernie Parrish seemed fearless on the field with his willingness to challenge coaches, and off it as he battled the NFL front office for the rights of players. But Parrish told me that "the worst thing anyone said to me came from Paul Brown." Over and over, Brown showed a tape of Parrish messing up a play. He didn't say a word for a while, he just replayed the mistake. Then he stopped the tape, stared at Parrish and said, "Don't tell me the great ones do it that way."

Parrish wanted to hide under his chair.

Defensive lineman Paul Wiggin told me: "No one had total respect like Paul Brown. Not Vince Lombardi. Not Tom Landry. None of them. I believe Paul Brown could have been a general in the Army. He could have run IBM or Ford."

He also could terrify them.

In 1946, the day before the championship game, Brown's starting center and team captain Jim Daniell was arrested.

According to Graham, the next day Brown asked Daniell if the story in the paper about his arrest was true.

Daniell said it was.

"Fine," said Brown. "Turn in your suit."

Daniell wanted to explain the situation to Brown, but the coach wouldn't listen.

"You're through," said Brown.

The players were shocked. But Graham said it wasn't until later that they realized Brown had a backup just as talented as Daniell. He was able to deliver a stern message about discipline, yet he didn't hurt the team.

In each week of training camp, Brown would summon six players to his office. They were usually rookies or veterans fighting to keep a roster spot. He'd hand all six an envelope. In three envelopes, there were bus tickets home as the players had been released. The other three were empty, meaning the players could remain at practice. It was pure agony as some players endured that week after week, but Brown believed it built mental toughness and the ability to perform under pressure.

When I was about 15, I was spotting pins at Marceline Bowling Alley. It was connected to a poolroom and bar on East 71st and Polonia Avenues. Frank (a Browns player, not his real name) lived over on Indiana Avenue, about five minutes away from Marceline. This was an old Polish neighborhood, and he felt right at home. He always had time to say hello and talk to us kids. He also liked Budweiser. Everyone bought him so many beers that he used to keep the extra cases in his own little corner. It was called Frank's Buds because he had so many beers that he couldn't drink them all.

He was a monster of a man with about 50-inch shoulders and about a 32-inch waist and everyone loved him. When it came to 9:45 p.m. or so, he would say goodbye to everyone and leave. He had such a high respect for Paul Brown, and the coach said everyone had to be in bed by 10. He would walk home and be in bed by 10.

He also brought a lot of the Browns to Marceline. They would shoot pool and have a few beers with Frank. It was great to talk to the likes of Forrest "Chubby" Gregg, Dante Lavelli, Max Speedy and many others. I never missed a home game from the first one played in 1946, before Frank joined the team, until I went into the service in 1958. We would walk downtown and back. We were young and didn't have a car, because that way we could have extra money for hot chocolate while we sat in the

bleachers. When the weather was bad, we would take the street cars and skip the hot chocolates.
—**Kenn Politowicz**

Yes, Paul Brown really did invent so much of what we take for granted as part of the pro game.

Start with the playbook.

Brown held team meetings where he'd scrawl X's and O's on the blackboard, and he expected the players to copy them down into their individual loose-leaf notebooks. Brown knew that if players wrote the plays down themselves, they were more likely to learn them than if the coach just handed the players the playbook. That was especially true since Brown collected the notebooks and graded them. He made notes, forcing players to rewrite them if the plays were recorded incorrectly, or if they were just too sloppy. He gave tests on the plays to make sure players had learned them. Some players cheated, but that didn't bother Brown very much. He figured if they went through all the effort to have sneaky cheat sheets, they still were learning the plays.

Brown had a degree in education from Miami and a master's in education from Ohio State in 1940. Brown once said: "A coach is a teacher, no matter what. The players must learn. No matter what you teach, you must get people to want to learn. People think there are great mysteries attached to the game, but there are not. It comes down to fundamentals, and they must be taught. If we tell (our players) 'why'—and I've always insisted on telling my players why . . . why we do everything we do, whether it's on or off the field . . . they are more apt to accept it and get in the spirit."

Dick Modzelewski claims that, when he was traded to the Browns in 1964, he received a playbook, that, even though he'd been with three different teams, it was the first playbook he'd ever had.

Paul Brown had been using a playbook since the 1930s. Brown wrote down his plays for two reasons. One was to help the players learn his system. Like the other great coach of his era (Lombardi), he had been a teacher, and he brought those principles to the

NFL. The other reason was so he could give copies to the football coaches at Massillon's junior high schools. That way, they could run the same plays he employed and use the same terminology. When the kids moved up from junior high to high school to play for Brown, they already would know his system.

This is what happens when you take a Rhodes Scholar—who also had considered going to law school—and put him in pro sports. Brown also worked harder than most coaches, who took vacations when the season ended. Brown rarely did. And he constantly looked for an edge. Brown also studied nutrition.

His pregame meals were the following:

A steak, no catsup.

A salad, no dressing.

A baked potato, no butter or sour cream.

"That stuff was so dry, it could choke you," Graham said.

But Brown believed it would not clog your arteries. It would not make you sleepy.

Brown's playbooks contained a dress code: clean T-shirts (not bare-chested) during practice, shirts and ties during trips. He spelled out the itinerary in minute-by-minute detail. Brown insisted his players leave the dugout in a group, not in a stream. He believed that the more a team acted as one unit, the better it would function.

Brown is credited with inventing the draw play, but it was sort of an accident. During an AAFC game, Otto Graham went back to pass. He tripped and fell. With the defense closing in, he handed the ball off to Marion Motley, who bolted past the defense for a long gain. Brown decided he liked the misdirection and began using it by design.

Desperation led to the development of the face bar on the helmet. In a 1953 game against the 49ers, Graham was whacked in the face on the last play of the first half, tearing open his lip and mouth. He needed stitches. In order to keep his star in the game, Brown had equipment manager Leo Murphy fashion a plastic face bar during halftime. A lot of people had done the same, and for the same reason. But after the season, Brown worked with an engineer from Riddell (the helmet manufacturer) to perfect the design. First he patented it, then ordered all his players to use it. Then he licensed his invention to Riddell and became a millionaire from the income.

At Ohio State, he put one of his assistants in the press box, figuring that the guy would have a better view of the opposing offense and defense. He installed a telephone in the press box and one by the bench, so the coach could give him reports on the game. This was the predecessor of the headphones everyone uses from high school on up during games.

Brown also began calling plays in the 1950s, sending them in by having one guard replace another on each play, carrying the call from the coaches to the huddle. In 1956, he decided to try something new. In order to get the plays in faster, he put a radio transmitter on the bench and a receiver in his quarterback's helmet. There was too much interference in the stadium, and it was scrapped. But it's how teams do it now.

He filmed his practice sessions and his games, so he could study them. He hired people to scout opponents' games, assigning them to write reports on their formations and plays. This had been done informally for decades, but Brown hired people and used a form. He approached the draft systematically, dividing the country into territories and assigning scouts to each region. For most teams, a coach would have buddies—other coaches, newspapermen, drinking buddies—who would tell him about players.

Another one of Brown's brainstorms is the 40-yard dash. People say Brown did it to figure out whom to draft. They're wrong. According to Dante Lavelli, Brown started doing it at Ohio State, where Lavelli was a receiver. He was trying to find the best players for his kick coverage team and figured the people who could run that distance the fastest were the right choices. He also thought the average punt was about 40 yards, so he made them run a 40-yard dash. It is a measure of the respect that the rest of the NFL had for Brown that times in the 40-yard dash became a standard for evaluating speed.

In 1945, Brown and others entering the new AAFC agreed to use white players only. The NFL had been doing it since 1933. But Brown changed his mind. It was 1946 when the Browns began to play, and Jackie Robinson had just been signed to play in the minors for the Brooklyn Dodgers. The NFL's Los Angeles Rams had signed two black players—Kermit Washington and Woody Strode. Brown decided to sign one of his players from Ohio State (Bill Willis) and one of the Canton McKinley players (Marion Motley). He brought in other minority players and treated them like everyone else—with lots of discipline, little patience and seldom a kind word.

One player who could convince Brown to bend a bit was Graham.

"He and Paul Brown would really butt heads," said Hal Lebovitz, who covered both for the *Cleveland News*. "But after Otto became a coach himself, then he turned into Paul Brown's biggest fan."

Graham said his teams won five consecutive titles with him calling the plays, then Brown decided he'd take over the offense.

"I didn't like it," Graham said. "But he was Paul Brown, so I did it."

Not always.

"They had a big game with Detroit," Lebovitz said. "The night before, several key players met with Otto at the old Pick Carter Hotel in Cleveland. They told him that he had to call the plays. Otto did, and they won."

Graham discovered something that day.

"If I changed the play and it worked, I didn't hear anything," he said. "'If it didn't, I never heard the end of it."

I was probably as shocked and disheartened as everyone else when the Modell family announced the move to Baltimore, but my father was not surprised. I was only four when Art fired Paul Brown, so I have no real memory of that. But to Dad, it was like his heart got cut out. Until his dying day in 2008, he NEVER forgave Modell for that. . . . He never really enjoyed the

Browns of the early- and mid-'80s either because Modell was actually successful. I'm sure that he felt that the Modell family orchestrated the destruction of the Browns beginning in 1963, and that day in 1994 was just the finale.
—**Mary Wolfe**

Why did Brown not win a title after 1955? He made the playoffs only twice more with the Browns (1957 and 1958). Brown was not a brilliant game-day coach. His keys to victory were practice, preparation and finding the right players. He also had tremendous assistants. Perhaps his greatest gift was an eye for talent, be it for players or coaches. After 1953, he lost two top assistants. Blanton Collier was offensive coordinator, and what we might call "assistant head coach." He left to become head coach at Kentucky after Bear Bryant. Weeb Ewbank was the defensive coordinator and had major input during the college draft. He left to be head coach of the Baltimore Colts. So many coaches trained by Brown (or disciples of Brown) were taking jobs elsewhere—and taking his system with them. Brown was losing his edge because his gospel (and football secrets) were being spread by his former coaches and players.

Consider that Hall of Fame coach Bill Walsh (three Super Bowl titles with the San Francisco 49ers) and two other great coaches—Ewbank (one Super Bowl win with the New York Jets) and Collier—were Brown disciples. Three Hall of Fame coaches played for Brown—Chuck Noll (four Super Bowl titles with the Steelers), Don Shula (two Super Bowl titles with the Miami Dolphins) and Bud Grant (one NFL title and three NFC titles with the Minnesota Vikings). Lou Saban played for him in Cleveland and won AFL championships in 1964 and 1965 as coach of the Buffalo Bills. Vince Lombardi never played for Brown or coached under him, but the two men were good friends. Brown recommended him for the job in Green Bay, calling him "the most qualified assistant currently in the NFL." After Lombardi was hired, Brown would offer to trade him players he couldn't use, sending future Hall of Famers Henry Jordan and Willie Davis to Green Bay. Bill

Belichick, who had won three Super Bowls as coach of the New England Patriots going into the 2010 season, has no direct connection to Brown, but his dad Steve was a close friend

Brown's last season in Cleveland was 1962, and the team had a 7-6-1 record. Brown's last championship was 1955. His last playoff appearance was 1958. He was not quite the power on or off the field, especially after Art Modell bought the team. But players also said Brown had lost an edge, and that may simply have come from being in the same place for 17 seasons. But when he left, many fans knew the Browns would never have a coach like him again.

History proves that to be correct.

The Browns Are Family

I was raised in a typical, suburban, white-bread, seven-kid Catholic family. Other than our religious traditions, we had no family traditions to speak of except for the Browns. You were not a part of our family until Dad took you to a Browns game (usually around second grade). You went to a game with a couple of his customers from his tool and die business. The scents of cigar smoke, beer and the spirits in the coffee thermos were just as memorable as seeing our heroes on the field. You knew it was a big customer if you had the Bond Court brunch before the game.

My mother and father were the oldest in their big families. The first place my oldest brother drove was to a Browns game. My widowed maternal grandmother called my brother, making him wear bread bags on his feet to pick her up for the game. They sat in the bleachers in December. Everyone in our family thought this was very normal.

Every Sunday, my widowed paternal grandmother had us all over for Sunday dinner, and the Browns game was required watching until the roast was ready right at 4:15 after the game. My father has owned Browns tickets for over 50 years. His father was an usher at Municipal Stadium for Browns and Indians from the day it opened to his death in 1963—the year I was born.

The five boys have all had season tickets over the years. When we were old enough, all of us Armstrong boys tailgated in the Muni lot every game . . . I asked my wife to marry me while at a Browns-Steelers game. She is a Steelers fan. Browns lose; no ring. Love is a funny thing. My son's first game was a heartbreaking loss to the Colts when Tim Couch threw an interception in the end zone to prevent a last-second win. He looked at me and cried.

—*David A. Armstrong*

I'm a retired Army officer with 24 years of service. I moved to Cleveland in 2000 when I was assigned to be the Administrative Officer for the Cleveland U.S. Army Recruiting Battalion. I grew up in Minnesota, a Vikings fan from childhood. I grew up with a passion for the Purple People Eaters . . . for Bill Brown, Dave Osborne and Jim Marshall wearing short sleeves in minus-20-degree weather, with no heaters on the sidelines at the old Met Stadium. I started losing that passion when the Vikings moved indoors to the Metrodome.

When I came to Cleveland, my office overlooked Browns Stadium from the 12th floor of the A.J. Celebrezze Federal Building. I noticed the passion this city had for their "brand new" Browns. Then, I met my future wife, Tracy. Her father, Bill Preston, had grown up in Cleveland, a product of the east side of town. He was a lifelong Browns backer going back to his childhood in the 1940s.

Her memories of Sundays with her father consisted of him throwing objects at the television, drinking a little too much beer and being red-faced most of the afternoon over the ups and downs (mostly downs in the 1970s) of his beloved Browns. Her dad died in 1992, but her description of him made him seem to be someone I'd have really liked to know. Passion for football was always in my veins. I had it as a child in Minnesota, then lost it for about 17 years. It came back here in Cleveland. My wife and I now have seven kids—four from our previous marriages, and three little boys we've had since we were married. It's too late for the older ones, but the little guys are Browns fans to the bone. Like Tracy's dad, my kids will remember me as the guy who, through thick or thin, *loves* the Cleveland Browns. I love their history, the loyalty of their fans and the fact that loving the Cleveland Browns is like being a member of a special club.

—John Hansen, Major (Ret.) U.S. Army

For my brother, Dave, and I growing up in Mentor, the Browns always meant Sunday afternoon at home with our dad. He grew up in Pennsylvania but was always a Browns fan. Mom tells us that he was yelling, "Run, Leroy, run!" for Leroy Kelly, long before we started cheering for Leroy Hoard the same way. When the move to Baltimore was announced, we agreed with the local sentiment that losing the Browns would be like losing a loved one. That lasted for just one week. On November 16, 1995, we lost our Dad, Dean Lenz, to congestive heart failure.

The two events were completely intertwined for us. Dave (in the ninth grade) was at a friend's house working on a school newspaper article about the Browns' move when he found out that Dad was in the hospital. The last conversation I remember having with Dad was about the Browns losing to Pittsburgh on Monday night and his promise to be home to watch the game Sunday against the Packers with us. It was a promise he was unable to keep.

Although the loss of the Browns paled in comparison to losing Dad, we were able to get some solace in the team's return. Mom, Dave and I still love watching the Browns. The Orange and Brown will still be part of what binds our family together.

—Richard Lenz

My first grandchild was born in 1995. I got him a No. 19 (Bernie Kosar) jersey and a football. We gave them to him while he was in the hospital. My daughter just rolled her eyes at me. Seth passed away three months later. We buried him in his Browns jersey. He never got the chance to develop the passion I have for the Browns—to live and die a little bit every Sunday throughout the fall with every score and every near miss.

—Keith Crabtree

I grew up in Elyria. Every Sunday during the season was the Cleveland Browns' day. My dad, Big Al, and I watched every game, even picking up the ones that were not televised on a Toledo station. The Monday morning *Plain Dealer* sports page was either the plague or the party favor—depending on the previous day's outcome. I was 10 when the Browns won the 1964 world championship. My first game in Cleveland Stadium was with my dad. I saw the greenest grass ever, and the events of the day will live as ones I will never forget, they were all with my dad.

I lost my dad when my son was 4 years old. But the Browns family bond was transferred to my son, Adam. He is grown now and lives in Washington, D.C. But every Sunday evening after the Browns game, we call each other and discuss the play by play. I know Big Al would love to have the last word in these reviews.

—*Ted Copeland*

In August 2008, my wife and I had a Cleveland Browns-themed wedding. We designed our own wedding invitations to look like a Browns ticket to enter the reception. We went as far as putting a seat number and having them sit in the Dawg Pound section. We found a Browns cake topper on eBay with the groom wearing a Browns helmet, kissing the bride with a goal post in the background. All the ushers and I wore tan suits with white shirts and chocolate brown ties. Also, we all had an orange lily pinned on our lapels. The bridesmaids all wore chocolate brown dresses as well. We decided to give everyone in the wedding party personalized Cleveland Browns jerseys. The guys were given the white road jerseys, the women were given the brown home jerseys.

At the reception, when it came time for us to be introduced for the first time as Mr. and Mrs. Ryan Burich, we picked the old Cleveland Browns marching band song, *High! O-H-I-O For Cleveland*, as the song to walk out to. We also had our Browns jerseys on as we were walking to the head table. To cap it off, as we were planning our honeymoon, we made sure to fly back home on Saturday and not miss the 2008 season opener against the Dallas Cowboys. After watching that game, maybe we should have stayed on our honeymoon for a couple of more days.

—Ryan Burich

Growing up in Parma in the 1980s, the thing I remember most is watching Browns games with my father and two younger brothers. On Sundays, my mother would leave around noon to visit my grandmother in Slavic Village. We would immediately move all the furniture to the sides of the family room. We removed all the cushions and placed them in a pile along the back wall (the end zone). We were told by my mother numerous times not to play football in the house, but we did so with my father's approval.

Dad would sit on the couch as "quarterback" as one of us would wait to hear "hike," receive a handoff or go out for a "pass" into the family room where the other two brothers (or sometimes Dad) would attempt to tackle him before diving on the cushions for a touchdown. We never kept score and almost never got caught. We broke a few lamp shades, and whether the Browns won or lost, it was always a great day for family room football.

—Jon D. Zapisek

It was Christmas Eve 1988, and the Browns were hosting a playoff game versus the Houston Oilers. I was a 15-year-old high school sophomore at the time and went to the game with my cousins (one of whom lived in New York and was home for Christmas) and uncle and dad. It was a good game, but the Browns lost. The best part of dealing with the loss was going to my uncle's house and spending Christmas Eve commiserating about the game over my grandma's wedding soup and other Italian Christmas favorites. This would be her last Christmas.

—A.J. Hite

Growing up in a divorced family since the age of 3, I can recall the many Browns games my brother and I would go to with our dad. It was extra special because we spent limited time with

our dad. We imagined we were Browns players while throwing
the Nerf ball in the front yard. We talked about the team over
dinners. We went to old Municipal Stadium to watch our beloved
team. It was something common we had during an awkward time
with our dad. One of the memories I will always have is helping
carry my brother to the car (age 7 at the time). It was so cold in
the stadium that the sole of his Zips tennis shoe froze to the floor
under his seat! He got up to try to leave—and his shoe ripped!

—*Matt Edwards*

The Cleveland Browns have made me realize that my best
friend in the world is my father. Through great times, trying
times, sad times and happy times—nothing has ever changed
with regard to my father and my love for the Cleveland Browns.
Sundays in my childhood were always special days as my father
and I would always devote the entire day to the Browns. The
neighbors would come over, and we would dress up in Dawg gear
and all have a great time watching the game. There would always
be a big bowl of dog biscuits in the room (especially during
the playoffs). The boys and their fathers would go out during
halftime and play Browns vs. Broncos in the backyard.

When I left for Bowling Green State University in the 1990s,
the Browns were always something that kept the bond between
me and my father strong. Kids tend to distance themselves from
their parents at this age, but the Browns kept my dad and me
close. Every Sunday, my dad and I would be on the phone during
the game, screaming and yelling at the TV just like we did at
home.

As an adult, I have lived in eight cities over the past 12 years.
Despite the geographical barrier, Sundays never changed for
my father and me. I would be at the local Browns Backers bar
and on the phone with my dad throughout the game. When
text messaging became popular, my mother said she would get
annoyed because my father's phone never stopped beeping as we
texted each other throughout every game.

—*Andrew Branham*

My mother and father's first date was at a Browns game in 1967. It was my mother who had the tickets. I was not there, obviously, but I guess it went pretty well as I did show up on the scene in October 1969. My family left Cleveland in 1973, but the Browns never left our hearts. We settled in Clarksville, Tenn. For years before the advent of cable television and the Internet, my father and I would leave church early on Sundays to rush home and see if the Browns game would be aired in our television market—only to be disappointed a vast majority of the time.

As I got older and my relationship with father became strained, we would always find a way to call a truce long enough to watch a game. Since his death in 1986, my mother and I continued to pour our hearts into our fanatical support of the Browns. While I was in boot camp, she would send newspaper clippings so I could keep up to date. Turns out I was able to curry favor with my company commander, who was a native of Findlay!

My mother has also passed away but not before saying to me in her last moments, "We're still going to the Super Bowl, son. It's only a matter of faith and time." I just hope it is within the time I have left. If not, I have passed on to my daughter the same fanatical devotion my parents were kind enough to entrust in me.

—*Jeff Sherman*

As my dad's health and hearing were failing toward the end, we would spend Sundays watching the Browns. He would yell at the television—not being able to tell how loud his protestations actually sounded to our much younger ears. His frustration with a Marty-ball move exploded one Sunday, and red-faced, he looked at me and said, "You want to make money, Jim? Take a hundred bucks every week and bet it against the Browns." He died in December 1985. And had I listened to his advice, I would be $6,000 richer. Dad was right. He always was.

—*James Sasak*

Living in a small community of Ottoville, Ohio, we were very loyal Browns fans. My dad, my brother and I would watch the

Browns games and then go out at halftime and play one-on-one football, with my dad being quarterback. I'm 38 now, and my father passed away 15 years ago. Those memories are so very vivid in my mind, and I wish I could tell my dad how much I really enjoyed those halftime games.

—*Kirt Martz*

My father now resides at St. Augustine Manor; a series of strokes has left him unable himself to share these thoughts himself. As a child of the 1970s, I had a difficult relationship with my father. One thing we could agree upon was our love of the Cleveland Browns. My dad was a season-ticket holder for many years; he lived and died with the Cleveland Browns.... We had a weekly ritual come fall: My dad and I got together to watch Browns football. This continued until they moved to Baltimore and left a huge hole in our lives.

The first year without a training camp, Hiram College hosted "The Boys are Back in Town." All the old Browns were back. My favorite memory was walking out of a campus building as my dad was sharing his memory of the first "Monday Night Football" game at Municipal Stadium. He looked up and saw former Browns linebacker Billy Andrews, the star of the night. My dad walked up to Mr. Andrews, shook his hand, and introduced me to him, "Son, this is the man who intercepted a pass from Joe Namath, and won that game." Caught in the moment, Billy Andrews was quiet, but I could see he enjoyed the moment almost as much as catching that ball.

—*Tom Donovan*

The first year the Browns returned, I surprised my father (a lifelong Browns fan from New Jersey) for Father's Day with a trip to Cleveland to see the Browns play in their new stadium. I figured I owed it to him since he had taken the whole family out to Cleveland for the very last game in the old stadium.

It was a very cold December Sunday, snow was blowing all around, the wind was howling, the wind chill was about minus 11.

The Browns lost to Tennessee. By the end of the game, hardly anyone was left in the stands. I think the third-string QB was on the field. But none of that mattered. I was with my father, and we had a great time together. I lost my dad to cancer four years ago, but a picture of the two of us taken that day in the stadium still sits on my desk—along with his replica of the old stadium.

—*Beth Rosenberg Sanders*

The only time I remember hugging my father was the moment when the Browns finally beat the Broncos with a last-second field goal in 1989. I can still remember seeing the ball barely make it over the crossbar. Being so happy that without even thinking, my father and I embraced. I was 11 years old, and it hasn't happened since.

—*Bill Pillar*

Growing up, Sunday Browns football was my religion—not Judaism. My father and mother both grew up on Browns football, going to the games at old Cleveland Stadium with their fathers. My dad's father was a season-ticket holder in 1946. He had two seats in Section 37. Over the years, the family had grown. Two tickets became four . . . and four became eight . . . and eight became 14.

By the time I was in the picture, we had 14 tickets. Our routine was the same every game. Uncle Kenny would pick everyone up at our house and pile us into his Suburban. Dad was always the driver downtown. Usually 10 people in the car—a mix of parents, cousins, aunts, uncles and friends. We would leave promptly at 11:30 a.m. for a 1 p.m. kickoff.

My mom was in charge of bringing the deli sandwiches from Davis Bakery. Uncle K always had the corned beef on rye with Russian. Dad bought the programs from our same program guy, and (the guy) always asked for a sandwich. Uncle Kenny bought the pregame hot dogs.

In close games, Dad, always the most unselfish guy, would go down to the car before the game ended. He would drive it up

to the top of the hill in the parking lot adjacent to the stadium
and have a cop sit in it to stay warm while he ran back into the
stadium to watch the finish. When the game was over, we all
sprinted to the car, our feet numb from the cold, and jumped into
the Suburban. Dad would take over there. Nobody was a better
aggressive driver out of the madness of traffic after Browns
games than him.

—*Todd Dery*

I fell in love with the Browns not because of the team itself,
but because it was something I could share with my father
and my grandfather. My dad is in many ways my best friend.
Cleveland sports—especially the Browns—have always been our
strongest common interest. Some fathers and sons work on cars
or go fishing together. We watch, read about and wring our hands
over the Browns. Through the years, watching the Browns has
been fun and has introduced me to many good friends, but most
of all, it's strengthened my bond with my father. My grandfather
is gone now, but one of his legacies is that a mutual love of
Browns football has kept me and my dad as close as the two of
them were. Watching your team win is great, but sharing the ride
with the people who you care about is what's really important.

—*Nicholas Allburn*

The Browns have been my team for the better part of 24 years.
But they also played a part in finding my soul mate.

On December 29, 2006, I went into Mandy Bartlett's
checkout line at the Wal-Mart in Ashland, Ohio. We struck up a
conversation because she had read my popular Browns columns
in the *Ashland Times-Gazette* for many years. A friendship
grew from that conversation. Then, eventually, we went out, got
engaged and got married on July 12, 2008. Mandy Sloan is as
big a Browns fan as I am, which makes Sundays in the fall very
interesting—and loud. But we are there every Sunday rooting
them on, dissecting each move made during the game, during
the week and in the off-season. And we will be there, together,

as rabid Browns fans until we both take our last breath here on Earth. God brought us together. But so did the Cleveland Browns.

—Dusty Sloan

My favorite Browns Stadium memory has yet to happen. My favorite memory will be the day I take my sons to their first game. Seeing the looks on their faces will stay with me forever. If their excitement is anything like mine was at my first game, it'll be hard to forget. That day will not only be my favorite Browns Stadium memory, but also one of my favorites as a dad.

—John A. Hykes

CHAPTER 7

Red Right 88 was the right call.

Before starting to explain a sports blasphemy that Red Right 88 was actually a good call, let's begin with another misconception—Oakland beating the Browns in that AFC division playoff game was not a huge upset, as some Browns fans believe.

When the two teams met at Cleveland Stadium on January 4, 1981, they both had a record of 11-5. Yes, the Raiders were the wild-card team, but they had the same 11-5 record as the AFC West champion San Diego Chargers. The conference title went to the Chargers on the *fifth* tiebreaker.

You can look at some other numbers to measure the two teams.

- Oakland had scored more points and also allowed fewer than the Browns. It was small: Oakland outscored Cleveland 364-357 and allowed 306 points to Cleveland's 310.

- Oakland had a better record against common opponents. In 1980, both teams had played nine games against six common opponents—Cincinnati, Denver, Houston, Kansas City, Pittsburgh, and Seattle. Oakland's record against them was 8-1, Cleveland 6-3.

- Oakland was 9-7 in 1979. After that season, it traded Kenny Stabler to Houston for Dan Pastorini. After five games, the Raiders were 2-3. They'd scored 99 points and had allowed 120—primarily because they committed 20 turnovers. Pastorini (61.4 rating, five TDs and eight INTs) looked terrible. In that fifth game, Pastorini broke his leg. The Raiders turned to Jim Plunkett, who'd been acquired in a trade several years earlier, but hadn't played at all in 1978 and had only thrown 15 passes in 1979.

- Oakland was 9-2 in the 11 games started by Plunkett. They scored 265 points and allowed 190. After making 20 turnovers in the first five games, they committed only 24 in the final 11 games. Suddenly, Oakland had become a powerful team under Plunkett, more dangerous than the overall 11-5 record would indicate.

- The 1980 Browns were winning close games in amazing ways. Week after week, they seemed to be juggling gasoline-lit torches, while Oakland was winning decisively. The Browns were 9-3 in games decided by seven or fewer points. Think about that, 12 of 16 games were decided by a touchdown or less. Oakland was 5-3 in those games. The Browns were 2-2 in games decided by at least eight points, Oakland was 6-0. Those six victories came in the last 11 games with Plunkett at quarterback.

- The Browns were an awful cold-weather team. From Cleveland's perspective, it would have been better to play in Oakland. The Browns were only 5-3 at home that season, 6-2 on the road. The 1980 Browns weren't the type of team that could play very well in cold weather as they finished 26th (out of 28 teams) in rushing yardage and 22nd in yards per carry. Of their 1,035 offensive plays, 436 were runs and 599 were passes. They won with Brian Sipe throwing the ball.

- The 1980 Raiders were 10th in rushing yards and rushing average. They had run the ball on 541 of their 1,044 offensive plays (51.8 percent). They were much better suited for a game played in icy weather and wild winds.

- The 1980 Browns had trouble with the kicking game. They ranked 16th in field-goal percentage and 22nd in extra-point percentage. One of the problems might have been the change in holders. The Browns always had used the backup quarterback as the holder. In 1980, it was rookie Paul McDonald. He grew up in Southern California and played at USC. The cold weather had to be a shock to him. Kicker Don Cockroft was having several physical problems, including two herniated disks. He later said he probably should have spent part of the season on the injured reserved list.

- Cockroft led the league in field-goal percentage in 1968, 1972 and 1974. He made all of his extra points in 1969, 1971 and 1973. He was one of the last of the "straight-ahead" kickers. They stood straight behind the ball and kicked it with the toe of the foot, rather than soccer-style, where you stand to the side and kick with the side of the foot. Cockroft was also the second-to-last "double-duty" kicker, as he also punted. In 1980, he was 16-of-26 on field goals, the 61.5 percent being the second-worst of his career. That season, he missed two field goals in the 19-16 loss to Denver and three field goals in the 16-13 loss to Pittsburgh at Three Rivers Stadium. He clearly was fading.

I was an 11-year old at the old Municipal Stadium on January 4, 1981. . . . Need I say more? It was a brutally cold day on the lakefront. My father and I were unfortunate enough to have seats behind one of the steel columns that held up the overhang above the worst seats. We still managed to have a perfect view of the Stadium's western end zone as Red Right 88 unfolded. I also remember clearly that was the day I first tasted whiskey. As we left the stadium, my father gave me a nip, presumably because I was freezing. But I'm fairly certain now that he simply couldn't justify anesthetizing himself, while letting me suffer through the ache of that particular disappointment.
—**Kevin C. Robison**

If I were ever to ante up the money for a jersey, it could only have the number 88 on it. The name over it would be RED RIGHT. I would wear that jersey. It symbolizes the most poignant football moment I've experienced. It sears in all the hope and pain all Browns fans feel in one play. . . . I would retire it with a Super Bowl appearance, if not a win.
—**Dan Orszag**

Fans will find this hard to believe, but Red Right 88 was the right call. The field goal was not a given, even before you consider the weather.

"We played the game a certain way that season," recalled then-Browns coach Sam Rutigliano. "We were bold. We knew we had to adjust the game plan to an extent because of the weather, but we had to be true to ourselves."

Game time temperature was 4 degrees above zero. Wind chill was *minus* 36 degrees. According to research by the Weather Channel, it was the coldest game played since the famous Ice Bowl in Green Bay on December 31, 1967. Cold, windy and a kicker with a bad back and a shaky season behind him.

Here was the situation:

1. Oakland had a 14-12 lead with 41 seconds left.

2. The Browns had the ball on Oakland's 13-yard line, second-and-9.

3. They were driving into the open end of the stadium, and they had one timeout remaining.

4. It would seem they should run the ball once or twice to chew up the clock, then kick a field goal. But there were problems. Oakland's Ted Hendricks had blocked the extra point on Cleveland's only touchdown, a 42-yard interception return by Ron Bolton. Paul McDonald said he struggled to handle the snap because the ball was like ice.

5. A field-goal attempt from 36 yards fell apart due to a bad snap. McDonald tried to run the ball and was tackled for an 11-yard loss. Cockroft also was short on a 47-yard field-goal try in the second quarter. He later was wide on a 30-yard attempt. So three previous field-goal attempts produced two misses and a bad snap.

6. Cockroft's supporters like to point out that he had kicked two field goals that day. But both came in the third quarter. He was booting into the closed end of the stadium where the wind was not as severe as at the open end. Kicking into the open end, he'd missed two field-goal tries and an extra point.

7. There was no reason to attempt a field goal until it was absolutely the final option. There was tremendous risk involved, far more than most fans remember.

8. Why not run the ball? Because they hadn't run the ball effec-

tively that day. In 27 carries, the Browns had gained 85 yards—3.1 yards per carry. Nearly half (42) of the 85 yards gained came on three plays—an 18-yard run by Calvin Hill, a 14-yard run by Mike Pruitt and a 10-yard scramble by Sipe. The other 24 carries gained a total of 43 yards. They really needed to get into the end zone.

9. Passing also was a problem. Sipe was 13-of-39 for 183 yards, with no touchdowns and two interceptions. He had been sacked twice and fumbled four times. The cold weather was also icing his game. But Sipe was the MVP. He made big play after big play. He was why the Browns were in this game.

10. Reggie Rucker dropped a pass in the end zone. He also caught another one in the end zone but couldn't get both feet in bounds. The field was like ice. All the receivers had trouble staying on their feet, remaining inbounds. So some of Sipe's poor stats throwing were due to the receivers battling the conditions. In the second half, Sipe was throwing a little better: 9-of-21 for 145 yards after being 4-of-18 for 38 yards in the first half.

After the Browns defeated the Bengals in the last regular-season game, the Browns announced tickets for the first playoff game would go on sale that Tuesday. At the time, I had a *Plain Dealer* route. After finishing my route, I decided I was going to cut school in order to get in line for tickets. I got down to the stadium at 6 a.m. (for an 9 a.m. sale start) and stood in line freezing in 20 degree temperatures for the three hours—knowing it would be warmer at the 12:30 p.m. start time, two weeks away.

The morning of the game, I finished my *PD* route and went over to my friend's house and helped him and his brother with their route. As we headed down to the stadium on the Rapid, everyone was in a jovial mood. Even with the minus-30-degree wind chill, nothing was going to stand in our way of going to the Siper Bowl!

At the stadium, there were no lines at the concession stands, but you couldn't get near the restrooms (the only place with any heat). The game itself was the usual Kardiac Kids game

played that season, and a victory was set in stone. But after
the interception by Mike Davis—78,000 people were suddenly
numb. The cold finally could be felt. The walk up the West 3rd
street bridge was a funeral procession. Nobody said a word.
The ride home on the Rapid was a funeral compared to the sure
elation five hours earlier. Realization had set in, and another
mid-winter Monday morning was just a few hours away.

   —Ken Vine

How did this happen to the Browns?

"One of the key decisions in that game was Oakland not taking
the ball (after winning the coin toss), but wanting to drive to the
closed end of the stadium in the second and fourth quarters," said
Rutigliano. "When we got the ball for that last drive, Brian and I
talked about that we had to do—pass, pass, throw the ball. We're
on our own 14-yard line."

With 2:22 left, Sipe drove the Browns downfield. He brought
them to the 13 with 56 seconds remaining.

"We ran Mike Pruitt for a yard on first down," recalled Rutigliano. "My plan was to throw on second down, then run on third
down. If none of that got us into the end zone, we'd kick a field
goal."

But Rutigliano was thinking of something else, of a couple of
field-goal attempts in the previous game from about the same
spot where Cockroft would have to kick.

"It was like the wind just blew them 10-15 yards to the side," he
said. "It was so tough to kick into the open end of the stadium with
the wind like that. At that point, I felt better about Brian throwing
than us kicking."

In Russell Schneider's *Plain Dealer* story the day after the
game, he wrote: "The play was called on the sideline during a
timeout by Rutigliano and quarterback coach Jim Shofner. Sipe
said he 'questioned' the selection of the play initially, but then
agreed with the strategy. 'I thought we would run the ball,' Sipe
said. 'Running the ball seemed to be the logical thing to do, but
the staff was adamant. I listened to them because they are smart,

they know what they are doing, and also, that play has worked often for us.'"

Thirty years later, Rutigliano talked about how Ozzie Newsome and Reggie Rucker would be running post patterns to the right of Sipe. How fullback Mike Pruitt would be available for a short pass. How all of this was designed for Dave Logan to end up open and covered by a safety on a cross pattern.

"He actually was open on the play," recalled Rutigliano. "But Brian saw Ozzie, and threw it to him first. I never blamed Brian; he made great decisions all season. You had to trust him."

Newsome was covered by safety Mike Davis. The pass was soft, a little behind Newsome. Davis picked it off.

After the game, Newsome told reporters: "I was behind Davis, and then Burgess Owens (the free safety) came back to me and forced me to take a couple of steps upfield. When I saw the ball coming, and felt Davis against my arm, I knew I was in trouble. I tried to knock the ball away from him, but I couldn't reach it. . . . It was a good call. A great call. Give Davis and Owens credit for beating it. We lived and died with the pass all year, and this time we died by it."

I was the founder and president for the first 15 years of the Southern California Browns Backers. . . . We had many banquets over the years. . . . At one, Brian Sipe related a story of how he and Sam studied Oakland films from every game, and how Mike Davis always broke to the right every time the tight end came across the middle . . . so he knew Ozzie would be open. But for the first time all year, Davis dropped back and stepped in front of Ozzie.

—Jeff Wagner

Don Cockroft had made two field goals, but missed two field goals. Brian Sipe had thrown two interceptions. . . . We'll never know if Don could have made that kick.

—Sue Wiedemer

Could Cockroft have indeed made the kick?

In his *Plain Dealer* game story, Schneider wrote: "Cockroft has been suffering with a left knee and sciatic nerve injuries since the fourth week of the season . . . He was disappointed that he didn't get one last opportunity to win the game, though he didn't complain about the strategy. 'Sam wanted to get it closer . . . you can't be critical of the call,' said Cockroft. 'I'd rather have had the opportunity to kick and fail than not to have had it at all, but I think what Sam said was very logical.'"

Sipe knew that he was supposed to—in Rutigliano's words—"Throw the ball into Lake Erie if no one's open." He later admitted he was more concerned about being sacked—losing yardage, making the field goal even harder—than throwing an interception.

"Sam took the entire blame for the call, but I threw the ball," Sipe has often said.

As he watched the play, Rutigliano was convinced the pass would go to Logan. He was watching Logan on the play, and Logan was indeed open. Sipe was a little impatient, then made a poor throw—two things he rarely did that season, or even on that final drive.

"I believe that we had to be true to ourselves," said Rutigliano. "I felt we had to take a shot at the end zone."

CHAPTER 8

The Drive didn't beat the Browns. It hurt. It drove fans to tears. It was almost inexcusable. But it isn't why the Browns lost to Denver.

Yes, I was there for "The Drive" with my dad in our seats. I've never felt such elation and desolation all within the same five minutes. My father, who was an accountant, was never one to show much emotion, so it was quite memorable to see him jumping up and down and giving me high fives in the fourth quarter. As season-ticket holders, with just seconds left on the clock, we were hugging and bounding up and down, shouting, "We're going to the Super Bowl, we're going to the Super Bowl," having vowed to find a way to be at the big game. Then John Elway quashed that dream as the Broncos marched downfield.
—Sam Siple

Every Browns fan remembers The Drive, the AFC Championship Game against Denver on January 11, 1987. Starting on their own 2-yard line with only a few minutes left, Denver's John Elway put on an amazing display of clutch passing, shredding the

Browns' "prevent defense," sometimes scrambling for first downs in fourth-down situations—delivering a touchdown to win the game.

Everything about what you just read is how most of us remember that game. Only most of what you just read is wrong.

Before diving deep into The Drive, let's look at another drive.

The Browns received the kickoff and started with the ball on their own 30-yard-line. Remember, they are playing at home. The score is tied. If they can just find a way to kick a field goal, they can beat Denver.

FIRST PLAY: The Browns had three receivers on the field. Bernie Kosar dropped back to throw, saw no one open, felt the rush coming and scrambled for a 1-yard gain.

SECOND PLAY: 2nd-and-9: Kosar dropped back to throw, didn't see anyone open deep, but still completed a pass for a 7-yard gain to Brian Brennan.

THIRD PLAY: 3rd-and-2: The Browns tried to be tricky, running a draw play to . . . Herman Fontenot? The same Herman Fontenot whose main job all year was to catch passes. The same Herman Fontenot who carried the ball only 25 times all season? They gave the ball to Herman Fontenot on the most important play of the season? And it was a running play, not a short pass? Yes, they did. And yes, he was stuffed at the line of scrimmage for no gain on a very slow-developing sweep against a defense that had stacked up on the line. "I was trying to get outside," said Fontenot after the game. He never got there.

FOURTH PLAY: 4th-and-2: Browns punt.

When did this series occur? AFTER The Drive. It happened in overtime. It happened because The Drive tied the game at 20-20, and the Browns won the coin flip to start the overtime. So when they began that drive, they were at home, on their own 30-yard line with up to 15 minutes in an overtime period to move down the field and set up for a field goal.

But they went three-and-out.

And Denver drove down the field again, winning it on a Rick Karlis field goal.

Somehow, all this is forgotten when remembering The Drive. Somehow, most Browns fans have blocked out the memory of the overtime period. Somehow, the Browns still could have won this game, despite The Drive. They were in decent position to do so.

But, they didn't.

Here's something else some fans may have forgotten.

The score was 13-13 with 6:40 left in the fourth quarter. The Browns opened that drive on their own 48-yard line. After an incomplete pass to open the series, they used four receivers and one back (Herman Fontenot) in the backfield. Kosar called what seemed to be an audible—a draw play to Fontenot. It gained 4 yards. Maybe that's why they returned to that call in the overtime period. Maybe that's also why Denver wasn't surprised by it—the Broncos had seen it in the previous Browns possession. Forgive me for dwelling on the Fontenot call, but when you need 2 yards and have one play to do it in a game that could lead to the Super Bowl—you just can't hand the ball to Fontenot.

This is not a knock on Fontenot, who was a productive receiver out of the backfield. In 1986, starting backs Kevin Mack and Earnest Byner combined to miss 13 games because of injuries. This created opportunities for Fontenot, who carried the ball only 25 times for 105 yards all season. But he caught 47 passes, second-best on the team. He is a class act, a guy who has been very successful in business after football. But this was just not the right call in the overtime period.

For the game, Fontenot had 3 yards in three carries, his 4-yard gain being the only positive rushing play.

OK, back to the middle of the fourth quarter. Back to the play after Fontenot did gain the first down. Kosar threw a pass to Brian Brennan, who faked a cutback, did a spin and utterly confused Denver safety Dennis Smith. Smith tried for the ball and missed. Brennan caught it at the 17 and waltzed in.

So as The Drive began, the Browns were in front, 20-13.

It was so cold, freezing, but I didn't care at all . . . 80,000 fans shaking orange pompoms and chanting "Super Bowl, SUPER

BOWL!" At the time, it was the greatest moment of my life.
Brian Brennan just scored the game-winner. "We are going to
the Super Bowl!" Ninety-eight yards of prevent defense later, my
moment changed. "Are you kidding me?" A little bit later, Karlis
kind of kicked a field goal. . . . My greatest moment became my
worst. I was 16 years old, and I was crushed. Not yet jaded, I
thought, "Maybe next year." Next year? Ugh.

—**Jack Savage**

As you read this, remember that The Drive didn't win the
game.

It wasn't a two-minute drive by Denver. Not even close. The
Browns kicked off with 5:43 left. The Browns had that 20-13 lead,
the Broncos had all three timeouts left. In fact, they only used two
on The Drive.

Big fourth-down plays? There were none by Denver.

The drive took 15 plays. Seven were on first down, five on second down and only three on third down. Of the three, only one
was long-yardage—as in more than 2 yards.

Elway didn't throw any long passes: "Long" is a subjective
term. Yes, Elway's passes on the drive traveled 22 yards, 20 yards.
14 yards, 12 yards and two 5-yarders. His longest pass of the day
was 28 yards. It was not like he was using that bazooka arm to fire
the ball downfield. Instead, he picked the Browns apart.

What about the so-called prevent defense?

Several times, they blitzed Elway. Once it worked, once it backfired. They couldn't get to him. They did go into the "nickel" or
"dime" defense during the drive with extra defensive backs, but
Denver had five receivers on the field for some plays, so they had
to use those extra backs to defend.

Before The Drive, Elway was a modest 14-of-26 passing for 116
yards. It had been a tremendous defensive performance by the
Browns for 3 1/2 quarters. But on The Drive, Elway was 6-of-9 for
78 yards. He ran twice for 20 yards and was sacked once, losing
8 yards. So he accounted for 90 of the 98 yards in a performance
that remains one for the ages.

And it all began so well.

With 5:43 left, Mark Moseley kicked off. He booted what NBC broadcaster Merlin Olsen called "a knuckleball." The ball landed on the Denver 23, in front of Gene Lang. It then skidded sideways, bouncing end over end. Lang—who looked terrified by the thought of trying to field the bouncing ball—finally put his paws on it when the ball was at the Denver 2.

Talk about the perfect kickoff at the perfect time—that was how The Drive began.

> I was with many of my younger brother's friends, in the end zone opposite the Dawg Pound, fairly close to the field. After we had pinned the Broncos on the 2 with less than 2 minutes left (actually, 5:32 left), we were all talking Super Bowl. Sheer euphoria turned to extreme nervousness and anxiety, to complete anger and frustration.
> **—Tom Kusmer**

> One minute I looked at my dad and said, "I can't believe we're going to the Super Bowl." . . . 98 yards later . . . well, we weren't.
> **—Brian Menoni**

You know this, but it's worth repeating: The Drive began on the Denver 2-yard line. When a defense has a team pinned that deep, when the quarterback has his feet on the goal line as he takes the snap from center—the first play means so much. It can mean a safety, pushing the offense back into the end zone. It can mean doubt, stopping the offense near the line of scrimmage. It can mean an off-sides or illegal motion penalty on the offense. They are on the road. The crowd is roaring. The linemen are anxious to get into their blocks, to keep the defense from gaining an advantage.

FIRST PLAY: In this case, it meant a 5-yard pass from Elway to Sammy Winder. After a faked handoff to Gerald Willhite, it was simply a quick toss from a two-back formation to the left sideline.

Maybe a brilliant play call if you thought the Broncos were going to run. Hanford Dixon stayed in front of Winder and kept him inbounds. The Browns were in their standard 3-4 defense, which had been working just fine all game. After all, the Browns had a 20-13 lead.

SECOND PLAY: Denver had three receivers and ran a sweep left to Winder for 3 yards.

THIRD PLAY: Now we have our first critical play—third-and-2. If the Browns hold here, Denver has to punt. Maybe Cleveland scores. Certainly they kill a little clock time. Denver Dan Reeves called timeout to figure out a play. Winder ran 2 yards for . . . a first down?! More than two decades later, there are people who claim it was a "bad spot" for the Browns, that Winder didn't gain every inch of the 2 yards needed. No matter what your opinion, the measurement gave Denver the first down . . . *But the Broncos were still 88 yards away!*

FOURTH PLAY: Winder gained 3 yards. If you're a Browns fan, you have to be thrilled by how the defense is playing. Denver has gone 13 yards, but it's taken them about two minutes do to it.

FIFTH PLAY: This was a game changer—for both teams. It also was a hint that the Browns were about to collide with greatness, that the stars were indeed lining up, but they were not about to spell SUPER BOWL over Cleveland Stadium. In its first four plays, Denver hadn't done anything to suggest any sense of urgency: One short pass, three runs. The Browns had six guys on the line. Elway faked a handoff, dropped about seven steps back—but the Browns had great coverage. None of his receivers were open. If only the Browns could get a sack, or at least an incomplete pass. Elway was truly a great passer, but time has erased the memory of how effective he could be as a runner. He was such a gifted athlete, he played minor-league baseball in the Yankees farm system during his summers in college. The NCAA had allowed athletes to be an amateur in one sport, a pro in another. Anyway, Elway saw nothing, and simply turned himself into a running back—bolting into an open area of the field—and sliding in front of Browns linebacker Chip Banks. . . . FIRST DOWN, 11-yard gain.

SIXTH PLAY: This was when the hearts of Browns fans began to pound in the same way when you are in school, handed a test and know you really didn't study for it. You look at the first page and begin to panic. You can barely write your name. You have a sense that whatever will happen, it won't be good. On this first down play, Denver's formation looked like a run. Only one receiver split out wide—Steve Sewell. In the first five plays, Denver has thrown only one stupid pass—for 5 yards. So the Browns were in their normal defense. Elway faked a handoff, dropped back 10 yards and unloaded a rocket to Sewell. It was not an impressive throw. Elway threw it high and to the right. The 6-foot-3 Sewell was open, but he had to leap to grab it. It was a superb catch. Browns safety Chris Rockins went for Sewell's legs when he was in the air, and Sewell flipped backward, landing hard on his back. He must have lost his breath when he hit the ground . . . but he hung on to the ball. It was a great catch for . . . 22 yards . . . FIRST DOWN . . . at the 50-yard line!

SEVENTH PLAY: Cleveland had a problem. Denver was at midfield with 2:20 left. Yes, the Browns were at home with a 20-13 lead, but it didn't feel that way. The crowd did more grumbling and moaning than cheering. When will the Browns ever blitz? They did on this play, with linebacker Clay Matthews pursuing Elway, along with three linemen. Matthews was pushed wide and then shoved aside—his momentum taking him out of the play and not bothering Elway, who connected with wide receiver Steve Watson for 12 yards. FIRST DOWN.

EIGHTH PLAY: Denver threw deep. Think about how long it takes to run 30 yards down and the width of the field—and then consider that not one of the Cleveland linemen could reach Elway. What about the blitz? The Browns sent linemen plus linebacker Chip Banks. Elway was hit by Bob Golic after he released the ball, and the pass was incomplete. So this was the second time the Browns blitzed with one linebacker.

NINTH PLAY: Here came the tease for Browns fans. Dave Puzzuoli made the play of his career. A backup nose tackle, Puzzuoli replaced a weary Bob Golic, and he sacked Elway for an 8-yard loss. Matthews blitzed again. It was the third time they sent a line-backer at Elway.

TENTH PLAY: This was the most important play of The Drive. It was third-and-18. Denver called a timeout, the ball on the Browns' 48-yard line. Cleveland still hadn't used the passive prevent defense that fans assumed they played the entire drive. The Browns sent four rushers (three linemen and Matthews), five guys were in man-to-man coverage and both safeties deep. But Elway's greatness emerged again. He fired a pass to Mark Jackson, who beat Hanford Dixon for a 20-yard gain. Something else happened on this play. Denver was in the shotgun. Steve Watson was lined up as the back to Elway's left. He ran in motion to the right. Just as he ran behind the center, the shotgun snap hit him in the butt and dived low and to the left. But Elway caught the snap before it hit the turf, then threw the pass for a 20-yard gain and a first down. No problem, he seemed to be saying. FIRST DOWN.

ELEVENTH PLAY: With the ball on the Cleveland 28 and 1:24 left, Elway heaved an incomplete pass, and the clock stopped.

TWELFTH PLAY: The Browns blitzed again, for the fourth time on The Drive. But Elway connected with Steve Sewell for 14 yards. The truth is, the Browns blitzed only one linebacker at a time—so it was not a total prevent defense—but it also was not a blitz with multiple players coming from different directions. The Browns just weren't able to reach Elway, who also had such quick feet, he could dart away from a rush to create extra time for his receivers to get open. FIRST DOWN, ball on the Cleveland 14.

THIRTEENTH PLAY: Elway nearly completed a pass to Watson in the corner of the end zone, but Frank Minnifield had excellent coverage, and Watson caught the ball out of bounds. Incomplete.

FOURTEENTH PLAY: The Browns blitzed again, Elway stepped up and ran for a 9-yard gain. They Browns just weren't fast enough to contain the future Hall of Fame quarterback.

FIFTEENTH PLAY: The ball was on the Cleveland 5. Denver had 39 seconds remaining. The Broncos lined up three guys right, one left. They had one back near Elway. The Browns had five defensive backs on the field. Denver's Mark Jackson was in motion, being watched by the Browns' Mark Harper. At the snap of the ball, Jackson bolted into the end zone, losing Harper almost immediately. Elway threw what looked like a 95 mph fastball at the knees. He said he wanted to make sure if Jackson didn't catch it, no one would. Jackson went down on his knees and caught it. TOUCHDOWN.

I was 11 years old and made a secret deal with God that I would forgo all my Christmas presents retroactively if the Browns went to the Super Bowl.

My dad had tickets to this game in Row Z. I will never forget the walk to the parking lot after the game, as though we fans were marching to our own funeral. My father and I said nothing during our next hour together. There was no reason to listen to Nev Chandler and Doug Dieken's postgame show on WMMS. There was just silence. Dreadful, awful silence.

I can tell you that my worst day at Cleveland Municipal Stadium was also one of my best days as a kid. When we got back to our warm home, my mother had chili waiting for us. Yes, I was mad at my dog. I was mad at my sister. And I cried for three straight days. But I was young. And I had a mom and a dad and a sister and a dog who loved me. We had a warm house. And chili. And each other. Browns fans know life does go on, even after crushing disappointments.

—Brian Kirk

My worst day was The Drive. . . . Before the game, we felt we could not lose. Before the game, I bought a Super Bowl Browns shirt. . . . After the game, walking out of the stadium, you could hear a pin drop.

—Scott Newcomb

At this point, I'm just sick of thinking about this game. Bet you are, too.

I opened the chapter stating The Drive simply forced an overtime. The Browns won the coin toss, then went three-and-out.

The ball was punted to Denver. I'll just say Denver drove down the field, kicked a field goal (some fans still swear it was a miss) and won the game.

FINAL SCORE: Denver 23, Browns 20.

Who cares about these details?

But thinking back, I wondered, "Why did they lose?"

It came down to offense, as much as the defensive collapse and Elway's bid for football infamy with The Drive.

The Cleveland-Denver game was the 17th AFC Championship Game since the AFL and NFL merged. In the previous 16, the winning team had scored 20 or fewer points or less only three times:

In the 1975 season, Pittsburgh's "Steel Curtain" beat Oakland 16-10.

In the 1977 season, Denver's "Orange Crush" beat Oakland 20-17.

In the 1982 season, Miami's "Killer B's" beat the Jets 14-0.

As I'm writing this, there have been 80 conference championship games. Only 17 of those 80 games were won by a team with 20 or fewer points. So the Browns were trying to do this the hard way.

I can talk about how the Browns offense turned the ball over three times, on consecutive drives. But I won't go into the painful details.

The offense committed two terrible penalties at the worst times, but I won't rehash all that horrible hash.

As for the defense, they were tired coming into the game. This was their second consecutive overtime game and the fourth of the season. The week before, they'd beaten the Jets 23-20 in double overtime—at the time, the third-longest game in NFL history. On November 30, they'd beaten Houston 13-10 as Kosar threw three interceptions and fumbled. On November 23—the week before the Houston game—Cleveland beat Pittsburgh 37-31.

Four of their last seven games of the season were in overtime.

But when preparing to blame the offense, consider the following:

• Earnest Byner couldn't run in Game 7. Byner suffered what

was originally reported as an ankle sprain. He ended up having surgery and missing the rest of the regular season. In his place, Cleveland used Herman Fontenot (who was really more of a receiver) and Curtis Dickey, who turned 30 near the end of this, his final season.

Byner was activated for the Denver game, hoping he could help as a blocker. He didn't have a single carry and he caught only one pass for 4 yards.

• Hall of Famer Ozzie Newsome couldn't play: Newsome's ankle had been injured in Game 1, and it never fully healed. Newsome caught 89 passes in both 1983 and 1984, and then 62 in 1985. But he had only 39 catches in 1986. He found a way to catch six passes for 114 yards in the playoff victory over the Jets the previous week, but his ankle flared up, and Newsome didn't catch a pass against Denver. He played but wasn't a factor as he couldn't move quickly enough to get open.

• Center Mike Baab was playing on a sprained knee. He endured it through the Jets game, and that double-overtime victory certainly wore him down.

• They had minor injuries. Kevin Mack was hit in the face with a helmet. In the Jets game, Kosar threw 64 passes and had been speared in the chest by Mark Gastineau.

• Yes, Elway was having trouble walking on his aching ankle, at least until he needed to make huge plays. At this point in the season, almost every team has people hurt. But if you are playing without a 1,000-yard rusher in Byner and the two guys who led the 1985 team in receiving (Newsome, 62 catches; Byner 45), it will have an impact.

• Bottom line: The Browns just ran out of gas, emotionally and physically.

My best/worst day at the Stadium was actually the same game: The Drive. We went down to the seats right next to the railing near the field. I looked up and saw all the bunting, and it felt different. We all know the history of that game and how it ended. But a lot of folks might not know how it really ended.

During those last few minutes we experienced a wide range of emotions with the highest HIGH . . . "knowing" we were going to the Super Bowl.

After the shock wore off, the players began to leave the field. We all stood . . . and gave them a standing ovation. I'll never forget that. Maybe it was just our section, but that's what I recall. We were shocked . . . defeated . . . a Super Bowl berth SNATCHED away from us, and the loyalty of the Browns fans put their extreme disappointment aside and thanked the players for all their effort.

—Dan Rubinski

A few years ago, I was sitting in a hot tub at an upscale resort in Maui. Sitting directly next to me was an older man and his young wife. The man noticed my Cleveland Indians tattoo on my left arm and pointed it out to his wife. He then said, "Hey there, are you from Cleveland?" I indicated that I was, and we began to chat. We talked about the Browns for a while, and the subject eventually came to The Drive and The Fumble. I jokingly told the couple that those two games "ruined my childhood."

While I knew that the man looked familiar, I did not realize who I was sitting with. I left the hot tub and went back to my beach chair. A few moments later, the waiter came up to me and said the man in the hot tub has purchased me a drink with the message, "Sorry I ruined your childhood . . . John Elway."

—Andrew Branham

Browns Fans in Exile

I have been in the military for the past seven years. From the first day in the Army, you feel increasingly separated from your family. It could be missing my mother's birthday several years in a row due to training events, or missing Christmas twice because I was deployed to Iraq or Afghanistan. I have had the misfortune of being deployed overseas for two Browns seasons. I say "misfortune," not because I was deployed. But because I was not able to watch any games while I was in Iraq or Afghanistan.

But every Sunday afternoon (Monday morning overseas), I would call my house and talk with my dad. In that 10-minute conversation, he would give me a play-by-play of the game.... Sometimes, I'd even wake up early and go to the computer lab just to see if there were any updates on the Internet about the Browns game. Every Sunday I would have a chance to connect with my family about something besides the war. Both times I deployed, my good luck charm was the "Browns Rally Towel" that I got at a game before my first deployment. I even taught the Afghanistan soldier that I worked with the "Here we go, Brownies, here we go" chant.

—*Michael Adzima*

I grew up in Bedford (class of 1971), and have been a lifelong Browns fan. I've lived in the Denver area (Loveland) since 1979.

While I have some great memories of going to games with my dad at the old stadium, my favorite memory was two seasons ago when my daughter and new son-in law surprised me with a trip to the Browns-Dolphins game at the new stadium. We drove around the outskirts of Cleveland looking at the leaves as they were turning and rode the Rapid Transit from Shaker Heights. We walked all around downtown and the Flats, etc. What a great day! I pastor a church here in Colorado.... Coming "home" reminded me once again how much I love Cleveland. I would move back in a heartbeat.

—*Kent Hummel*

I'm from Baltimore. The day after my Colts skipped town to move to Indianapolis, I chose to become a Browns fan for several reasons: They were in the AFC, it was close enough so I could go to games when I got older (I was 14 at the time), I already liked the players like Ozzie Newsome, Clay Matthews, Brian Sipe, Greg and Mike Pruitt, etc. The team and city hated the Steelers as much as I did.... But the real reason I've remained a fan after all of these years is the friends I've made along the way. The Baltimore Browns Backers took in this football orphan and made me one of their own. We would watch games together, go on road trips, have events outside of football and really became close.

—*Stephen Bochenek*

I'm 56 years old and have been a loyal Browns follower all my life, even though I never lived year-round in Ohio after high school. I've lived in Kentucky; Virginia; Chicago; Istanbul, Turkey; and Long Island, New York. When I lived in Istanbul, one of my oldest and dearest friends used to send me videotapes of all the Browns games after the season.

When I was at Asbury College, which is a Christian liberal arts college near Lexington, Kentucky, Rev. Bill Glass, a former Browns defensive end, came to speak. I was assigned the job of driving him back to the airport. I had a ton of questions about Blanton Collier and guys he had played with on the Browns. He was gracious and kind but was more interested in speaking about things of the Lord.

Then there was January 18, 1988, about 3 a.m. I was living in Turkey, listening to the Browns-Broncos game on a very faint short-wave radio signal of U.S. Armed Forces radio. I was so excited when Earnest Byner was going in for the score. When he fumbled, I let out a scream that woke my dear wife, who was sleeping in the next room.

—*Erol Altug*

I'm a longtime Browns fan and president of the North Texas Browns Backers club, which started in 1999 with the return of the Browns. The Backers around the country are as true fans as those who sit in the seats each game and over the years. The Backers come back every week. They then channel their energies into community projects under the banner of the Cleveland Browns. My club has worked with the St. Vincent de Paul Society to feed 12 families at Thanksgiving each year. At Christmas each year, we have found four families to give them a complete Christmas and all of this under the banner of the Cleveland Browns.

—*Mike Mango*

I'm 61 years old, and thanks to my dad, who is no longer alive, I've been a lifelong Browns fan. A number of years ago, I met Ozzie Newsome at a Browns Backers Banquet in Dayton. He had retired but was not yet with the Ravens. Some time earlier, I had bought a pair of Ozzie's shoes at a charity auction. I stood in line so he could autograph the shoes. There was a buzz around me as people were saying, "She has Ozzie Newsome's shoes!"

When I handed him the shoes, Ozzie said, "Hey, these look like my shoes!" I was so excited. "They are your shoes!" Each football season, I bring them out to display on the sports shelf in my office.

A good memory was December 11, 2009, the day after the big win over the Steelers. I went to the Salvation Army to drop off some donations. The man helping unload the car was wearing a Browns jacket. We spent several minutes reliving the excitement of finally beating the Steelers. When I drove away, I thought of how neat it was to connect like that with another human being, especially a Browns fan. In southern Ohio, there are a large number of Bengals fans. When you talk football, some of them say, "I used to be a Browns fan." I try to gently correct them, reminding them that a true Browns fan does not change teams ever. Once a Browns fan, always a Browns fan.

—Debbie Badonsky

CHAPTER 9

The Browns almost didn't draft Jim Brown . . .

> In 35 years of watching sports in Cleveland, I have seen
> only two superstars who combined power, speed and grace into
> one awesome package—Jim Brown and LeBron James. When he
> wasn't running people over, Brown could dance his way down
> the sidelines, eluding tacklers. It took at least two of them
> to bring him down. If needed, he could carry the team on his
> shoulders.
> **—Lloyd Ettkin**

I thought I knew everything about Jim Brown's career until my researcher, Geoff Beckman, took a long look at the draft that brought the greatest running back in NFL history to Cleveland. Where do I begin? The year was 1956. Otto Graham had just retired as the quarterback. Can you imagine Graham and Jim Brown on the same team coached by Paul Brown? Never would have happened. That's because the Browns *never, ever* would have started the 1956 season at 3-6 had they still had Graham—and then they would not have had a high enough draft pick to select Brown. Graham retired after the 1955 season with his seventh title, including back-to-back championships in 1954 and 1955. In Graham's last three seasons, the Browns had lost a *total* of six games.

The unusual thing about Graham's retirement is that he was showing no sign of aging. In his last year, he led the league in four categories—completion percentage (53.0), yards per attempt (9.3), touchdown percentage (8.1) and passer rating (94.0). He could have played at least one more year. He was 34, had won those last two titles. His salary was $25,000, which would be about $200,000 in 2010. But he almost retired after 1954. His body was feeling all the sacks, late hits and stress of being a championship quarterback. So Graham going out of the dressing room door allowed Jim Brown to come through it a year later. In Graham's last season, the Browns scored a league-leading 349 points. In 1956, they dropped to 11th with 167 points. The Browns used three quarterbacks, who had only eight touchdown passes compared to 18 interceptions. Can you imagine how Paul Brown handled all this? The Browns had replaced Graham with Tommy O'Connell, George Ratterman and Babe Parilli. All that did was make fans long for Otto. The Browns had the sixth pick in the 1957 draft because they were 3-6 at the time—on their way to their first losing season in franchise history.

Get this: In the 1950s, the draft was held during the season. The 1956 draft took place on Monday, November 26—the day after the Browns played their ninth game of the season, losing 20-17 to Washington. Consider that by holding the draft on Nov. 26, the draftees hadn't finished their senior years. They hadn't played in the bowls or the several All-Star games. There was no NFL Combine, where the top prospects are gathered to be interviewed by NFL teams and also scouted as they run through some drills. There were pro workout days at colleges. No players visited NFL teams at their facilities. Teams didn't have months after the season to evaluate the top college players. They just played a game on Sunday, then went to work Monday drafting players—with the memories of what happened the day before fresh in their minds. The draft order was based on the current standings, not last year's. If it were based on that 1955 championship season, no Jim Brown in Cleveland. But with no Otto, the 3-6 Browns had a shot at a very good player, and Brown was not the only star at the top of this draft.

My favorite Brown is the greatest running back of all time, Jim Brown. No one will ever average over 5 yards per carry for their entire career as he did. When the Browns returned in 1999, I joined the Legends Club, above the end zone for pregame and postgame festivities. I came up at halftime, and the lady running the club told me I had just missed Jim before the game when I left to go to my seats. Lo and behold, here he came again at halftime. I almost never ask for autographs, but I asked for his. At that time he was older than 60, but he was still like a rock when I touched his shoulder and shook his hand.

—Dennis Pinkozie

Paul Brown was not looking for a fullback. He needed a quarterback, another Otto Graham—and there were some very good quarterback prospects in this draft. But first, they had to flip some coins.

And just like the lottery ping-pong balls bouncing the right way enabled the Cavaliers to be awarded the draft rights to LeBron James in the 2003 NBA draft, if the Browns had won a couple of the coin flips—no Jim Brown. The NFL didn't use strength of schedule or head-to-head records or any of that other stuff to break ties. If two teams had the same record, the NFL settled the matter by flipping coins. And they flipped a lot of coins back in the day. There were three teams with 3-6 records: Green Bay, Pittsburgh and Cleveland. To break the tie, all three teams flipped coins. If all three teams got the same result, they flipped again. If two teams got one result and one got the other, that team would pick.

Then the two remaining teams would keep flipping coins.

Paul Brown liked John Brodie, a star quarterback at Stanford. But Brown doubted Brodie would be available, as the San Francisco 49ers had the No. 2 pick and wanted Brodie. Brown also liked Len Dawson, a star quarterback at Purdue. But Paul Brown ended up with Jim Brown because

1. Green Bay won the first flip and took Ron Kramer, an end.

2. That left the Steelers and Browns to flip coins. Pittsburgh called heads. Pittsburgh won. Pittsburgh took Len Dawson, a fu-

ture Hall of Fame quarterback. Losing this coin flip broke the heart of Paul Brown, who wanted Dawson to be his next Graham.

3. Three quarterbacks were selected in the top five picks. Top pick Paul Hornung was a quarterback in college at Notre Dame and in his first two pro seasons before switching to running back in the pros with Green Bay.

4. Losing two coin flips, a quarterback-hungry Paul Brown sighed and wisely didn't try to force yet another quarterback into the top of the draft. Instead, he called the name of Jim Brown, a fullback from Syracuse, at No. 6 in the 1957 NFL draft.

This was one of the best drafts ever. Four of the top eight eventually made the Hall of Fame: Jim Parker, Hornung, Dawson and Brown. Pittsburgh later traded Dawson to Cleveland along with Gern Nagler in exchange for Junior Wren and Preston Carpenter. Dawson played only nine games and threw 28 passes before being released. He started one game in 1961, when Milt Plum was recovering from a broken thumb. Dawson hardly looked like a Hall of Famer as he completed only 6 of 12 passes for 68 yards and two interceptions. After being cut by the Browns, Dawson went to work with the Dallas Texans, who a year later became the Kansas City Chiefs in the new American Football League. He played until he was 40. When you think about all the turmoil the Browns had at quarterback in the 1960s and early 1970s, this makes you weep.

Still not convinced that Paul Brown's first draft target was Dawson? Hall of Fame sportswriter Chuck Heaton wrote in his book, *Browns Scrapbook*, that Brown indeed preferred Dawson over Jim Brown. But Paul Brown also was smart enough to grab "the best athlete available" after his quarterback choices were gone.

My best day as a fan has to be watching Jim Brown set the then-single-game rushing record against the Rams in 1957 . . . 231 yards in a 45-31 victory. We knew then that we had something truly special.
—**Gerry Prokupek**

Jim Brown finished fifth in the Heisman Trophy voting. Think about that, how can this be true? What did Brown do at Syracuse? He gained 986 yards (on 158 carries; a 6.3 average) in eight games. He added another 132 in the Cotton Bowl. He scored 13 touchdowns (three more in the bowl game). Since everyone played both ways back then, he played middle linebacker. He was also the kicker.

There's so much more about Brown. In high school. Brown earned 13 high school letters in five sports. He averaged 38 points per game as a high school senior in basketball. He broke records in track. He averaged 14.9 yards per carry in high school! Brown was such a gifted lacrosse player that he dominated the sport at Syracuse and is a member of the College Lacrosse Hall of Fame. At Syracuse, he also averaged 13 points in two years of varsity basketball. At 6-2 and 232 pounds, Brown was the strongest, fastest and most frightening back that college football had ever seen. Or as *New York Times* columnist Red Smith once wrote: "For mercurial speed, airy nimbleness, and explosive violence in one package of undistilled evil, there is no other like Mr. Brown."

Brown was named to the All-America team—and the reason was because most of the teams were chosen after the bowl games. Syracuse lost 28-27 to Texas Christian in the Cotton Bowl. Brown gained 132 yards on 26 carries and scored three touchdowns. He completed a pass for 20 yards. He kicked three extra points. That same game, the entire TCU team gained 133 yards rushing— Brown had 132. Paul Brown already had drafted Jim Brown and really knew that he had something special.

Heaton wrote: "When he arrived at the club's Hiram College training camp in the summer of 1957, he drove into the sleepy town in his fire-engine red convertible—after an all-night run from Chicago where he had played only a so-so College All-Star game the previous night. There was silence in the Browns' dressing quarters when Brown stripped down, displaying his classic physique, which should have been captured in bronze and displayed in an art museum. Paul Brown, eagerly awaiting the appearance of his first-round draft pick . . . saw Jim run only a few plays in the morning workout. But he was so impressed, he told Brown after practice, 'You're my fullback.'"

He was more than that—Jim Brown was Paul Brown's star. Jim Brown would become the greatest running back in NFL history—in his second season! That's when Brown rushed for a league-record 1,527 yards and 17 touchdowns. Remember, this was 1958, when teams played only 12 games. In fact, he gained 387 more yards than anyone—ever. No one had ever run for 17 touchdowns. Now, teams play 16 games, and 1,000 yards is considered a special season, Brown ran for more than 1,400 yards in six of his nine seasons, including four of his last five with the Browns. This was when they played 14-game seasons.

> My hero back then was Jim Brown. He would run around and through would-be tacklers. It was not uncommon to see Jim Brown carry several tacklers on his back for large gains. Then he would get off the ground and walk ever so slowly back to the huddle. It appeared that he was totally gassed. However, the burst always quickly returned when his number was called again.
> **—Larry Holden**

> I remember Jim Brown and how he used to get up from a tackle slowly only to run harder on the next down and needing twice as many players to stop him.
> **—Robert Busby**

Is he the best running back in NFL history? I'm hardly the only one who thinks so. He changed the way we view running backs, his combination of power and speed and utter disdain for the defense trying to tackle him. He also had no interest in blocking, which gave his critics something to complain about.

"Brown is a great athlete, and he could block, but he doesn't," said Otto Graham. "This is ridiculous. If I were coaching a pro team, I'd have everyone pulling together."

Was the former star Browns quarterback a bit jealous of the attention that Brown was receiving? Did it make Graham feel as if he were being forgotten by the fans? Or was Graham trying to send a message to Brown, a message that coach Paul Brown wanted his fullback to hear?

Graham was right, and Graham was wrong.

He was right: Brown didn't like to block.

But he was wrong: Anyone would want Jim Brown on his team. When I was writing *Browns Town 1964*, players told me Brown not only played in every game—he never missed a practice! Sure, he sat out some plays and a few drills. But there was never a practice spent in the trainer's room, never a full practice spent on the bench. He may have looked like Superman with his 47-inch shoulders, his 32-inch waist on his incredibly defined 6-foot-2, 230-pound frame . . . but the man did get hurt. After Sunday games, he'd show up Monday at 6:30 a.m. to be treated by the trainers. He knew no one else would be around.

"Now I see guys run the ball a few times, then raise their hands to come out of the game . . ." Brown told me a few years ago, so disgusted, he couldn't even finish the sentence.

Former Browns lineman John Wooten insists Brown played the entire 1962 season with a broken left wrist. Brown was his roommate, and Wooten said he had to tie Brown's shoes because Brown couldn't use his left hand. That also was part of the reason Brown carried the ball even more "like a loaf of bread in one hand" as several of his teammates recalled. He couldn't use the left hand.

"Everything is mental," Brown once told me. "If you are always in the trainer's room, always getting rubbed down, you get too comfortable. . . . If you were a marked man like I was back then, you had to be tough. You had to take the pain. If you broke a toe but could still walk, you played . . . you needed a strong mind."

Brown also said that he wanted his teammates "to go to the Pro Bowl and tell guys from other teams that Jim Brown never goes in the training room. Man, he's crazy."

Browns trainer Morrie Kono insisted Brown never drank water

during games and refused to wear a coat when it was cold—unless Kono came up behind him and draped the coat on Brown's shoulders. He wanted his teammates and the league to believe that he was Superman—that he never got hurt, never was tired. Yes, he seemed to drag himself back to the huddle after being tackled, but then he hammered into the line as if it were his first play from scrimmage.

"The defense is always looking for a sign of weakness," said Brown. "You can't show it. You have to do everything the same way, every time. I never changed how I went back to the huddle, no matter how I felt."

Former Browns defensive end Bill Glass began his career in Detroit, and he said once when he tried to tackle Brown, "He dropped his left arm on top of my helmet. It felt like I got hit with a lead pipe." Other players said when they tried to grab Brown's face mask, he'd bite their fingers if they were near his mouth.

When you score a touchdown, don't celebrate.

"Just hand the ball to the official; act like you've been there before," Brown said.

But it's believed he picked up that quote from another Brown named Paul. No matter where the words came from, Jim Brown followed that personal code of honor.

I can talk about some of Jim Brown's legal troubles, but this is not that type of book. I can dwell on how it was disappointing that he supported Art Modell when the owner moved the Browns to Baltimore—of course, he was on Modell's payroll at the time. I can talk about his movie career and some controversial statements he's made over the years.

But I won't.

I'll simply say that when Jim Brown walked away from the game at the age of 30, he truly was at his peak. I'm not going to get into the old debate about how Modell may have forced Brown to retire early because Brown was going to miss training camp (and perhaps a game or two) because he was acting in the movie *The Dirty Dozen*. I don't feel like digging into that old stew as I dealt with it in depth in my book, *Browns Town 1964*.

But these days, Jim Brown is on a cane. He walks slowly, as if his entire body aches. He now looks like an old man, although his voice remains strong. But I'd rather remember him going out in his prime, as I imagine most of you would, too.

So I'll end this with the words of you, the fans, about the greatest running back . . . ever.

I was born in 1949, so I was 8 in the fall of 1957. I remember watching Jim Brown on a small, black-and-white TV on Sundays with my dad and brother. Watching Jim Brown, even as a neophyte fan, I could see something special. The moves, the speed, the power; he had it all. He generated excitement. The patented sweeps behind Gene Hickerson and Dick Schafrath were something to behold. I became a big fan. However, his retirement after the 1965 season brought anger and disappointment. I guess I thought that my hero would play forever. Looking back, what a smart man he was! He went out on top, the best in the game, the best of all time.

—John Anderson

He's the mold of everything you want in a player. He dominated like no other running back in NFL history. He fought for every single yard and didn't do it for the money. He played every single down of football like it was the last down he would ever play, and as a result, the fans loved him for the effort that every single fan wishes they had the opportunity to show if they got to be out there on the field.

—Nick Paparodis

I attended school with James Brown in junior and senior high school, the Class of 1980 at Shaker Heights. My Dad knew Jim Brown when he was a player. Brown and my dad used to fish together. My Mom and Dad were guests of Brown at Hiram College once during camp. My parents had a photo of Brown kissing me as an infant.

— Bill Beck

In Solon Little League in the summer of 1965, my manager happened to be a long-standing usher at Municipal Stadium. He took our team to Hiram to watch a practice. After the practice, he called Jim Brown over to say hello to us. I remember like it was yesterday (instead of 45 years ago) shaking Jim Brown's enormous hand. He was my hero, and he smiled and was very gracious to us. It was an unbelievable experience for me as a 12-year-old fan of the Browns. Although I left the Cleveland area and moved to California in 1979, I will always be a Browns fan, and Jim Brown remains my hero to this day.

— **Tim Corbett**

I remember jumping onto the field at the last home game in 1965 and running up to Jim Brown and thanking him for all he had done for the team that season. That was his last home game with the Browns. He was gracious to allow my friend, who had his camera, to take a picture of me with the greatest running back ever.

— **Tom Nowel**

I was about 14 and loved to play golf. My mom had dropped me off at Highland to play a round. As I was walking toward the clubhouse, I noticed a limousine pull in. As a kid from Euclid who didn't see many limousines, I stopped to see who might emerge. Three men stepped from the backseat, and one of them was Jim Brown. As he made his way to the clubhouse, I fell in beside him. There wasn't much said between us, 'Have a nice round, Mr. Brown.' 'Thanks, kid.' Something like that, but just to walk with the man, see his size, sense his strength, well, many memories have faded over the years. But not that one. I think that's when I became a lifelong Browns fan.

— **Chris Reece**

CHAPTER 10

Clay Matthews made the fans proud.

My favorite Brown? Pretty easy question. Clay Matthews. I loved his workmanlike attitude. Driving his old Mercury Capri to work every day even after he had "made it." He embodies the Cleveland area and what Browns fans are about. He may not have been the most gifted athlete on the field, but you knew he was going to bring his lunch bucket and play 60 minutes, and there would be no mental mistakes. A class guy. I remember a game late in his career where the announcers said he looked like he had lost a step. On the next play, he intercepted a pass, sealing a victory, causing the announcers to say what a wily veteran he was. A winner who *wanted* to play in Cleveland.

—Jim Ousley

He was with the Browns from my earliest memories of watching the Browns until I was in my late teens. Clay epitomized hard work and consistency that defined the people of Cleveland during that time period. It was a joy to watch him play football.

—Michael Hartley

"That kid from Notre Dame," said Sam Rutigliano. "He was a defensive back, and we were ready to take him instead of Clay Matthews."

Luther Bradley?

"That's right, Bradley," said Rutigliano, the Browns coach during the 1978 NFL draft. "If he had been there, we'd have been happy to take him at No. 12."

But in a *Plain Dealer* story after the draft, Art Modell said the Browns had Matthews rated No. 4 in the entire draft. No one said anything about Luther Bradley.

"That's not true," said Rutigliano, laughing. "That was just Art talking. We really liked Clay, especially (assistant coach) Dick MacPherson. He went out to USC and talked to Clay; he really wanted us to take Clay."

Rutigliano paused for a moment.

"We should be real happy Luther Bradley didn't fall to us," said Rutigliano. "Because I don't care what anyone says, Clay Matthews is a Hall of Fame player."

Even the Browns fans who loved the team and consider Clay Matthews one of their favorite players may not fully appreciate what he did in his 16 years with the Browns. Start with that fact, Matthews was with the Browns for 16 years, from 1978 to 1993. He played three different linebacker positions. He played for five different coaches. He played for teams that were 123-124-1, making seven trips to the playoffs in those 16 years.

He finished his career with three seasons in Atlanta, meaning he played in the NFL for 19 years.

Of his 278 games, he started 248. More significantly, of his 30 non-starts, 13 were in his rookie season, 14 in his final season.

In 10 of these 19 seasons, he started every game. The only time he was out with a significant injury was in 1982, when he broke an ankle.

At first, Matthews said he played so many games for so many years because "it's the genes."

His father was a pro football player. His brother played pro football. His son is with the Green Bay Packers. The Matthews family plays football and plays for a long time.

But then Matthews said, "The NFL is a grind. It's Week 12. The game still looks bright and shiny on TV, but you are banged up, the weather is miserable and you're playing in Buffalo or Cleveland or Pittsburgh. At this point, football is not fun. It's about being a professional, wanting to do your job the right way. It's a test of wills—who wants to do the best over the long haul."

And Luther Bradley?

He was picked at No. 11 by Detroit, where he played for four years—two seasons as a starter. He then went to the United States Football League and set the league record for interceptions. He had 36 NFL starts, 32 in his first two seasons—only four in his final two seasons.

While Browns fans can whine about their team and its draft miseries, it could be worse. You could be a Lions fan, the only team with a worse record than Cleveland since the Browns returned in 1999.

Matthews came from California, but he seems more like a kid from Cleveland, Canton or anywhere that people grow up being told, "Life is hard, so you better keep your mouth shut and work hard. Don't expect anyone to give you anything."

On draft day, Matthews told the Cleveland media: "My strong point is that I'm consistent, but I'm not a flashy type. I feel I played well against all facets of the game—passing, running, all of it."

The same could have been said of Matthews when he retired in 1996, after being the oldest player in NFL history—40 years, 282 days—to be credited with a sack.

Clay Matthews, in the middle of Chip Banks' holdout and public whining, said something that will always endear him to Browns fans: "They won't have any trouble signing me. I'm a Brown." He is a quintessential Cleveland guy.
—**Andy Janovsky**

My all-time favorite Brown . . . Clay Matthews. At one point, he started more games at linebacker than anyone in the history of the NFL. A warrior, a low profile, a hard worker. . . . I loved the locks of hair out the back of his pumpkin orange helmet while the wind swirled inside Municipal Stadium.
—**Ryan Phillips**

Matthews is grateful that he was picked by the Browns. Thirty-two years after he was the Browns' top pick, he talked about the culture that he found with the Browns.

"The young players and new players come to a team and see what players dictate the culture," said Matthews. "They say, 'I want to be like that guy.' So you need the right culture. When I came to the Browns, they had two linebackers that most people don't remember—Gerald Irons and Charlie Hall. But those guys did all the right things in terms of how to work. They were at the end of their careers, but they were true professionals, and they took me under their wings."

Matthews paused, then explained, "If your highest-paid players don't work out, don't pay attention in the film room—that sends a message to the rest of the team. It means all that matters is talent, not character. But if your best players do the extra work in the summer, do the film study, stay around after practice—then it carries over to the rest of the team."

Matthews said one of the Browns coaches showed him tapes of the Steelers.

"They were our main rivals," said Matthews. "But I studied Jack Lambert and Jack Ham—their linebackers. I wanted to play like them. The Browns were developing the right culture when I came to them."

In 1977, the Browns were 6-8. Coach Forrest Gregg was fired. Rutigliano was hired, and immediately was impressed by Matthews: "Almost anyone could coach Clay. He's a guy who only needed to hear something once. Then, he got it. After Clay's rookie season, [assistant coach] Dave Adolph sat down with him. I was there. But it was Dave who told Clay, 'Don't you realize that with your talent, you can do anything you want at linebacker?' Clay just listened. You could tell that he was taking it all in."

In 1979, Matthews' second season, he became a starting linebacker.

Matthews had the type of career that legendary USC coach John Robinson predicted in a 1978 draft day story by *The Plain Dealer*'s Russell Schneider:" Clay is a very good player, a very consistent player. He has good speed, but not fantastic sideline-to-sideline speed. . . . He also is a very good human being, and the fans in Cleveland are going to appreciate him."

Then Robinson added almost as an afterthought: "I've got to rank him as our greatest linebacker ever."

Wow!

And Browns fans would probably say the same: "Yep, Clay is probably the best we've ever had."

Asked to name a single big play by Matthews, and most would hesitate and then bring up the final game of the 1989 season. He recovered a fumble against Houston and then threw it away, nearly costing Cleveland the game. He was trying to lateral it. Most people don't remember his game against Buffalo, two weeks later in the playoffs, where he intercepted Jim Kelly at the goal line with three seconds left. If that doesn't happen, Buffalo plays Denver in the AFC Championship Game, probably beats them and goes to five straight Super Bowls.

> In the late 1980s, I went to a store in Lorain to see Clay Matthews, who was making an appearance to sign autographs. He walked in all by himself. He was dressed in plain clothes with his hands stuck in the front pockets of his jeans and a grin on his face that said, "I'm kind of embarrassed to be here and receive all of this attention." He didn't have the attitude or act like a great football player. If I didn't already know what he looked like, I wouldn't have given him a second glance. I was so impressed by his humility and "regular guy" attitude.
> **—Roger Whitacre**

Is Matthews worthy of becoming the first Browns linebacker to make the Hall of Fame? He made the Pro Bowl four times in a five-year period ('85, '87, '88, '89), at two different linebacker spots. You can claim it should have been five times in six years. In 1984, Matthews was named first- or second-team all-NFL by three sets of voters, but he didn't make the Pro Bowl. That makes no sense. It's as if the Pro Bowl voters forgot about him.

Which is why he often was underrated. Matthews doesn't have a single drop of self-promoting blood in his veins. When you ask him about the Browns, he talks about the players and coaches who helped him—and the fans who loved him and the rest of his teammates.

"Playing in Cleveland was a great experience," he said. "There are not many distractions, which is good. It's all football. People love the team. They know the game. It really is close to life and death to them. Other teams have good followings, but there is something unique about football in Cleveland, the way the fans embrace the team. I ended my career in Atlanta. I'd go out, and a few people maybe would recognize me. They sold out every game, but it was not like Cleveland. The players mean a lot to the Browns' fans."

Why isn't Matthews receiving more consideration for the Hall of Fame?

Pro Football Hall of Fame voters say, "Four Pro Bowls in 19 years—good but not great."

But they need to look deeper at his career:

• Matthews played for bad teams for much of his career. His team had a winning record eight times in his career and went .500 two times. Writers and award voters don't pay much attention to players on losing teams. There was one five-year period in his career where the Browns were at or above .500 every season—making the playoffs all five years and going to the AFC Championship Game three times. That was from 1985 to 1989, and he was named to the Pro Bowl four times. Why? Because the team was good, not because his performance improved that much from the early 1980s, or even that he declined that much in 1990 or 1991.

• He played 75 percent of his career on the strong side: This is a critical issue. Right (strong-side) linebacker in a 4-3 defense is known as "Sam" in the coaches' playbooks. He lines up on the strong side—the side where offenses normally put both their tight end and the fullback. It's called the "strong side" because you have two extra blockers facing the linebacker. It's a thankless job.

On running plays, "Sam" has to wade through two extra blockers. His job is usually to force the play to a spot where someone else—possibly the left defensive tackle or the middle linebacker ("Mike") can make the tackle. On pass plays, he has to either worry about those guys as receivers, or if they stay in to block, he has to get past them. Most quarterbacks are right-handed. That means they look and often throw to the right—so "Sam" is always in the quarterback's field of vision. They can see you coming if you rush. If you leave a man open, they can pass to him.

• For most of Matthews' career, he was in a spot where you don't pile up a lot of stats. Two of the linemen (left defensive end and right defensive end) along with the left-side linebacker (the "Will") rack up most of the sacks, tackles and fumbles.

• Matthews also was the right-outside linebacker when he played in the 3-4 defense. He had the same responsibilities and same issues as in the 4-3. You have even less chance to rush the passer, because the two defensive ends and the weak-side linebacker usually blitz. Tackles on running plays are the responsibility of the inside linebackers. Matthews spent nine years—the heart of his career (80-88)—at this thankless job.

• Left (weak-side) linebacker in a 4-3 defense is the glamour spot of the linebackers. You're lining up on the quarterback's blind side. You usually don't have two extra blockers in your way. Matthews played there only five years (1989-90 with Cleveland under Bud Carson, and 1994-96 in Atlanta). He never got to play the "Will" spot in a 3-4 (weak-side outside linebacker), which is where all the linebackers who get double-digit sack totals play.

• When Matthews played the weak side, he did so with the unselfish attitude of a strong-side linebacker—the spot where he was used by coaches such as John Robinson, Marty Schottenheimer, Sam Rutigliano and Bill Belichick. As a weak-side linebacker, it was hard for Matthews to ignore everything else that was happening and concentrate on chasing the quarterback He worried far more about the entire defensive picture than his own statistics. In 1984, he had 12 sacks—which, for a right-side linebacker, is an insanely high number—but didn't make the Pro Bowl.

The same unselfish virtues and natural humility that made
Matthews a great player and teammate probably will keep him
out of the Hall of Fame, which is a real shame.

One last story about Matthews, something he told me recently:
"After my career was over, I went to my local high school—Oaks
Christian High," he said. "I asked if they needed any help with the
football program. They asked me what I knew. . . . I said I knew a
little football. They said they needed an offensive line coach, so I
coached the offensive line. It was like playing defense, only you
turn it around . . . look at it from the other side of the ball. Then I
became a defensive line coach and coordinator. I help out where
they need me."

CHAPTER 11

Fans still can't get enough of Bernie Kosar.

Bernie Kosar is a rare case of someone wanting to come to Cleveland. He grew up in Boardman, Ohio, had a very successful career at the University of Miami and actually wanted the Browns to draft him. He and his agent even went around the rules and skipped the NFL draft so he could be taken by the Browns in the supplemental draft.
—Steven McCann

Bernie Kosar personifies Cleveland—an awkward underdog who seemingly doesn't have the tools to make it, but does anyway through sheer will and all the intangibles that money cannot buy. He was a true long shot who succeeded on the highest level among great athletes. Oh, and he's a local boy who went out of his way to play for his hometown team.
—Tom Brice

An elderly woman said, "I've got to meet Bernie—he's on my bucket list!"

It was about an hour before the Cleveland Gladiators of the Arena Football League were to play a game at Quicken Loans Arena in the summer of 2010. A consultant for the team, Bernie Kosar was signing autographs for fans.

They lined up, and like the 70-something lady in the Kosar jersey, they just wanted to shake his hand. They want him to sign a program or a cap. Most of all, they wanted to thank him for what he did for the Browns . . . and the fans.

At this point in his life, Kosar was 46. He had not played for the Browns in 17 seasons. He recently had been through a nasty, public divorce. He had filed for bankruptcy. He was no longer the football knight in the shining helmet coming to rescue the Browns.

He was a middle-aged former player who sometimes limped on a sore, surgically repaired ankle and had an aching back. His reputation was no longer prefect.

No one cared.

That's because when the subject is Bernie Kosar, Browns fans always start with this fact: He chose us. He wanted to play for the Browns. He schemed to play for the Browns, graduating a year early and letting the world know that this quarterback from the Youngstown area wanted to leave Florida and come back home. It seemed amazing back in 1985, and even more improbable in 2010—especially after Akron product LeBron James not only left the Cavaliers for Miami, but did so in a self-absorbed, utterly disrespectful ESPN special. James seemed to care less about the impact of such a display of arrogance to the fans of his hometown team who cheered for him for seven years.

Kosar said he watched the show and wept.

Yes, he cried.

He cried because he knew how it would hurt the local fans. He cried because James seemed to be so distant, so hard-hearted to the people who loved him so much as a player. Kosar cried, because not only did he choose us . . .

In so many ways, he is one of us.

Remain loyal to Cleveland teams and the fans of Northeast Ohio, and they will stand behind you. All the people lining up to see Kosar that day were witnesses to that fact. Kosar's Cleveland career lasted only slightly longer than that of James—8 seasons to James' seven years with the Cavs—but it was the Browns who cut him.

"I never wanted to leave," he said.

Heck, he never even wanted to play at the University of Miami. His first choice coming out of Boardman High School was Ohio State.

"But (coach) Earle Bruce was running the option back then," said Kosar. "He really didn't want a non-athletic passing quarterback like me."

The same for Notre Dame, another school on Kosar's wish list. Ditto for Pittsburgh and Penn State, two more schools that interested him. He was the 1981 Ohio Associated Press high school football player of the year when his team was 8-2. But there was no state title. Even more significant, Kosar seemed to come from out of nowhere to some college recruiters. He was injured most of his sophomore season. As a junior, his school system was on strike, and he played only six games. This was before the era of big-time summer football camps being held at major colleges for high school players. Nor were there as many recruiting and scouting services as today.

But there was something else. Yes, Kosar stood 6-foot-5 and about 200 pounds in high school—he just didn't look or move like an athlete. His shoulders hunched. His knees and elbow seemed to jut out at strange angles.

Sports Illustrated's Rick Reilly wrote: "If you stood them next to each other, Kosar would look like the 'Before' to John Elway's 'After.' Elway is muscular. Kosar is built like a CPA whose health club membership expired. Elway is beach-boy blond. Kosar looks like a mattress salesman. Elway's throwing motion would make (pitcher Sandy) Koufax envious. Kosar throws, as Jim Murray of the *Los Angeles Times* once said, 'like a guy losing a bar of soap in the shower.' Elway's passes arrive so angrily, they leave marks on receivers' palms. You could catch Kosar's passes with a beer in each hand."

Now understand that Reilly wrote that in 1988, the height of Kosar's powers as a pro quarterback. Now imagine what he looked like in high school. Consider that he often threw the ball sidearm, not even close to the motion that you'd want from a big-time passer. His passes floated rather than flew, and some scouts had to wonder if those soft high school completions would turn into college interceptions when Kosar faced faster defensive backs. Even with his ideal 6-foot-5 height for a quarterback to see over the line, it took a coach with imagination and gumption to consider Kosar a blue-chipper. That coach was Miami's Howard Schnellenberger. He loved pure passing quarterbacks and believed in throwing the ball. He preached a gospel that football intelligence and instincts are just as important as talent. In fact, the mental part of the game is part of what makes an athlete gifted. Schnellenberger coached Joe Namath and Kenny Stabler at the University of Alabama when the program was run by Bear Bryant. In the NFL, Don Shula hired Schnellenberger to install his special passing offense for the Miami Dolphins.

While it would have been fun to see Kosar at Ohio State in the early 1980s, there was no better place for a quarterback of his type to play than Miami under Schnellenberger. It was a program designed to send quarterbacks to the NFL because of the superb coaching. It was more than just Schnellenberger. One of the Hurricanes' assistants was Earl Morrall, who spent 21 years in the NFL. The quarterbacks coach was Marc Trestman, who later was an offensive coordinator in the NFL. Schnellenberger was head coach of the Baltimore Colts when Bert Jones was the quarterback. So Kosar was surrounded by a former NFL quarterback (Morrall) and coaches with NFL experience. The offense was pro style; the approach was as much intellectual as physical.

But there was something else—the special bond between Kosar and Schnellenberger.

"He was like a father to me," said Kosar.

Schnellenberger redshirted Kosar for the 1982 season. As 1983 loomed, he was intrigued by Kosar but had another prime prospect of a quarterback. Yes, it was Vinny Testaverde. File this under the headline of "You can't make it up." Long before Bill Belichick brought Testaverde to the Browns to replace Kosar in 1993, they were together in Miami—where Schnellenberger was trying to pick a starter. Like Kosar, Testaverde also didn't play for the Hurricanes in 1982. Unlike Kosar, he had a bazooka arm, the ideal throwing motion and moved with such grace, it was easy to look at the Brooklyn-born Testaverde and say, "He just looks like a quarterback, a Heisman Trophy winner." And Testaverde indeed won that award in 1986.

According to *Sports Illustrated*, 10 days before the 1983 opener against rival Florida, Schnellenberger still had not decided between Kosar and Testaverde. "I could have gone either way," the coach said. "The night before I announced my decision, I went to church and prayed. I finally picked Bernie because the game was at Florida with 70,000 fans against us, and I figured Bernie would handle it better if we lost."

Another report said Schnellenberger polled his coaches, and all but two of them voted for Testaverde to start that game. The two for Kosar were Trestman (the quarterbacks coach) and Schnellenberger. At one point when Kosar was a redshirt freshman, he was No. 4 on the quarterback depth chart and wondered if he'd ever get a chance to start. But Schnellenberger didn't fall into the trap of judging his quarterbacks by their high school honors or even first impressions in early practices. He waited and watched, and Kosar grew on him. A year later, it was Kosar whom the coach trusted the most. He picked Kosar to start for the same reasons he recruited Kosar—the quarterback's maturity, confidence and poise. And by the way, those were the attributes that were slow in developing for Testaverde, who struggled trusting his own talent and needed more time to grasp offensive concepts than some quarterbacks.

Miami won the national title that 1983 season, Kosar throwing for 300 yards as the Hurricanes upset Nebraska 31-30 in the Orange Bowl. He broke school records for completions and touchdowns. Schnellenberger would say the premier quarterbacks would throw to the right receivers about 75 percent of the time. With Kosar as a freshman, it was 90 percent. The coach told *Sports Illustrated* that Kosar made the correct call at the line of scrimmage "92 percent of the time" when opponents lined up to blitz.

After Kosar's freshman season, Schnellenberger began to tell reporters that he was "better than" some starting NFL quarterbacks right then—at the age of 20. Schnellenberger left the Hurricanes after the 1983 season to coach in the United States Football League. Kosar was taking extra courses in the spring and summer, aiming for a degree in finance and economics, and graduated in three years . . . with honors.

Why go through all the Miami background on Kosar? Because it explains so much about him. Yes, he was smart, but he never would have been so advanced in terms of his football knowledge had he attended almost any other school. And he went to Miami not because it was his first choice, but because the Midwest football powers didn't want him. There, he was surrounded by some of the nation's top coaches for quarterbacks, and that accelerated his development. He played only two seasons at Miami, the second for coach Jimmy Johnson. Armed with his degree, he entered the supplemental draft, where the Browns pulled off a trade with Buffalo—giving up two first-rounders (1985, 1986), a third-rounder (1985) and a sixth-rounder (1986) for his rights. Buffalo already had another Hurricanes quarterback—Jim Kelly—so it didn't need Kosar.

For Browns fans, everything fell into place so Kosar could play in Cleveland. Of course, Kosar also made sure the right pieces were in the right spot so he could come home.

Bernie Kosar was the epitome of what Cleveland was all about at a time when the city needed a figure to rally around. Cleveland has been the butt of many jokes through the years, some justified but many more not. Kosar was the same way. He'll never be accused of having blazing speed or coordination . . . but how can we forget him crouching under center with the right leg back so he wouldn't trip over the center after the snap? He graduated in three years with two degrees, outsmarted the NFL and entered the supplemental draft just so he could play for his home team at a time when no one wanted to come here. He played in the dilapidated Municipal Stadium, and he

found a way to win on the green dirt they called a field. He was very hard-working, intelligent, an all-around nice guy and playing for a city like Cleveland, what more can you ask for?
—Jerry Kendig

When Kosar won the national title at Miami, he was 20 years old. When he joined the Browns and became their starting quarterback on October 13, 1985, Kosar was only 21.

And when the Browns cut him on November 9, 1993, he was only 29.

Now you know why Kosar sometimes has said, "I'd like to play just one more game."

And why he has told active players, "It goes by so fast."

And why it's still hard, even for Browns fans, to truly appreciate what Kosar did in his career.

Kosar always sounded older, felt older and player older than the calendar. Think about jamming a double major of finance and economics into a degree in three years, with a 3.27 grade-point average. Challenging enough for even a full-time student, but remarkable for the starting quarterback of a national championship team.

Think about playing only two years of college, then coming to the pros in your hometown. The blessing for Kosar was the Browns had a capable veteran in Gary Danielson to open the season at quarterback. They were coming off a 5-11 record in 1984, but Marty Schottenheimer had taken over in the middle of that season and coached them to a 4-4 mark in the second half. He had two punishing running backs in Earnest Byner and Kevin Mack. He had a future Hall of Fame tight end in Ozzie Newsome, a reasonably talented offensive line with Cody Risien, Dan Fike, Rickey Bolden, Mike Baab, Paul Farren and George Lilja. Kosar did not come to an expansion team.

But the expectations were outrageous. Kosar received a five-year, $5 million contract, making him the highest-paid player on the team before taking his first pro snap. He was the hometown hero arriving to save the hometown team.

Few Browns fans remember that Kosar actually was nervous in his first pro game, completing only 6-of-22 passes for 97 yards. It was an exhibition game against the New England Patriots, and it helped Schottenheimer stick to his decision to open the 1985 season with Danielson. But Danielson was injured in the fifth game of the season. Kosar trotted onto the field—and promptly fumbled his first snap. But he completed his first seven passes, mostly short and safe throws. The Browns beat New England, 24-10. The next week, Kosar started and Cleveland was a 21-6 winner over Houston.

The Browns finished that season at 8-8; Kosar was 4-6 as a starter. They made the playoffs, then blew a 21-3 lead, losing to Miami, 24-21. Mostly, Kosar handed the ball to Byner or Mack that season, both rushing for 1,000 yards. His stats were humble: eight touchdown passes, seven interceptions, a 69.3 passer rating and what would be a career-low 50 percent completion mark. He was not named to any all-rookie teams. That distinction went to the Rams' 34-year-old Dieter Brock. Yes, he was a rookie at 34.

Give Schottenheimer credit—something rarely done—for wisely working Kosar into the lineup and then protecting the young quarterback. Kosar was sacked only 19 times and rarely put in a position where he had to carry the offense on his young shoulders. So, just as Kosar was in the right place at the right time with the right coach in Miami's Howard Schnellenberger, you can say the same for Kosar once he came to the Browns.

In 1986, it happened. Lindy Infante was hired as offensive co-ordinator, and the Browns were transformed from a physically punishing running team to one that had a complex offense taking advantage of Kosar's football acumen.

Gary Danielson told *Sports Illustrated*'s Rick Telander: "(Kosar) has this ability to accept all surrounding stimuli and utilize it. I don't understand it, but he can focus on everything and not overload. I'm not just talking about blocking schemes and coverages. I mean things like how many people are in the stands, how many timeouts are left, where the stadium speakers are and why we have Gatorade and not Coke. He won't just know who the refs are, but where they are from. He'll take in all this stuff, feed it in and use it to find an angle, something to help us win."

As you consider 1986's 12-4 season, remember that Kosar played most of it at the age of 22. His birthday is November 25, 1963. When it appeared the Browns would beat Denver (Yes, the dreaded Drive game), the network television broadcasters were discussing how Kosar was on the verge of being the youngest quarterback ever to take his team to a Super Bowl. They didn't say how Kosar still could have been playing quarterback for the University of Miami—he did have two years of eligibility left. Or how the quarterback of the Hurricanes that season—Vinny Testaverde—is 12 days older than Kosar.

The point of all this is to demonstrate simply how so much happened so fast for Kosar, and how he handled it so well.

"I never felt that young," he said. "But I knew I was one of the youngest guys on the team, so I was very careful with what I said in interviews. I didn't want to take any credit. I wanted to praise my teammates. I worked at giving very boring answers."

Which is what older quarterbacks always tell young ones to do.

> The way Bernie played . . . using his intelligence because he was not fleet of foot . . . throwing the ball at any angle to get a completion . . . because protection had broken down . . . even drawing a play in the dirt and have it going for a touchdown . . . struck a chord with Browns fans. Bernie was willing to use all of his God-given gifts, both positive and negative, to win. He showed what it means to be from Cleveland and be proud of it.
> **—Jon D. Zapisek**

The point of this chapter is not to replay Kosar's career, but it is to put Kosar into context of someone who played his entire Browns career in his 20s but usually acted as if he were 40. From the Browns' 1993 media guide, here is just part of the list of his charity activities:

- Donated $10,000 to the University of Miami to be split between the business school and athletic department.
- Gives two scholarships each year at $5,000 each award to Miami students on the basis of need.
- Donated a "substantial sum" to the Miami Project designed to help find a cure for paralysis.
- Helped pay the medical bills of a local college baseball player severely injured in a game.
- Tennis shoes for inner-city Special Olympic competitors.
- Honorary Chairman of the Mahoning County American Heart Association and the Rainbow Babies & Children's Hospital "Light up a Life" campaign.
- Donated $25,000 to benefit those with cystic fibrosis.
- Donated $10,000 to Project: LEARN.

There were far more charity activities than these, many that Kosar did not want made public. He is so loved by most Browns fans today nearly as much for what he did off the field as the success playing for the Browns. He signed countless autographs, shook thousands of hands and posed for endless pictures with strangers.

"It takes about 20 seconds to be nice to most people," he said. "I try to always do that."

Kosar spoke those words when he was 46, still signing autographs, still posing for pictures, still being Bernie.

And yes, still wishing he could pull on an orange helmet and play one more season—even one more game—for the Browns.

So what happened to Kosar that his Browns career was over before his 30th birthday?

Yes, Bill Belichick happened, cutting Kosar in favor of Testaverde in 1993. But Kosar was never a starter after leaving the Browns, backing up for three more seasons in Dallas and Miami. By the time he was 30, his body was feeling 50 after all the hits.

In 1988, he missed seven games because of two different injuries—strained knee ligaments and strained elbow ligaments in his throwing arm.

In 1990, he fractured his right thumb.

In 1992, he played the entire second half against Miami with a fractured ankle. He missed nine games, came back and broke the ankle again against Pittsburgh.

These are the injuries listed in the media guide.

At the age of 46, Kosar is paying some major physical dues for his willingness to stand in the pocket until the last split second, giving the receiver just a little more time to get open—then throwing the ball just as a defender decked him. He can't just stand up from a low chair; his surgically repaired ankle and aching knees aren't strong enough. He needs to pull himself up a bit with his hands on the arms of a chair. Nor can he hold his right arm straight out.

"I've had surgery on my ankle to get a screw taken out," Kosar said. "I had surgery on my right elbow to have spurs removed and on my left elbow to have a ligament fixed. My back hurts sometimes. The ankle still isn't great. But I'm doing OK, I really am."

Kosar also has dealt with the aftermath of concussions suffered. There are some headaches, some brief memory loss, some occasional involuntary twitching.

"I don't know how many concussions I had . . . a lot," he said. "We just played through them. It was like a badge of courage. No one was counting when I played. I kept smelling salts in my pouch (around his waist) when I was out there, because I'd get hit and feel dizzy."

He paused.

"We played at Pittsburgh, Cincinnati and Houston every year," Kosar said. "That awful (artificial) turf, the worst fields. It was like cement. The initial hit wasn't the worst, it was when your head banged down on that turf. I have friends that I played with who are worse. They have short-term memory loss; I don't."

"But in the morning, I sometimes feel slow. At night, I get tired. I struggle sometimes to say exactly what I want when I'm tired like that. But I have been treated; I am doing better."

Kosar said all that without a trace of pity. It was as if he was reading off his work schedule for the day—no emotion, just a fact of life.

"I've gotten to know some of Bernie's friends from the Browns," said Tami Longaberger, Kosar's close friend. "Most of them have real physical problems from football that they'll deal with the rest of their lives. But they are like Bernie; they say they'd go through it all once more if only they could play again."

The sudden cut of Bernie went to the heart of each fan. Here was a young man who personified that work ethic, so when he was "dismissed," it was as if a close friend of each fan had been fired.

They loved him then and they love him now as one of their own.

—VernAnn McConnell

In 2009, Kosar quietly made a call to Baltimore.

"I needed to see Art," said the former Browns quarterback.

He meant Art Modell, the former owner of the Browns who moved the franchise to Baltimore after the 1995 season.

"We hadn't talked since I was cut (by the Browns in 1993)," said Kosar. "I heard that Art was in a wheelchair and not doing well. I know that Art thinks he can't come back (to Cleveland), so I went to Art."

All Kosar ever did was make Modell a lot of money from 1985 to 1993, when Kosar quarterbacked the Browns. With Kosar, the Browns went to the playoffs five years in a row, from 1985 to 1989. Since 1990, they have been to the playoffs only twice (1994, 2002). Kosar also led the Browns to the AFC Championship Game three times, and they haven't been close to that level since. Modell talked about a "lifetime" contract for Kosar in the late 1980s, but that didn't stop Modell from allowing Belichick to cut him.

So why visit Modell?

"Because it was something I should do," said Kosar. "Why not make up with him? Life is too short. We had a great visit."

Then there's Belichick.

"Bill and I made up not long after he got the New England job," said Kosar. "I was interviewed about it, and I told the writers that

I thought Bill would make a good coach. I really meant it. He's a smart guy. Bill then called me to thank me, and we've been friends ever since. I have never been one to carry grudges for long."

For real?

"I got whacked by Bill, but stuff does happen," said Kosar. "You can't change history. You can't be negative or bitter about it. I didn't want to carry that around when it came to Bill. When reporters asked me about how Bill would do in New England, they figured I'd slam him. But I said what I really believed. Bill is fantastic when it comes to organization and discipline. His strength is defense. He really knows his X's and O's. He could learn offense, and he'd learn from what happened in Cleveland."

But there's more.

"People won't believe this, but when we were talking about coaches for the Browns in 1999, I mentioned hiring Bill to Mr. (Al) Lerner and (Browns President) Carmen Policy," said Kosar. "They about laughed me out of the office. They thought I was crazy. I thought Bill would be perfect for a team on a tight timeline because of his incredible organizational skills. We'd needed a special coach for an expansion team."

Kosar had to know the public backlash for bringing Belichick back to Cleveland—remember, he had yet to revive his career at New England—meant it was impractical. But the fact that he'd mention it says two things about Kosar: 1) He is a very creative thinker and risk taker when it comes to football. 2) He really hates grudges.

Asked to discuss Kosar, Belichick responded with this e-mail: "I have always had a lot of respect for Bernie—his football intelligence and passion for football. I appreciate the support he has shown me through the years. I have always admired his preparation and commitment to the Browns—before, during and after Bill Belichick. I have enjoyed my communications with Bernie through the years."

It sounds very formal and sterile, but the facts are that Kosar has reached out to Modell and Belichick over the years, two guys who were part of the worst season of his life.

In the fall of 2010, Kosar was 46 years old. He saw the world not through the eyes of the confident quarterback but from the perspective of a man who knows life can be hard. It's not always fair. We also can make some dumb decisions.

"When I was playing, I never thought it would end," he said. "I knew it would happen, but I never thought it would, you know what I mean? I didn't think I'd get hurt. I didn't think I'd get divorced. I didn't think I'd go bankrupt. I thought the money would always be there. No athlete when he's young or in his prime ever thinks it will end."

But end, it did.

The divorce was very public, very ugly.

The money disappeared due to some family issues and some poor investments. Kosar also forgot he was an honor student with a finance degree from the University of Miami. He allowed some people to handle his money, and he simply didn't pay attention to where it went.

"I know how to make money, and I know how to spend money," he said. "The saving part never worked for me. My dad was a steelworker. My brother's company closed. Things happen; people needed help."

He paused.

"I was into a lot of Florida real estate," he added. "Anyone who had a lot of Florida real estate and says they didn't get killed in the last few years is lying."

Kosar started over.

At press time, he was dating Tami Longaberger, the CEO of The Longaberger Company of Newark, Ohio. It has been nationally known for its handmade, quality baskets and enthusiastic, Avon-like sales force. Longaberger published a business book called *Weaving Dreams*, and she is on the board of trustees at Ohio State.

"The rumor is we're engaged," said Kosar. "I act like we're married. Just say that we're good friends. Her impact on me is phenomenal. She is an amazing person."

Longaberger was helping Kosar get organized. He was represented by Neil Cornrich, one of NFL's most respected agents. He was working through his bankruptcy issues and working with Longaberger on selling products with NFL licensing.

"Bernie is a person who is honest and has the courage to express his opinions," said Longaberger. "He's not self-absorbed. He is generous and kind. He has a hard time being mad at those who haven't been nice to him. It's not in his heart to hold grudges."

Kosar has four children: Sara (age 18 in 2010), Rachel (17), Becky (13) and Joe (10).

"I spend a lot of time as Mr. Mom," he said. "The kids live in Florida, but they spend a lot of time up here with me. I coach my son's flag football team. It's so cool. We have a kid named Michael Stolzenberg. He plays with artificial legs and arms. He's unbelievable, so tough. When I feel bad, I think about him. I get real thankful. Then guess what? He runs faster than me."

Kosar loves to play catch with his son, both pretending they are quarterbacks.

"I still have a juvenile streak in me," he said. "If one of us makes a bad throw or drops a pass—usually, it's me—then we later play a game called Gastineau. I stand by the bed, and my son blindsides me. Hits me hard. He's about 5-4, 125 pounds. He lifts weights with me. He's strong."

Most Browns fans will remember when the Jets' Mark Gastineau hammered Kosar in a game. Now, it's what Kosar calls it when his son tackles him.

Kosar was not dwelling on the past, but he was thinking about it.

"I still talk to (Denver quarterback) John Elway," he said. "We never talk about The Drive or The Fumble. He knows it's still too painful for me. We talk about guys we played, games we saw—even some individual plays in games. He owned the Denver franchise in the old Arena League, and we talk a lot about Arena League players. But we don't talk about those (AFC playoff) games."

Kosar did receive a Super Bowl ring as a backup with Dallas in 1993, "but my goal was to win a Super Bowl for Cleveland. It's why I wanted to play here in the first place. It's home."

So what was worse, The Drive or The Fumble?

"Can't say," he said. "They both sucked. But I felt the worst for Earnest (Byner, who fumbled). He's such a good man. I think about him every day. I admire how he handled all that."

There are nights when Kosar feels as if he's still the Browns quarterback.

If you say, "In his dreams," you're right.

"I have dreams where I'm still playing," he said. "Not dreams about whole games, just plays. I may be watching film of certain blitzes or defenses, then I go to sleep—and suddenly I'm in a game, facing that defense. I've had dreams about 2-minute drills. I still watch a lot of game films. Arena League, the Browns, whatever. I remain fascinated by it, I love to study it."

"Bernie is brilliant when it comes to the game of football," said Longaberger. "He tells me what is going to happen with a play as soon as the teams are on the line of scrimmage. His vision for the game is absolutely amazing. Sometimes, he will talk about his playing days . . . a specific play that he would want to do over, how coach (Howard) Schnellenberger, coach (Gary) Stevens and coach (Marc) Trestman influenced his offensive philosophy and his life. He misses the locker room environment that no one really understands but the players. He still appreciates the loyalty and love he receives from the guys he played with."

Just as Kosar was incredibly young when he led Miami to the NCAA title and the Browns to all those second-half victories in big games, he's still under 50, still young enough to make another comeback.

"I'm 46, in the second half of my life," he said. "I feel better than I have—physically and emotionally—probably since I played. I work out about every day. I eat better. I do a lot of stretching. I have stopped making long-term plans because I have learned how it all can change. I want to make the most of every day. I really am content where I am right now."

Why We Love Bernie Kosar

I remember listening to (Cleveland radio talk show host) Pete Franklin going hog-wild bananas on the radio that we would have this supplemental pick to grab a young Bernie Kosar. Franklin was beside himself with excitement, and I would soon find out why. Kosar, as well as Brian Sipe, had a special ability to almost always have the game within his grasp (or at least have you believing that it was all possible). Their teammates rallied around both of those players. They could always convince the huddle that they were only one play away. That, to this day for me, defines great leadership. The intelligence of both players was palpable on the field, as well as on the sidelines. Kosar's last touchdown play that he drew up in the dirt was a great example, to me, of leadership (even if coach Bill Belichick was upset).

Initially, I was not totally sold on Kosar. Perhaps because we were led so close to the Promised Land, only to fall short, got the better of me. He was always a step slower than I had wanted him to be. He is only slightly older than I am, so he was not in the "beyond reproach," revered status of a Sipe. My father and uncles had talked of Otto Graham and Frank Ryan. Bernie was not as mythical as they were. I had always held him to impossible standards to save my city from its sports doldrums. I needed him to be mythical to me, and he wasn't that.

One day, after he had retired, my in-laws and I went down to

Saint John's Cathedral (Roman Catholic) for a Sunday Mass in downtown Cleveland. I had spotted Kosar. He was with his wife, his kids and what looked to be either his parents or her parents. After the Mass, everyone was mingling out on East 9th, just like thousands of other times. Kosar was out front talking with a number of people and families who had wanted to wish him well. . . . Everyone was dispersing. I watched as Bernie slowly made his way east to where he and his family had parked. They were talking and laughing and taking their time. His kids and parents were not making it a quick trip for him. Bernie was about out of sight, when I suddenly saw him turn around and sprint back west toward the northwest corner of the cathedral.

Suddenly he stopped.

There was a very old man standing there, who had been motionless the entire time. Bernie reached into his pocket and gave the very old man some money. The man had been asking for money from people who had been in earshot. Bernie had waited so that no one else was around to see it. . . . *Bernie turned around*! There was no one who witnessed this except for me from a very long distance. This story is very important to me because my faith grew a little bit witnessing that moment. Bernie, even retired, had still somehow found a way to draw up that play in the sand and, yet again, found a way to make a Sunday thrilling for me.

At that very precise moment, to me alone, Bernie Kosar became mythical.

—James Geither

Like most any other Cleveland kid, Bernie Kosar was my idol. It was the first true taste of success for Cleveland sports in my lifetime, and as far as I understood, it was all about Bernie. I spray-painted my shoes orange, and I listened to *Bernie, Bernie* on repeat. Then, in the summer of 1987, I was at a Cleveland Indians game and fortunate enough to have been invited into a suite in left field by family friends. It was one of those games where the attendance was 5,000. Every suite was empty, save the adjacent one from which a group of large, athletic-looking folks finally emerged in the fourth inning or so.

One of those large, athletic-looking folks was none other than my hero, Bernie J. Kosar. I was awestruck and giddy. They were friendly and waved, and greeted us politely. My dad, never bashful, went over to the railing maybe an inning later. I don't know what he said exactly, but moments later, I heard Bernie say, "Michael, c'mon!" as he was waved me over.

I was grinning ear to ear. I tried to climb over the railing, and Bernie lifted me over. I can't exactly remember what I said or even what he said, because I was in a state of disbelief. But he put me on his lap. I sat there for an entire glorious inning. At the conclusion, he took our address from my dad. One month later, a signed poster from Bernie Kosar showed up at my house, and it said: "To Michael, Best Wishes, Bernie Kosar." Along with the poster were sweatbands, a sweatshirt and a typed letter also signed by Bernie saying how nice it was to meet me. I still have it. To this day, I have hung this poster in every place I've ever lived.

—*Mike Albainy*

I was 8 years old and started to get into Cleveland sports when Bernie was the quarterback. The Browns were winning with this QB who looked like a normal steelworker living next door. He played through injuries and gave me the first taste of what Cleveland sports was all about. I got married August 4th, 2007, and wore a Bernie Kosar jersey when I threw the garter to the single guys. The song that I had playing? It was *Bernie, Bernie* by The Bleacher Bums.

—*Brian Truskot*

Bernie Kosar is the reason I went to church from 1985 to 1993. At that time we lived in Rocky River and used to attend St. Christopher's Saturday Mass at 5:30 p.m. Why this specific Mass? That is the one that we could sit near Bernie Kosar and wait with baited breath for the handshake of peace. It was somewhat comical to see the congregation, in a less than crowded Mass, encircle Bernie as if he were Bruce Springsteen belting out *Jungleland* in the Meadowlands. He would take the time to shake all the hands around him, and he even stayed after Mass to talk to his adoring fans.

The most memorable Masses were the ones that Bernie and Brian Brennan attended. Even the most pious parishioner's focus would wander from the pulpit and wonder how Bernie was going to elude the rush of Mark Gastineau and find Brennan on a seam route during the next day's game. Bernie was the kind of guy who was loved by all people and touched the lives of everyone he met. So I apologize to my parents, grandparents, and priests; I went to church to break the first commandment and worship another god. This one wore number 19.

—*Matthew Grady*

The ONLY time in my 60 years that I cheered for the Dallas Cowboys in the Super Bowl was in the 1993 season, when Bernie got his ring. I am forever grateful to the Cowboys for giving our beloved quarterback what he so greatly deserved. Bernie was so gracious to my son Justin when he signed a helmet that Justin had painted and striped to look like a Browns helmet. He even asked Justin where he got it. Now my son is gone, but I still have that helmet and memories of Bernie at quarterback.

—*Mike Miller*

Bernie's young fans knew if they didn't remain in church until the end of Mass, he would not sign an autograph for them. The Browns playoff game on Saturday, January 3, 1987, remains in my mind forever. It and what occurred postgame speak highly of Bernie. The Browns were down by 10 points to the New York Jets with 4:14 to go. With a furious rally led by Bernie, who set playoff records, the Browns tied it with seven seconds remaining and won it in the second overtime. Coach Schottenheimer said, "I have never experienced or seen a comeback like that." Tackle Paul Farren said, "It's incredible the way he brought us together as a unit, one play at a time."

The following Monday, a reporter asked him how excited he felt after the victory. Bernie told him that he went to Mass Saturday evening after the game and was so keyed up from the effects of the game that he could not concentrate on the liturgy, and therefore he went to Mass again on Sunday!

—*Joe Smorowski*

Every Christmas, the Cleveland Public Schools' special education department would sponsor a party for all of the students featuring current and former Browns as guests. Bob Gain, Doug Dieken and Steve Everitt were a few of the players who showed up every year to sign autographs and mingle with the kids. The joy and excitement that these Browns brought to the kids was apparent. Bernie Kosar would buy tennis shoes for the entire group so that they could participate in the Special Olympics. No fanfare, publicity stunt or photo-op, just giving from the heart.

—*Ernest A. Fronczak*

The most striking memory I have of him was at the Hall of Fame Game in Canton in 1999, when the new Browns first took the field. Bernie was there, patiently signing what must have been hundreds of autographs. He didn't charge a dime to us, the fans. That's why we love Bernie.

—*Geoff Elliott*

Bernie Kosar represented all that was "good" about the Browns. He wanted to play here and had an overwhelming desire to lift the organization onto his shoulders and put the team back on the top shelf, so to speak. You gotta love a guy who wants to do the right thing and does it through his performance, not just his words. He wasn't just satisfied with the team being labeled as a "contender," he wanted the team to be called a "champion."

Leadership qualities are difficult to find in most people, but Bernie Kosar had a ton of it and showed it every Sunday. His work with charity organizations outside of the game was also

extremely impressive, and still is today. Bernie lived and died
with the team's success and failures, much like we do every week.
We related to him so well because he was more like "one of us,"
and shared our hopes and dreams for the franchise. He didn't just
play for the money. He played for the city, and most of all . . . .the
fans.

—*Bob Mori*

CHAPTER 12

Only the players and the fans could have created the Dawg Pound

My favorite Brown is Frank Minnifield. I was born in 1967, and Minnie is the best Browns player in my lifetime. A lockdown CB who was awesome against the run. What more can you ask for?

—John Jaeger

The Dawg Pound wasn't invented by any marketing firm or by some genius in the Browns front office. Nothing was planned to convince Browns fans that what they needed to do was bark like dogs and bring Milk-Bones to the games.

It all started one day in practice, almost by accident.

In 1984, Frank Minnifield had just joined the Browns as a free agent from the United States Football League. He came to the Browns as a starting cornerback and showed up with the nickname "Sky," because he could jump. He told *The Plain Dealer*'s Tony Grossi that he could jump. Really jump. Leap to the stars, as he told Grossi: "My standing vertical leap has been measured at 44 inches."

If true, that put him in the same orbit as Michael Jordan, Julius Erving and LeBron James in their primes. Maybe was it was true, as Minnifield was 5-foot-9 and 160 pounds when passed over by the NFL and instead signed with the USFL, a league willing to overlook his size. Even after Minnifield emerged as a star in the USFL and the Browns were starving for a cornerback, they almost didn't sign him because of his height.

"I liked Minnifield, and so did our scouts," recalled Sam Rutigliano, the Browns coach when Minnifield signed. "But I had to lobby with (owner) Art Modell. He never saw Minnifield play, but he had talked to (Oakland Raiders owner) Al Davis—and Davis said to forget Minnifield, he was too small."

Exactly why Modell would trust Al Davis in the 1980s is something that Rutigliano and others in the organization wondered. Davis was infamous for looking for an edge. Given how often he moved his franchise between Oakland and Southern California and some of his other business dealings, it would not have been a surprise if Davis told Modell to forget about Minnifield—and then signed the defensive back to a contract with his Raiders.

> I've met several Browns players over the years. One experience that stands out was meeting Frank Minnifield. It was the off-season between the 1989 and 1990 seasons. Minnifield and Hanford Dixon were at their peak as shutdown corners. My wife and I were living in Lexington, Ky. We attended a Jaycee event at which Minnifield made an appearance. After the event, I went up to him to wish him and the Browns well and to shake his hand. What shocked me was his size. I'm not a big man at 5-foot-11, but I towered over Minnifield. . . . I could not believe he was as short as he was and still was one of the best in the business.
> —**Stan Sak**

Minnifield was a walk-on at Louisville as a freshman because he was 5-9 and 140 pounds. Yes, that's correct, 140 pounds. He played well enough as a freshman to get a scholarship for the next three seasons. He became a starting defensive back and the Cardinals' top kick returner. As a junior, he led the team in punt returns—and the entire nation in kickoff returns (30.4 yards per attempt). But he was still 5-foot-9, even if he gained a few pounds and was listed at 160 his senior year.

We can't be sure, but Minnifield probably wouldn't have been taken in the first eight rounds in the NFL draft (if at all). So when the USFL's Chicago Blitz (whose front office consisted of former NFL head coach George Allen and his son Bruce) drafted Minnifield in the third round, he didn't wait for the NFL.

After one game of the 1983 season, Minnifield injured his knee and went on injured reserve for the year. After the season, the Chicago owner (who lived in Phoenix) decided to trade franchise territories with the Arizona owner. The Arizona owner thought that was a fine idea, because he'd drawn only 25,000 fans. For some reason, nobody in Arizona wanted go to an outdoor stadium to watch football in 116-degree heat. This is why Minnifield's career record shows that he played 15 games for Arizona in 1984. He intercepted four passes, recovered two fumbles and blocked a couple of kicks. He helped Arizona make the 1984 USFL Championship Game. By that point, he'd moved onto the NFL's radar screen. And someone in the Browns front office took notice.

There was much complaining and gnashing of teeth when the Browns signed Minnifield. The USFL wasn't happy. Some other NFL teams were not happy. But Minnifield was thrilled to sign what was said to be a four-year, $1.6 million deal. It actually was four contracts—one year each. About $400,000 was guaranteed. But that still was a lot of money to Minnifield, and it was also more than many of his new teammates were making.

"We had two first-round draft choices (cornerback Hanford Dixon and safety Don Rogers) in the secondary," said Minnifield. "Then I came along with a big contract."

In 1981, Dixon was the 22nd pick in the NFL draft. According to a story by *The Plain Dealer*'s Russell Schneider, the Browns gave Dixon a signing bonus of $150,000. His three-year deal paid him an average of $115,000 annually. In 1984, safety Don Rogers was the team's first-round pick, selected 18th overall. His contract was worth more than what Dixon received, but it still didn't match Minnifield's deal.

Minnifield realized that "with two No. 1 draft picks and me as a high-priced free agent, we could have problems."

There could be jealousy. There could be other problems off the field, especially as Dixon and Minnifield were natural leaders, very vocal, extremely outgoing. Minnifield made a point to get to know his fellow defensive backs, especially Dixon.

"You need to be close as a team," Minnifield said. "It has to be a choice. You have to choose to get along, you choose to build chemistry. You are going to need it with all the stuff that happens in a game and during a season. You get to know their wives, their kids, their family situations. It's more than just football. It takes extra effort to care about people, to talk and listen to them—but it's worth it."

The 1984 season was a tough one for Minnifield and the Browns. He battled various injuries. The team started 1-7, and Rutigliano was fired. Marty Schottenheimer took over at midseason, and the team was 4-4 under the new head coach. But Minnifield and Dixon knew there were times when the team was ready to fall apart in 1984. They avoided a total collapse, but the team desperately needed chemistry.

> With no symbol on the helmet, Hanford and Minnifield
> brought us the Dawg Pound and everything that goes with it.
> They helped define what the Browns should be: overachievers,
> hard workers leaving it all on the field.
> **—Jason Provchy**

So exactly how did every Browns fan start barking like a Dawg?

"A big part of our success was that we were very close as a unit," said Minnifield. "It began with the defensive backs. We started going out to dinner at the same places. We helped each other on the field, in the film room. Then we started barking in practice. It was just something that we did, me and Hanford. We used to say the quarterback was a cat, and we're the dogs. The cat has no chance against the dogs. Soon, other guys on defense started barking. It brought the group closer. You can't make up something like this; it comes out of a group hanging together, getting to know everyone's personality. We were like that, barking dogs. We didn't want to be vanilla. We wanted our own identity. We wanted to show our enthusiasm. The fans caught on to it, and soon, all the Browns fans and players were barking."

That is what Minnifield told me, and it matched Dixon's version.

Here is a letter that Minnifield posted on the Blanton Collier Foundation's Web site:

"The 'Dawg Pound' started during the 1985 training camp at Lakeland Community College in Kirtland, Ohio. Hanford and I started the idea of the pound to try to get more pressure on the quarterback. We had the idea of the quarterback being the cat, and the defensive line being the dogs. Whenever the defense would get a regular sack or a coverage sack the defensive linemen and linebackers would bark. This attitude carried into the stands at the training camp, where fans started barking along with the players. We then put up the first 'Dawg Pound' banner in front of the bleachers before the first preseason game at old Cleveland Stadium. The bleacher section had the cheapest seats in the stadium, and its fans were already known as the most vocal. They adopted their new identity whole-heartedly, wearing dog noses, dog masks, bone-shaped hats and other outlandish costumes. Woof. Woof."

> I wish they would come up with more T-shirts, hats, etc., with a Dawg Pound logo on it. I love the phrase: *Bark loud! Bite hard! Leave a mark! Go Browns!*
> **—Sidney Johnston**

The Dawg Pound caught on because it was a bit silly and lots of fun. Going to a football game dressed up as a dog and barking during key plays is so unlike how most of us must act during the week—it had tremendous appeal. It was a way to blow off steam that comes from the pressure of everyday life. It also was a way to bring fans together, along with a way for them to connect with the team. That's because the defense was barking during the games, too.

In a 1985 *Plain Dealer* story, Tony Grossi wrote how Minnifield and Dixon "pointed to each other from a distance, ran full speed at each other and splashed the first official High 5 of training camp. . . . 'Boom,' screamed Dixon. 'We are the best.'"

For a few years, the defense was indeed just that. In 1985, the Browns were 8-8 with a rookie quarterback named Bernie Kosar mostly handing off to a pair of 1,000 yard rushers—Kevin Mack and Earnest Byner. The Browns actually made the playoffs that season, but blew a 21-3 lead and lost 24-21 to Miami. In the summer of 1986, Rogers died of a cocaine overdose. Because he played only two years, many forget that Rogers seemed on the road to the Pro Bowl. In his second season, he led the team in tackles. He was blending into the hard-hitting secondary that Schottenheimer wanted and was being fashioned by Minnifield and Dixon. Rogers died a week after Maryland star and Boston Celtics first-round draft choice Len Bias overdosed on cocaine. He died less than two days before he was to be married. He seemed to die needlessly and shockingly, because he didn't give the usual hints of drug use—being late or missing practices or zoning out in team meetings.

"Coming after that loss to Miami, what happened to Don really shook us," said Minnifield. "It was the turning point. We could have folded. It showed us that tomorrow wasn't promised to anyone, that we had to stick together more than ever."

Dixon and Minnifield set a goal—they didn't just want to go to the Pro Bowl, they wanted to go there together.

People used to ask me why I sit in the Dawg Pound. I always said, "That's where the real fans sit." In the Dawg Pound, everyone is up and cheering, and God help you if you're for the other team! I've had some good times in the Dawg Pound and earned my nickname, "Dawg Pound Girl!"
—**Laura Urbanek**

Fans loved Dixon and Minnifield because they seemed and played like underdogs.

"One of our goals was not to act like high draft choices or guys making big money," said Minnifield. "We wanted to be regular working guys."

What it made work was they were sincere.

Cocky for sure, but sincere.

"Our antics ain't taunting," Minnifield told *The Plain Dealer*'s Tony Grossi in 1985. "With our bump and run, we stand there and we talk to those receivers. We talk about their shoes, their uniforms. Then we go out there and bump 'em. We ain't gonna hurt anyone this year and point at them. We're just gonna hurt them to get them out of the game. After that, we hope they recover and have a good season."

There was a game in 1984 when Minnifield blasted into Cincinnati's Chris Collinsworth, and then several players celebrated as the receiver remained on the field, obviously in serious pain. He didn't play the rest of the season. The Browns coaches told the players to cut out the antics after a player is hurt, but Schottenheimer wanted them to keep barking.

"I'd be afraid they'd bite me and I'd get rabies (if he told them to stop)," said Schottenheimer in 1985, praising "the enthusiasm they created."

"We approached each play with a can't-lose mentality," said Dixon. "Have no fear, get right up on the receiver and jam him up. You not only want to win each battle (with a receiver), but know why you won it. That means you have to prepare for your opponent. You watch tape together at the facility. You take tape home, and watch some more."

For all the barking and charisma displayed by Minnifield and Dixon, there was another element—preparation.

In 1986, *Sports Illustrated*'s Doug Looney wrote that Dixon and Minnifield were "two of the orneriest, cockiest, brashest—and don't forget best—cornerbacks in the league. Schottenheimer says he wouldn't trade them for any pair in the NFL. Every time there's action, these guys seem to be a part of it. . . . There's more to stellar defense, says Dixon, than dealing out physical abuse. And he has the evidence. At his condo is a filing cabinet filled with manila folders. They contain information on opposing receivers and backs, and their playing habits. These folders get constant attention. So do the videotapes of rival teams that he brings on trips, with special emphasis on how teams work when they are within 15 yards of the goal line."

In a 2001 interview with Chuck Murr of *The Orange and Brown Report*, Minnifield recalled, "We scratched. We held. We bit. We pushed. We intimidated. It was a much more physical game (than today). . . . The defense was built around Hanford and me. We put a lot of guys in the box (up on the line) and that allowed us to play man coverage. We forced teams to throw against us. We could get away with it then because the rules were not as strict."

Give Minnifield credit for mentioning how the change in rules has made it harder for current defensive backs. Few retired players in any sport are willing to admit anything is more difficult for the modern athlete. But the bottom line on Minnifield and Dixon was they had at least three seasons—1986, 1987 and 1988—when they were unquestionably the best cornerbacks in the NFL, at least that's the three years they both went to the Pro Bowl. But they also were outstanding in 1986, when Dixon was picked for the Pro Bowl while Minnifield was ignored. In 1989, both players also made the Pro Bowl—three years in a row together—but Dixon was slipping a bit—still very good but not an elite defender.

Cornerback is such a demanding position, especially how Dixon and Minnifield played it. This was not zone coverage, it was man-to-man. If the defender stumbled or was slightly faked, everyone saw it. The result could be a touchdown, a long gain, a critical first down.

"We hated even the thought of playing a zone, and I'm not sure we even knew how to play it," insisted Minnifield, 21 years after making his last Pro Bowl team.

Dixon and Minnifield each played nine seasons, but Dixon (who had fewer injuries) appeared in more games: 131-122. Dixon also had more interceptions, 26-20. The players vote for the Pro

Bowl, and Minnifield was honored four times, Dixon three. The writers—who picked the All-Pro teams—preferred Dixon 2-1. Minnifield was the superior to Dixon in coverage, while Dixon was a stronger tackler. You can spend a lot of time debating who was better, but this much is certain—the Browns have not had a cornerback even close to this pair since 1989, their final season together. Before them, you can talk about Warren Lahr, Erich Barnes, Bernie Parrish and maybe some others as being very good cornerbacks, but never in their history did the Browns have two at the same time approaching the talent and leadership skills of Dixon and Minnifield.

"Before I was drafted by the Browns (in 1981), I watched the Red Right 88 game on TV," recalled Dixon. "It was snowing, and all those fans had their shirts off. I remember thinking that those people are crazy, that's the last place I wanted to play. Then the Browns drafted me, and I loved it. There was so much good about the Browns of the 1980s, but the fans were the best."

CHAPTER 13

Art Modell is just not a Hall-of-Famer.

Three things have made me cry as an adult: 1) The passing of my father in 1985. 2) The passing of my mother in 1994. 3) The news the Browns were leaving for Baltimore. I guess one would not think that a sports happening would equate with the loss of a dear loved one, but I know for a fact that I wasn't the only adult male shedding tears when that news broke.

—Bill Beasley

The move still stings knowing if the Browns had stayed in Cleveland, we likely would have a Lombardi Trophy and a consistent playoff-caliber team. Instead, we are in a constant rebuilding mode.

—Larry Forrer

Does Art Modell belong in the Hall of Fame?

Most Browns fans have an answer to that one, but what they have to say usually isn't printable. And when it is, it doesn't make a lot of sense. "MODELL, IN THE HALL OF FAME??? ARE YOU KIDDING ME??? FIRST HE FIRED PAUL BROWN!!!! THEN HE STOLE OUR TEAM AND LEFT US WITH THIS CRUMMY EXPANSION FRANCHISE!!! THE MAN BELONGS IN JAIL!!!!"

Browns fans should be able to make a rational—or at least a very emotional but logical—argument against Modell being enshrined in Canton, Ohio.

Let's begin with a cold, hard fact that some people still refuse to accept. Except for in Green Bay, Wis., the fans don't own the team. From March 21, 1961, until Modell moved the team to Baltimore after the 1995 season, the Cleveland Browns were owned by Art Modell.

In 1999, when the Browns returned as an expansion team, owned by the Lerner family, the city welcomed them. Everyone was delighted to be rid of Modell and happy to have a fresh start with the front office team from the San Francisco 49ers. But Modell wasn't responsible for any of the problems the team faced over the first 11 years the return.

There's a good case to be made against Art Modell. But it usually isn't the one that Browns fans sputter about.

Some Browns fans will open their case against Modell by saying, "He fired Paul Brown, the greatest pro football coach ever. He doesn't deserve to be elected just for that!"

In this book, the argument is made that Paul Brown is the greatest Cleveland Brown . . . ever. People in Green Bay may tell you that Vince Lombardi was greater than Brown. But when he was a young assistant with the Giants, Lombardi asked Brown for advice. People from San Francisco will mention Bill Walsh, but Walsh, who was an assistant for Brown, called Brown the greatest coach in NFL history. Chuck Noll and Don Shula played for Brown and considered him their mentor.

New Englanders make their case for—who ever would have believed this—Bill Belichick as being this generation's Paul Brown. When I contacted Belichick for this book, he declined to discuss some topics. But he did e-mail me his feelings on Paul Brown. Belichick believes Brown is the greatest pro football coach . . . ever.

But Art Modell was right to fire Paul Brown!

There, I wrote it.

When I began the research for *Browns Town 1964*, I dug deep into Modell's decision to fire Brown. I began writing the book in 1994, when the Browns were still here. I didn't finish it until 1996, after they moved. There was every reason to hammer Modell for his decision. But I couldn't do it.

The man who invented so much of modern pro football, the man who coached in Cleveland starting in 1946 had simply run out of gas by the early 1960s. Even the best coaches can suffer a bit of burnout. They can become inflexible. They can become stale in the same city with the same team, the same fans, the same set of expectations and history of disappointments. Player after player on the 1964 team said that Paul Brown had to go. They said he seemed to be losing touch with the players. Jim Brown was frustrated that Paul Brown continually ran his star fullback between the tackles—there were no sweeps, there was no creativity. Both his longtime starting quarterbacks—Milt Plum and even the great Otto Graham—said they were given no real freedom to change plays that Brown called from the sidelines. Veteran sportswriter Hal Lebovitz and players, such as quarterback Jim Ninowski, said Brown refused to criticize Jim Brown.

"The truth is Paul was scared of Jim Brown," Lebovitz told me when I interviewed him for the book.

Remember, from 1959 to 1962, Paul Brown's last four seasons with Cleveland, the team failed to make the playoffs. His final four records were 7-5, 8-3-1, 8-5-1 and 7-6-1.

Brown was even becoming isolated from his friends. Blanton Collier first met Paul Brown during World War II when Brown was coaching at the Great Lakes Naval Training Station. Collier was a high school coach before the war, and he began hanging around Brown's practices—just to watch and learn. Soon, Brown put Collier to work as an assistant. After World War II, Paul Brown took the Cleveland job and brought Collier along as an assistant.

In 1954, Collier left Paul Brown to become the head coach at the University of Kentucky. In 1958, when Green Bay was looking for a new head coach, they asked Brown whom to hire. Brown told them to choose Collier or Lombardi. When Kentucky fired Collier after the 1961 season, Brown hired Collier back as an assistant. But in 1962, Modell was the owner. At the time, Modell was 37, only a little older than his players. When players began to come to Modell with complaints about the coach, Modell was flattered. He was too willing to buy them drinks and listen. Brown began to feel threatened.

During the 1962 preseason, Brown permitted Collier to make some changes to the offense. Collier began giving quarterbacks two or three options to pick from when they arrived at the line of scrimmage, rather than the one play that Brown had insisted be used. The Browns looked sharp in the preseason and won all their games. Reporters began writing about Collier's new "Check-off System," and how it revived the offense.

"Paul read those and put Blanton in the corner (of the office)," said Lebovitz. "The check-off system was junked. That was the beginning of the end of the relationship between these two men who had been such close friends."

Ninowski said the quarterbacks were stunned to see the little bit of freedom taken away.

During the 1962 season, there was a practice right after a blizzard when there was about a foot of snow on the field. Usually, Brown kept workouts in those conditions very short. He also was on the field and in the cold with the players. But on this day, he sat in his car, about 20 yards from the practice, and watched.

"The quarterback would go to Paul's car after every play, and Paul would roll down the window, tell him something, then roll up the window," recalled Ross Fichtner, a defensive back. "The players were freezing, but Paul never left his car."

Collier shared most of Brown's philosophies and strategies, but he didn't rule by fear. He had a knack for making the players think that his idea was really their own. He had long conversations with Jim Brown, Gary Collins, Frank Ryan, Bernie Parrish, Jim Ninowski and other key players. He took some of their suggestions and then made a few suggestions of his own. In many ways, Collier was a modern coach, working with players rather than them having a sense that they were nothing more than worker drones. Collier's approach worked because the players already knew him as an assistant—and he was a change from Brown. If you are going to fire a coach, then bring in one with a different personality. Collier was the best and perhaps the only coach who could have replaced Brown and immediately been successful.

The Browns were 10-4 in 1963 . . . up from 7-6-1 in Brown's final season.

Sports Illustrated wrote, "There can be no doubt about it, the major factor in the improvement of Jimmy Brown and his teammates is the absence of Paul Brown."

Paul Brown did return to the NFL after five years, when the AFL gave the city of Cincinnati an expansion team. Brown coached the Bengals from 1968 to 1975, going 55-56-1. He made the playoffs only three times and lost in the first round every time. This was a strong performance for an expansion franchise. It also happened because Brown had five seasons away from the game to recharge emotionally and reconsider some of his tactics.

Yes, Paul Brown was the greatest pro football coach . . . ever.

But Modell got it right by replacing Brown with Collier.

> I'm still not completely healed from the dagger wound to the heart that Art Modell inflicted when he ripped my beloved Browns out of Cleveland. I cannot look at my Kardiac Kids button, my Brian Sipe rookie card or the photo with me and Dave Logan without drifting back (to when the Browns moved). . . . On that day, I cried like a girl. Well, I am female, so I guess that's not too weird. I went to work with swollen eyes and a sullen disposition.
> **—Carrie Kinnison**

The case for putting Modell in Hall of Fame, or any owner, should be based mostly on what his teams did on the field. Modell was certainly better than average. He had 21 winning records in his 35 years of owning the Browns and a .519 winning percentage in the regular season. In those 35 years, Modell's teams went to the playoffs 17 times. In 1964, his team won the last championship—as of 2010—that any Cleveland fan has seen. The Browns went back to the NFL Championship Game in 1965 and lost.

Browns fans often point out that the Browns never won a Super Bowl—never even made it there under Modell. Since the Super Bowl wasn't played until the 1966 season, this isn't entirely his fault. Most people remember the Browns came one game short of the Super Bowl in 1986, 1987 and 1989. But the team also reached the NFL Championship—also one game short—in 1968 and 1969.

In the 1960s, a case can be made that Modell was not just a good owner but an outstanding one. He made a daring decision to fire Paul Brown and promote Blanton Collier. Collier was a better coach for the Browns than Paul Brown was at that point.

Paul Brown's final four records were 7-5, 8-3-1, 8-5-1 and 7-6-1.

Collier's first four records were 10-4, 10-3-1, 11-3 and 9-5.

From 1962—Art's first season as owner—through 1969, the Browns went to the NFL finals four times in eight years.

After the 1960s ended, Modell's team began to stumble. In 1970, Collier was 64. He had battled hearing problems for his entire coaching career. In 1970, he went 7-7 and retired at the end of the season.

In the 1970s, the Browns made the playoffs only twice (1971, 1972), losing both times. They had five winning records in that decade, along with some real stinkers such as 4-10 in 1974, 3-11 in 1975 and 6-8 in 1977. Nick Skorich had a winning record (30-24, from 1971 to 1974), but everyone else went 42-46.

In the 1980s, Modell's Browns had a good decade. They made the playoffs seven times (1980, 1982 and 1985 to 1989). But they also had two 5-11 seasons.

In the 1990s, the Browns had one winning season and five losing years under Modell. After he moved to Baltimore, he had one 8-8 record and three losing years.

Due to financial difficulties, Art had to sell his team in January 2004. From 2000 to 2003, the Ravens had three winning seasons. They made the playoffs three times and won the Super Bowl at the end of the 2000 season.

So what can we say about all this?

If anything, the case for Art Modell to be enshrined in Canton really looks like more of an argument for Blanton Collier (74-34,

.688 percentage from 1963 to 1970). Collier ran the team in his own fashion, but he used many of the methods and plans that he and Brown had developed over the years. Many of Collier's assistants were men who had been hired and trained by Brown. Modell deserves credit for making the coaching change. At the time, Brown's firing was unthinkable. In the days before big TV contracts and luxury suite sales and the pressure to win every year, teams let a coach who won a title stay until he felt like leaving.

The firing seemed to convince Modell that he could run a football team as well as Paul Brown. The seamless transition to Collier deceived Modell into believing that he really knew football, that he did not need a strong general manager.

So, in 1970, the Browns traded Paul Warfield to Miami for a draft pick and used the pick to take Mike Phipps.

From 1971 to 1995, the Browns' final 25 years in Cleveland with Modell, the team went 187-188.

That's one game under .500 for a quarter of a century after Collier.

It's 12 winning seasons in 25 years after Collier.

It's 4-10 in the playoffs after Collier.

It's seven coaches (including two interims) after Collier, and only two with winning records: Skorich (30-24) and Marty Schottenheimer (44-27). Modell hired two coaches who eventually took teams to the Super Bowl, Belichick and Forrest Gregg, but he fired both. After that, they won a title.

It's hard to see how his performance in Cleveland—or his 63-64 record with the Ravens—qualifies Modell for the Hall of Fame.

Art Modell does not belong in the Hall of Fame, and I will carry that torch for as long as I live for what he did to us . . . . The move was not about football, *it was about my family!* My family owned season tickets for more than 50 years. His father was an usher at the old Stadium from the day it opened until he died in 1963. . . . Art Modell stole our team . . . Paul Brown's team . . . he stole our family!

—David Armstrong

When watching the press conference to announce the Browns move to Baltimore, I thought, "These guys are stealing my childhood. *They're stealing my childhood!*"
—**Jonathan Leiken**

Modell's supporters want to see him inducted to the "Contributors" wing in the Hall of Fame at Canton. The only way to make a case for Modell is based on the mediocrity of some of the previous selections. Art won one Super Bowl title (2000) and one League Championship (1964). Most of the other inductees have much stronger credentials:

CURLY LAMBEAU (six titles): He spent 30 years as a player, coach, general manager and founder of the Packers.

WELLINGTON MARA (six titles): His father, Tim, founded the Giants in 1933. Wellington was given a share in 1937, and he owned the club until 2005.

GEORGE HALAS (six titles): He is the Papa Bear of the Chicago Bears.

TIM MARA (four titles): Founder and then majority owner of the Giants for the first 34 years of their existence.

ART ROONEY (four titles): He owned the Steelers from 1933 to 1988, but the franchise was a joke until the late 1960s. In 1965, Art made his son Dan the general manager. That's when the team began to make smart moves. Dan is far more worthy than Art, but the Rooney family does belong in the Hall of Fame.

TEX SCHRAMM (three titles): He was a team president who started with the Rams in the late 1940s and won a title in 1951. He was fired late in the decade and then joined the expansion Cowboys.

AL DAVIS (three titles): He has owned the Oakland/Los Angeles Raiders since 1966. He also served as AFL commissioner and is credited with forcing the AFL-NFL merger. He also moved the Raiders all over California.

RALPH WILSON (four Super Bowl appearances): He won two AFL championships and four AFC titles with the Buffalo Bills. Lost in four Super Bowls.

GEORGE PRESTON MARSHALL (two titles): Owned the Redskins from 1932 to 1969 and is credited with being the guy who convinced the other owners that they needed to play a standardized schedule and a championship game. Both were revolutionary football ideas at the time.

DAN REEVES (two titles): Owned the Cleveland/Los Angeles Rams from 1941 to 1971. The 1945 title was in Cleveland. He moved the team to Los Angeles the next year for the money. You can argue this is a man after Modell's own heart.

LAMAR HUNT (one title): Hunt founded the American Football League and served as its first commissioner. His decision that the AFL would share revenues of ticket receipts and have a national TV contract with every owner sharing equally was promptly "borrowed" by the NFL. It's a major reason the league has prospered.

JIM FINKS: Finks was a very well-liked man who served as general manager for three clubs that achieved very little: Minnesota, from 1964 to 1973 (one league and one conference championship); Chicago from 1974 to 1982 (nothing); and New Orleans from 1986 to 1992 (nothing, although the Saints did have their first winning season in team history under him). Finks served on the rules committee for many years.

CHARLES BIDWILL (one title): An incomprehensible pick. He founded the Chicago (now Arizona) Cardinals, whose only title was the 1947 NFL championship.

BERT BELL: Owned the Eagles from 1933 to 1940 and co-owned the Steelers from 1941 to 1945. His teams never won a thing. He was elected because he served as commissioner from 1946 to 1959.

PETE ROZELLE: The NFL commissioner from 1960 to 1989. He is credited by everyone with turning pro football into the big-time business that it is today.

HUGH "SHORTY" RAY: He served as supervisor of officials and technical advisor on rules from 1938 to 1952. He is credited with pushing through all the rules changes during his tenure. He also insisted that the league hire referees. Until then, they were hired by the teams. He required the referees to learn the league rules and pass tests on them. He also would show up at games unannounced, to make sure referees were enforcing the rules as written.

JOE CARR: The first commissioner of the NFL, who served from 1922 to 1939. Carr's admirers credit him with professionalizing the league, by pushing reforms like "Let's not count pickup games in the standings."

*   *   *

There are at least three owners whose teams outperformed Modell's: Carroll Rosenbloom of the Colts and Rams (three titles, two leagues); Joe Robbie of the Dolphins (two titles, three leagues); Jack Kent Cooke of the Redskins (three titles, two leagues).

Art Modell's biggest "contribution" is the money he helped his fellow owners make. In the 15 years since Modell moved the Browns to Baltimore after the 1995 season, there have been 12 new stadiums built for NFL teams. Almost all of the money came from taxpayers. Maybe the owners of these teams should vote Modell a cut of their profits, but not a spot in the Hall of Fame.

> Following the Browns was a way to escape life's trials. . . .
> Whatever I did, I had the Browns on my mind. When the move
> was announced, I told a friend (also a pastor of the church
> where I worked) that I had the same feeling when my mother
> died when I was 9 years old. He said they were feelings of grief.
> **—Phil Devaty**

So what is the case for Modell in the Hall of Fame?

Of the owners in the Hall of Fame, Marshall, Bidwill, Hunt, Reeves and Davis all moved their teams. Yes, Modell was in financial trouble, but it was not all his fault. In the 1970s, when the City of Cleveland had financial problems, Modell signed a contract to operate and maintain Cleveland Stadium, in return for all the revenues. This was a phenomenally poor business move as the ballpark was falling apart and the Indians were losing and their attendance was terrible. He took out a line of credit with an adjustable rate. In the middle-1970s, and the rate went into the stratosphere during the Carter administration. At one point, he was paying 21 percent. Modell refinanced several times, but it didn't bring relief in the long run. Twenty years later, as the Indians were on the verge of a good team, the county built a new stadium to lure them and all their fans away. Modell lost the rent, the concession and parking. He was stuck with upkeep on a stadium that had been opened in 1931.

Modell said he didn't need a new stadium, then changed his mind and moved the team to Baltimore. His supporters admit that was bad, but no worse than what his fellow two owners did. The county built the baseball stadium for the Indians because Dick Jacobs threatened to move the team. The Cavaliers' owner, Gordon Gund, moved a franchise twice. Gund brought the California Golden Seals to Cleveland, and then moved them to Minnesota. He pulled NHL hockey out of two cities. Gund bought the Cavs at a bargain price. He refused to move downtown unless the city gave him an arena and found creative ways to avoid having to pay even the minimal rent the county charged him. Modell was the worst businessman of the three, but he cost the taxpayers of this region far less than the other owners.

But I still think, *Modell was a lousy businessman.* The question is not how he compares to Jacobs, Gund or any of the other franchise owners over the years. It's what he did with the Browns.

> In the 1960s, my father and I watched games together. . . . He reiterated to me over and over that one day I would understand that Art Modell was not an honorable man and did not deserve any credit for the success of the Browns under his ownership. It turns out that he was completely right about Art Modell, although I didn't understand it at the time . . . .
> **—Brian McKendry**

> I have to know why Art Modell had no choice but to move. Does he realize that he's a pariah? Does he care about his legacy? Was it worth it? Could his wife have talked him out of moving? Did Al Lerner advise him to move? Couldn't Art live off

the proceeds of selling the team? Does he have any regrets?
Does he miss Cleveland? Can he fathom the hurt he caused?
Does this bother him?

   —Tony Pono

Here's what bothered me the most about The Move: There was
no need for it to happen.

For at least 10 years, Modell watched his team play with Al
Lerner. They were very close friends. Lerner was like Jacobs, a
man tied to the Cleveland power structure who knew how to get
deals done. He also was very aware of Modell's financial situation. Modell reportedly was $70 million in debt by the time of the
move in 1995.

Let's think about this for a moment. Modell spent 10 years with
Lerner at the games. The two men considered themselves "close
friends." They both supposedly were committed to the city of
Cleveland. What was the obvious solution to Modell's problem?

Sell the team to Al Lerner!

I once asked Lerner why this didn't happen. Why did Modell
have to move, and why did you help him? After all, the final details of the move were agreed to on Lerner's private jet. Lerner
had the connections with the bankers in Baltimore.

"Art said he wanted to keep the team for his family," Lerner
told me. He meant that he wanted to turn the team over to his
son, David Modell.

"Why did you help him move the team?" I asked Lerner. "You
had to know how angry it would make the fans."

"I viewed it as helping a friend," Lerner said. "That's what I was
doing, helping a friend."

That was the end of the discussion, at least from Lerner's
view.

But aren't there times when a friend has to say, "Art, I am not
going to help you move the team to Baltimore. That's just not
right."

Lerner saw this as a business deal. Maybe he believed that the
NFL would award an expansion franchise to Cleveland. Maybe

he believed the move was the shock needed to convince the city to build a new football stadium. Maybe he even believed that he'd end up as the owner of the expansion franchise. Lerner clearly was the league's favorite to own the expansion Browns. They knew he had to cash to buy it and believed he'd do a good job running it.

But had Modell sold to Lerner, he could have retained a small interest in the team and been some type of president emeritus. He could have gone around town giving speeches, shaking hands, being *Art Modell, Owner of the Browns* . . . even if Lerner supplied the cash behind the franchise. He could have been a very respected figure, given credit for bringing in Lerner to save the team for Cleveland. And like Dick Jacobs did for the Indians, Lerner would have found a way to muscle the city into a new stadium. Unlike Modell, he was the kind of guy who knew how to get big deals done.

If you want to really play What if Art sold to Al? then you'd have a situation where Ozzie Newsome is running the Browns in Cleveland with Lerner's checkbook. Newsome led the Baltimore Ravens to the Super Bowl in the 2000 season, and they have been a regular playoff team for a decade.

Yes, all that and more could have happened here.

Here's my point for Modell being a terrible businessman.

He moved the team into a rent-free facility in Baltimore. He received every imaginable perk that a city could give a new owner. He sold out every game. But in January 2004, he still ran out of money and had to sell the franchise to Steve Bisciotti to deal with all his financial complications.

In a *Baltimore Business Journal* article written by Daniel Kaplan after Modell's sale, the former Browns/Ravens owner said: "The quality of ownership is not what it was in yesteryear. The people in football today, and maybe they have to be because of the amount of money they spent to buy their franchises, but the owners today are bottom-line-oriented—profits, give me profits, revenues, profits."

The article is very sympathetic to Modell. Many media stories credit Modell with surrendering the team's nickname, colors and history to Cleveland right after the move. But when I was writing *False Start*, I found stories in the Baltimore papers stating the new team would be "The Baltimore Browns."

It was only after the fans screamed and protested and filed law suits and pressured the league that Modell gave up the name, colors and history.

Modell explained moving the Browns to *Baltimore Business Journal* this way: "I wasn't greedy . . . it was survival, not greed."

But in the end, he didn't survive as an NFL owner. He didn't keep the franchise in his family. He failed in his main goal and lost respect in his adopted hometown in the process. That hardly sounds like a Hall of Famer.

Meeting Browns Players

In the 1960s, all the games were nearly sold out. If you wanted a seat, you had to be prepared to stand in line. . . . One day, I was in line by Gate B with 300 or more fans. I stood there with my mother, who came along even though a few months earlier she had gone through major surgery. She wanted to see why I continually bragged to her about the enthusiasm of the Browns fans. Mom was a Clevelander through and through, but didn't know the difference between a football and a baseball. As we got inside the door of Gate B, Mom felt faint and sick. I helped her sit on one of the steps. Then I heard a voice behind me politely saying, "Ma'am, can I help you?"

I turned around, and I couldn't believe my eyes. This polite man was Jim Brown. With my mouth wide open and in some sort of shock, I stood there and listened to this best player ever to run with a football say to Mom, "Can I get you some water, or would you rather have me assist you up the steps? You can sit on a chair, and I will bring you the water."

Mom decided to go up the steps with Jim. Then he says to Mom, "Is that your son?"

Mom said, "Yes," and he proceeded to tell me to follow them to the top of the steps. He had her sit down and got the water. Every person on those steps knew who was supporting my mother. Everyone except my mother, who had no idea who Jim Brown was. I will never forget the kindness Jim Brown extended to my mother.

—*Randy Barle*

I was 15 years old and at University Hospital in December 1987 for a brain tumor operation. It was a day after surgery, and I was in ICU. I heard that several Browns (Bernie Kosar, Brian Brennan, Kevin Mack, Earnest Byner, Bob Golic and Mike Baab) would be visiting the hospital that day. I really wanted to go, but the doctors wouldn't let me out of bed. I was devastated. My parents went down to talk to the players and try to get me a couple of autographs. Amazingly, they came back not only with an autographed picture signed by all of them, but with Mike Baab and Bob Golic in tow! They spent maybe 10-15 minutes chatting with me, and I was in heaven. It really lifted my spirits at a low point in my life.

—*Mic Starick*

Bob Matheson and Joe Taffoni were two Browns players on my *Cleveland Press* paper route (East 130th) in 1969-70. At 10, I knew a lot more about delivering papers than I knew about football. The first Monday night while collecting at the Mathesons', a giant of a man with a cut across the bridge of his nose and two black eyes answered the doorbell. I couldn't speak.

Mr. Matheson kindly deferred to his wife Pam to deal with the mute kid at the door. She explained to me the rough day at the office he had had the day before. Mrs. Matheson always offered a hot chocolate, asked how things were going and even gave a standing invitation to swim in their apartment building pool.

Going forward I read everything I could about the Browns and Bob Matheson. I was devastated the following year when the Browns traded Bob Matheson but reveled in his success with the Dolphins. His 53 defense, three Super Bowls and an undefeated season with the Dolphins were somehow a source of pride. Many years later, reading of his untimely death (complications from Hodgkin's disease) brought a tear to my eye, but it was then that I reflected and realized I had been cheering for Mrs. Matheson, she was my hero, and the tears were for her.

—*Andrew J. Dietrich*

In 1999, I sent three footballs to Otto Graham through the Cleveland Browns, requesting his autograph. When I didn't hear anything back for a while, I sent Mr. Graham a letter asking if he received the footballs, and could he please sign them for me. His wife actually called and said they never received them. I found out later that the Browns just put them in storage.

I called back expecting to leave a message on the voice mail, and Otto answered! I told him what an honor it was to speak with him. We spoke for about 15 minutes about the old days, Art Modell and the return of the Browns. Soon after, I received all three footballs back signed, including one for my oldest son that was born that January.

When our second son was born in 2001, I sent another football to Otto for him to sign. Otto sent the signed football back with a note, joking, "By the way, there's a 10 kid limit per family." When I sent him a thank-you note, I told him my wife was glad to hear about the 10-kid limit!

—*Bill Haney*

Lou Groza spoke at my church's father-son breakfast in the '60s and gave out photos that he would personally autograph for you. That was cool enough, but one year Indians catcher Ray Fosse was to be the honored guest. The day before he was called up for National Guard duty. Guess who showed up with a smile on his face...? You got it, one of the greatest kickers of all time.... Groza even signed my baseball! I still have it.

—*Gary N. Zupancic*

I was sent to a kicking camp at Baldwin-Wallace when I played football for Normandy High School in 1994. I had no idea where to begin or how to get started kicking. I was a better kickoff headhunter. From a crowd of people, Matt Stover noticed

my inappropriate foot apparel. He loaned me his shoes to wear
for the day. What a dramatic difference in my kicking!

—*Kevin Gearing*

I was probably 6 or 7 years old when my father spotted
Hanford Dixon at a Cleveland-area restaurant where my family
was dining. It was probably 1988, a Pro Bowl season for Dixon.
My father told our waitress that I (a young kid, of course) wanted
to buy Hanford a drink. He asked her to pass the message along.
The waitress returned a few minutes later to let us all know
that Hanford graciously accepted my offer. But he wanted me,
specifically, to know that he was ordering a Coke. Later on during
dinner, Hanford even came over to personally thank me. Years
later, my dad told me that the actual drink may not have been a
Coke. When I learned that as an adult—I thought it was a class
act by Hanford to act as a role model even when he was out
enjoying himself on his own time.

—*Mike Belsito*

I wanted the opportunity to meet the field-goal battery of
Ryan Pontbriand, Dave Zastudil and Phil Dawson so I could
obtain their autographs for a special Cleveland Browns football.
I attended the "Dawson Bar" game in Baltimore in November
2007. I was always impressed with the high degree of excellence
and consistency displayed by the field-goal unit of Ryan, Dave
and Phil.

I spent some quality time chatting with each of the three
players. For a few minutes, it was just the four of us in a little
group. They happily signed my ball and actually gave me the
sense that they were flattered by my request. We are talking
about three Pro Bowl-caliber players who are each among the
best at his position.

After Phil Dawson signed my ball, he and his family walked
out onto the practice field to spend a few moments together by
themselves. It was then that I realized what a great idea it would
be to have had Phil sign the words "Dawson Bar" underneath his

signature. I mentioned this to Dave, who promptly took my ball back out onto the field so Phil could fulfill my request, which he happily did.

—Eric McBurney

The year Art Modell moved our beloved Brownies to Baltimore, I worked as a security guard for the Browns, specifically as a member of the Courtesy Squad. One of our additional duties for the final few games—after the announcement to move the team was made—was to walk the players from the locker room to their cars. One game I drew Steve Everitt. He was the Browns' first-round draft pick in 1993 from Michigan, played center and was as tough as they come. He had long, scraggly hair, wild eyes and looked like someone from the Hell's Angels. To get his "game face" on, he would come on the field before most other players, sit on the bench by himself and start rocking back and forth. He was a flat-out scary-looking guy.

I said, "Steve, I'm going to walk to your car with you."

He never looked up, grunted at me and kept walking. There were a few dozen fans crowded around the exit, many yelling to get the attention of the various players as they left. When Everitt walked slowly toward them, no one said anything—they just parted a way for us to walk though.

About 100 feet from the exit, there was a small girl with her dad. I saw the dad bend over and say something in her ear. As we approached, she said, "Mr. Everitt, may I please have your autograph?"

I started to say something like, "No autographs today," but before I could, Everitt stopped, got down on one knee and looked the girl in the eyes. He said in a very soft, clear voice, "What's your name, little girl?"

She said her name, and he signed her big Browns Number One foam finger. She said thank you—so did her dad—and we began to walk to the parking lot again. As we crossed the street and approached the players' parking lot, I said, "You're a class act, Steve."

Without so much as looking up, he grunted at me and kept walking.

—Rick Gucwa

In 1980, I was 5 years old, and my mom and dad just got season tickets. He decided that summer we would go to training camp at Kent State. My mom loved Brian Sipe. I liked Lyle Alzado. I thought he was tough, crazy and he played to win. He also looked a lot like my dad!

At training camp, I was on a mission. I was going to meet Lyle and get his autograph. My mom was on a mission to take a picture of Brian Sipe and maybe get close to him. My dad was into the actual camp. We got there early and had to wait for a while; it seemed like years to me. The players were coming out of the tunnel. . . . I left my mom and dad's side, without telling them my plan, and headed up to the tunnel. I waited for Lyle, who was the last person to come out of the tunnel. I asked him for an autograph. He asked where my parents were. I told him they were down there, with the crowds of people, My mom was losing her mind with me being gone!

Lyle asked me if it would be all right to take my hand and go and find them. Of course it was! This was better than just getting the autograph! He escorted me back to my parents. They thought it was pretty cool. I should've gotten in trouble, but they let it slide since I got to have a player bring me back—he gave me an autograph, too.

—Jenna Skidmore

As a rabid young fan, I knew the Browns were quarterbacked by Frank Ryan, who had a Ph.D. in mathematics from Rice University and was a part-time faculty member at Case Western. When my grade school math class began discussing basic numerical concepts, including the identity that any number divided by itself would equal one, I was convinced that zero divided by zero should also equal one. My teacher told me I was wrong. With the blissful naivety of a grade school student, I chose to write to Dr. Ryan and pose this question to him.

Several weeks later, my mother appeared at school with an envelope from Case. Dr. Ryan had set this matter straight.

—*David W. Loring, Ph.D., ABPP-Cn Professor*

I grew up in Chesterland, and my friends and I had the pleasure of meeting Jim Kanicki. His backyard and my friend Tommy's abutted each other and were separated by a row of pine trees. We sometimes played baseball in the backyard. A home run was over the trees and into Mr. Kanicki's backyard. One day we were playing, and Tommy hit a home run. To our surprise, the ball was returned to us by Mr. Kanicki himself. Not only did we get our ball back, but we got to meet and talk to Mr. Kanicki. What an honor and thrill for a bunch of teenage boys to meet a real Cleveland Brown. I'm 50 yrs old now, and it still gives me goose bumps when I think of it.

—*John VanDerLinden*

One day after the game we are all walking out to the bus to head back to Akron. We were walking through the players' parking lot. I was walking by a car, and I saw Tommy Vardell getting into his SUV. I was wondering if I should say anything. He was limping, and his hand was bandaged from getting smashed. I decided it was my once-in-a-lifetime shot to meet a famous athlete. I knocked on his window. He rolled his window down. I said, "Mr. Vardell, Mr. Vardell . . . can I please get your autograph?" He started laughing and gave me the autograph.

—*Shawn Starcher*

I traveled to Platteville, Wis., with my two sons (11 and 12) and other Windy City Browns Backers in 1993 and 1994 (for a scrimmage during the Browns' training camp). We drank, laughed, talked, played pool and hung out with the likes of Bernie Kosar, Ozzie Newsome, Steve Everitt, Vinny Testaverde, Tommy Vardell, Eric Turner, Eric Metcalf and on and on. We were treated like family by the players. My one son was allowed on the sideline during the scrimmage by Michael Jackson and Keenan McCardell. A running play was coming right at him. Michael Dean Perry and Eric Metcalf scooped him up out of harm's way. Bill Belichick and his staff asked him to leave, and they gave him a set of receiving gloves and a ball.

—Russell E Sutherland

My mom is a huge Browns fan. She used to go to Westlake Holiday Inn on Monday nights to meet players. Doug Dieken was always there. One night, he bought her a drink. She was so excited she stole the glass so she could have it forever!

—Tom Coy

CHAPTER 14

Old Municipal Stadium may have been a dump, but it was our dump.

I know that Cleveland Municipal Stadium had to go. Even in the summer, it was cold and dark and dank and arguably ugly. About 20 percent of the crowd had to deal with a large girder obstructing their view at some point. The restrooms were inexcusably wretched, at least the men's rooms were. But there is one thing that the facilities that replaced it don't come close to as far as a fan's experience. . . . At old Municipal Stadium, when you've managed to hike up those serpentine ramps to the upper deck, past the eternally gray structure of dirty steel and concrete, and then you walk up that last stretch that seems better described as a dark tunnel to where you find your seats, your world very suddenly opens up to an unbelievably green vista. It's greener than one is used to seeing. It's breathtaking. It brings a tear to your eye. You're not in Kansas (or Cleveland) anymore, you're in Oz.

—**Gary Peck**

As I read Gary Peck's e-mail, it so reminded me of my youth at Cleveland Municipal Stadium. While I came from a baseball family, and most of my visits to the stadium on Lake Erie were to watch the Indians (we averaged about 20 games per season), my father probably took me to a dozen Browns games over the years. The impact was the same. As a child, I remember walking over the West 3rd Street Bridge with my little hand in his huge paw. Then he'd lift me up on his shoulders as we approached the stadium; it seemed my head was in the clouds. The blue lake loomed beyond the park in the distance. Sometimes, I could see a huge freighter; other times, there seemed to be small, dainty sailboats.

And the stadium was a monster. The stadium was a palace. The stadium always looked bigger as we approached it, no matter how many times I'd been there before.

When the crowd was large . . . for Browns games . . . everything seemed louder. The vendors selling programs outside the gates. Inside, the guys hawking beer, hot dogs and peanuts. More than 45 years after my first trip to the stadium, I can close my eyes and smell the hot dogs on the grill, the popcorn freshly popped. I can remembered what seemed like the endless hike up one ramp after another, almost like being lost in an old-fashioned Erector Set that someone had assembled while they were at the end of a three-day bender.

But as Ken Flint e-mailed: "Municipal Stadium was a dump, but it was OUR dump—there was no doubt where the game was being played. Cleveland Browns Stadium is a homogenized stadium which could be in Nashville, Jacksonville or anywhere else. I'm not saying I enjoyed having the plumbing leak on me, but the flavor (maybe the wrong word!) of the place was Cleveland-specific."

The old stadium especially means a lot to Northeast Ohio fans who remember a world of three-channel, black-and-white televisions, when most houses were small boxes without air conditioning. Games on TV looked so gray—another reason the grass at the stadium was so green. In the summer, heading to Lake Erie was a way to cool off. Maybe you didn't go in the lake, which was extremely risky back then due to pollution and a certain river going up in flames. But the winds off the lake were nature's air conditioning . . . at least during certain parts of the baseball and football seasons.

Those same winds also made the stadium feel like Santa was about to come down the chimney—assuming he could find it in the middle of all the blowing snow. I know it's truly a romanticized memory, but I do recall some absolutely beautiful days at the old stadium—some of them in August when my father secured tickets to watch preseason football doubleheaders—that's right, *two* meaningless football games—played like a twi-night baseball doubleheader. This was in the 1960s, when I lived in a shoebox of a house in Parma and there was no air conditioning. It was nice to just be at the stadium with my father watching a bunch of guys from four different football teams who seldom (if ever) would play in the regular season.

Art Modell launched the football doubleheader idea, the Browns hosting one from 1962 to 1971. On August 30, 1969, a crowd reported to be 85,532 saw the Chicago Bears face the Buffalo Bills in the opener, while the Cleveland Browns lost to the Green Bay Packers, 27-17. They also drew crowds of 83,736 (1964), 83,118 (1965), 83,418 (1966), 84,236 (1967), 84,918 (1968), 83,048 (1970) and 82,710 (1971) for those doubleheader games. So fans liked them. I also believe my father got free tickets for several of those dates, and that may also explain the big crowds—Modell wanted people in the stadium, spending money, even if they didn't pay their way through the gates.

In the 1960s, Municipal Stadium was considered a good place for baseball and sensational for football because of all the fans in the seats. It also was before fans expected stadiums to look like the newest mall or the lobby of the Ritz-Carlton. It was a place to watch a game.

As Gary White e-mailed: "The moment you entered the stadium, you could take a deep breath and smell an air like no other. A combination of Lake Erie, the salt mines, the steel mills, urine, beer, concrete, steel and sweat. To know we were going to watch 'Our Browns' fight for pride and honor! Not for money! There were 80,000 fans screaming and yelling, fights in the bleachers (the *real* Dawg Pound) . . . win or lose (but mostly win, of course), *every* Sunday!"

That was so true from 1946 (when Paul Brown gave birth to the franchise) through 1970, the final season of Blanton Collier.

My dad, Herb Schaffner, was an early season-ticket holder. He worked for Brush Electronics in Cleveland and, encouraged by their president, he met and was escorted by a Browns employee to Section 27, Upper Deck, where he agreed to buy a block of about 14 seats in the first and second rows. We kept four, and family friends took the rest. Those were "our seats" from 1955 through 1983, when Dad retired and I left the area and could no longer keep them. I took Dad to the second home game of 1999, when the "new" Browns lost to the Patriots. We sat in the Dawg Pound, and as exciting as it was to be in the new stadium, I think we both longed for the old seats in the old stadium. We missed our old pals in Section 27. It was funny—outside of our immediate circle (our tickets), we never knew the names of those who sat around us. But whenever we arrived at a game a few minutes late, they always filled us in on the kickoff and first series or two—and we did the same for them. If we missed a game, they were concerned, and we missed them if they didn't show up on a Sunday. Dad and I gave them all nicknames, and I can still see their faces.

—Bob Schaffner

Municipal Stadium was the idea of William R. Hopkins, Cleveland's first and only city manager. Until 1924, Cleveland had been run the way it is now—by an elected mayor and an elected city council. After a series of scandals and controversies in the late teens, the city had a referendum, and they voted to adopt a "city manager" system of government. Hopkins was the business guy, the CEO of the city. He was concerned about urban blight, so he built parks for the people and playgrounds for the kids. He was behind the public library (1925) and the music hall (1929). Hopkins widened most of the city's major streets to allow for more automobile traffic. But because he was worried about smog, he pushed for laws about air pollution. By 1925, he finished an airport—which is named after him. He also had a hand in the Terminal Tower, train lines coming into the city and other significant projects.

If Paul Brown made the Browns a true professional sports franchise, then you can say Hopkins had a Brown-type impact on the city. William Rowland Hopkins was a genius in urban development. His next project was going to be the creation of a gigantic entertainment complex—the centerpiece of his newly reclaimed lakefront. It would host about any event, not just baseball games. College football teams often played games on neutral sites to raise money, and Hopkins wanted a piece of that action. The same with boxing, wrestling, track and field—even skating. Here's a critical fact that people often get wrong. Cleveland Municipal Stadium was not built to try to attract the 1932 Olympics. There is absolutely no doubt about this. The August 1, 1928 edition of the *Los Angeles Times* has a headline about the Olympic Games being awarded to Los Angeles. Cleveland voted on the bond issue in November 6, 1928, for the new stadium—more than two months after L.A. was named as the Olympic city.

Here's something hard to believe today: According to the 1920 census, Cleveland was the fifth-largest city in the country— behind only New York, Chicago, Philadelphia and Detroit. The stadium's proponents noted that because Cleveland (population 796,841) did not have a stadium of sufficient size to host the Olympics, the bid had gone to the country's 10th-largest city (Los Angeles, population 576,673).

Hopkins wanted the facility to be owned by the public. There were concerns that baseball owners were gouging fans on ticket prices and concessions. The city couldn't own a team. But if the city owned the ballpark, it could hold down the prices by means of a lease. Teams didn't move from city to city, and Cleveland was a major market in the 1920s and 1930s. Hopkins always dreamed big, and he wanted the new facility to seat 100,000! At the time, the Indians played at League Park with 21,000 seats. Fans complained that they couldn't buy a ticket ... or secure a good seat ... and that ticket prices were too high. A big stadium would take care of that.

Stadiums often caught on fire back then—most were made of wood. Cleveland Stadium would be built entirely out of fireproof materials—steel and concrete. He wanted a roof to protect people from inclement weather. Because of the roof, there was a need for so many girders on the second deck. But the roof kept people from being exposed to snow, rain and wind. The scoreboard was large for its era. While the first baseball night game would not be played until 1935, Hopkins insisted that lights be installed.

*   *   *

When ground was officially broken on June 25, 1930, some critics were already calling it "The Mistake on the Lake". Engineers, quickly realizing they would be way over budget, saved some money by cutting the seats from 100,000 to 80,000. Still the project still went $500,000 over budget. And remember, the budget was $2.5 million, so that's a whopping 20 percent.

Cleveland Municipal Stadium was officially dedicated 370 days after groundbreaking on July 1, 1931. The very first event held in it—on July 3, 1931—was the World Heavyweight Championship between Max Schmeling and Young Stribling. But there were no other events. The Indians didn't play their first game in Municipal Stadium until a year later, July 31, 1932. In that day's papers, there were stories about Adolf Hitler becoming a political power in Germany and Franklin D. Roosevelt running for president, promising to end the Depression and legalize beer sales. Babe Ruth took one look at the outfield and proclaimed, "You need a horse" to cover all the ground because the center-field wall was . . . 463 feet . . . that's 463 FEET from home plate!!! Baseball Commissioner Judge Kennesaw Mountain Landis attended the first game and insisted, "No barrier to block anyone's view . . . comfortable chairs . . . look at those people in center field, they can see every play . . . it's the greatest baseball plant in the world."

The judge either had some very bad food or, even worse, eyes to miss all the poles and not notice that the center-field bleachers appeared to be in the middle of Lake Erie when at home plate.

Mel Harder and the Indians lost 1-0 to Lefty Grove of the Philadelphia A's in front of 80,184 fans. The crowd for the second game was 21,218 (12,000 students admitted free). After seven games, the average attendance was 12,270. In 1933, the Indians played all their games at the stadium, barely averaging 6,000 fans. By 1934, they were back at League Park. It cost too much to play in front of 74,000 empty seats on the lakefront. The Depression killed any plans for development around Municipal Stadium. During the 1930s and through World War II, the stadium was mostly empty. The Indians did play some weekend games there, but that was about it. Only when Bill Veeck bought the team did the Indians make the stadium their home, the first full season in 1947.

My first Browns game at the stadium was in the early 1980s. My last game at Municipal Stadium was December 17, 1995, the Browns' final game ever at the old, beat-up, out-dated, gray dungeon along Lake Erie. The place where 80,000 Browns faithful gathered eight Sundays a year to show support for our team that we lived and died for. This was the place where every restroom had two inches of urine along the floor, and you'd never heard a complaint from any of us fans. This was the place where when 1 p.m. rolled around, the fans had made their way from the tailgate parties in the Muni Lot—and brought their party around the mud field which was painted green to look like grass. This was the place where the Dawgs were let loose each Sunday. The place where blue-collar Clevelanders came together with white-collar Clevelanders, all races, all creeds. We all became one. We all wore our hearts on our sleeve to show our passion for our city, our team and even our beat-up stadium. This was our football culture.
—**Joe Chmielewski**

The first football game in Cleveland Stadium took place on November 19, 1932 when the annual Notre Dame-Navy game came to Cleveland. The stadium also hosted the game 10 other times— in 1934, 1939, 1942, 1943, 1945, 1947, 1950, 1952, 1976 and 1978. The average attendance was over 69,000, and the 1947 game attracted

84,000 fans. Cleveland Stadium probably could have been the home of the local college football power—but there wasn't one. Ohio State played in the stadium four times: 1942 (against Illinois), 1943 (Purdue), 1944 (Illinois) and 1991 (Northwestern).

They tried to start the "Great Lakes Bowl" on December 6, 1947. Kentucky (coached by Bear Bryant) beat Villanova, 24-14, in front of fewer than 15,000 fans. The low attendance along with trying to convince college teams to play in frigid weather destroyed that idea.

In 1936, Cleveland finally got a pro football team. The Cleveland Rams joined the newly formed American Football League and went 5-2-2, finishing second in the league. They played four home games in the stadium in front of more than 70,000 empty seats for most games. Cleveland was supposed to play the Boston Shamrocks in the AFL Championship Game . . . but the game was cancelled when the Boston players (who hadn't gotten paychecks in more than a month) refused to play unless someone paid them.

Shortly after the season ended, NFL President Joe Carr told Rams owner Homer Marshman (one of the few AFL owners to meet payroll every week) that if he wanted to switch leagues, he'd be welcome. Marshman joined the NFL. Cleveland went from 5-2-2 in the AFL in 1936 to 1-10 in the NFL. After the season, the Rams said part of the problem was the lack of enthusiasm shown by the fans. They also said it was impossible to build any excitement in huge Cleveland Stadium. So the Rams played the 1938 season at . . . Shaw Stadium. Yes, this is the same Shaw Stadium where high schools such as Shaw, Benedictine and Cleveland Heights played. That lasted only a year.

Then, the Rams bounced around:

- 1939-41, back to Cleveland Stadium
- 1942, League Park
- 1943, citing problems related to World War II, the Rams didn't play at all
- 1944-45, League Park

In 1945, the Rams were 9-1 and won the NFL championship.

They played all four regular-season home games at League Park, drawing a total of 77,000 fans. Since League Park held only 21,000 people—they could only have sold 84,000 tickets. For the championship game, they moved to Cleveland Stadium and drew 32,178 fans for their 16-15 victory over the Washington Redskins. After the season, owner Dan Reeves said Cleveland couldn't support a pro football team. He also suggested the city needed a much better stadium than the one they had and moved the Rams to Los Angeles.

Then came Paul Brown and a new franchise in the All-American Football Conference. Brown had played in Municipal Stadium in 1942 and 1943 when he was coaching Ohio State. Yes, the stadium was big, but Brown had coached at Ohio State. He knew what it was like to play in a stadium with huge, screaming crowds. If he built a championship team and drew crowds, Brown was convinced Cleveland Stadium would be a great place to play. In their first home game, the Browns drew 60,195 fans to watch them beat Miami 44-0. Their lowest attendance of the season—37,054 on November 24—was higher than the Rams' best crowd in 1945. The season high in attendance was 71,134 fans. Paul Brown coached the Browns to 10 consecutive championship games from 1946 to 1955. The Browns were always in the top 10 in attendance but never led the league. In 1954, the NFL Championship Game attracted only 45,000 people. In 1949, a mere 22,500 were there to watch the Browns win the title game. Part of the problem was Paul Brown's approach to marketing the team. He didn't. He won games, opened the gates and sold tickets. He hated the idea of promotions or massive discounts, so there were none.

In 1960, the Browns went 8-3-1 and drew 56,328 fans per game—behind Los Angeles, New York and Baltimore. In 1961, the Browns fell to 8-5-1 and did not make the playoffs. Attendance improved to 60,983, which led the NFL. The difference? Art Modell bought the team in 1961 and began to promote. There were fireworks and giveaways and discounts and players making lots of public appearances.

Before the 1963 season, Paul Brown was replaced by Blanton

Collier. The assumption is the firing of a legend and the father of the franchise would hurt attendance. But the Browns led the league by averaging 69,320 fans—almost 10,000 more than in 1962. A 10-4 record was the real reason. In 1964, the Browns led the NFL again. And they became the first NFL team to draw more than half a million fans to their regular-season home games. Their 549,334 fans—78,476 fans per game—shattered the NFL record. It remained that way for nearly three decades.

There were players who grumbled about the locker rooms and writers who didn't care for the press box. But everyone else, even those who knew the stadium was turning into a bit of a dump by the 1980s, still insisted it was a great place to watch a game.

*   *   *

The stadium was a gutsy idea but extremely flawed for several reasons:

1. Because it was built for many events, it wasn't especially suited for any of them.

2. It was the worst for baseball, which was the game played there the most. Too many seats were too far away from the field for the fans. The original fences were ridiculously far away.

3. The first concert held at the stadium was in 1966 (the Beatles); there were very few over the decades. The Schmeling match was the only boxing event.

4. The stadium was a good place to watch a football game—but there was virtually no college football played there. Pro football took up no more than 10 dates per year, counting exhibitions.

5. After being built in 1931, the stadium did not receive any major renovations until the city spent $5 million in 1967 to add box seats. Because the box seats weren't set at the right angle, the field needed to be lowered. Removing the topsoil destroyed the drainage and made it impossible to keep the grass in good shape. Cleveland Stadium was considered one of the best infields in the American League in the 1940s until the addition of box seats and the need to lower the field in 1967. After that, they never could fix the infield. The city lacked the cash to keep it up.

6. Modell took over the stadium. He spent $3.6 million in 1974 to add loges and a new scoreboard with more space to sell ads. He didn't really have the money for more upgrades. He couldn't raise the rent on the Indians, who were owned by men with no money. They put lousy teams on the field, attracting small crowds.

7. No municipally owned facility can be anything but a drain on the finances. Cleveland Stadium was one of the first. If the city falls on hard times, they won't be able to keep the place up.

Losing the old stadium and its special blue-collar atmosphere and replacing it with the new, modern Cleveland Browns Stadium does not really fit the emotional and social demand of Browns fans. I was in both stadiums. I was born and raised in Europe, but I still knew that with the demolition of old stadium, the hearts and souls of many Browns fans were also ripped out.
—**Martin Hubmayer**

I was working as a TV news photographer in Erie, and we covered the trio of the Steelers, Browns and Buffalo Bills. Being from Buffalo, I had the privilege of shooting their games, as well as plenty of Browns games. The one thing I loved about that old stadium the most was the noise. I don't believe I've ever heard a place so loud in my life. Combined with the old-style feel and look of the stadium, not to mention the history, and it was (and still is) one of my favorite sports venues I've had the pleasure of shooting in.
—**Mike Brown**

The Browns' last game at Cleveland Municipal Stadium was December 12, 1995, a 26-10 victory over Cincinnati. You had a team started by Paul Brown beating another team founded by Paul Brown—before Art Modell (who fired Brown) moved the Cleveland Browns to Baltimore. After that last game, people were removing their seats. They had come to the game with tool belts and pounded away—so they could walk off with the same chair where they had sat for decades. Others just stood and stared at the field, tears in their eyes, unable to say a word. Now, when fans talk about The Move, it doesn't take long for them to sound as if they have lost a close friend.

Elizabeth Armstrong wrote: "The Lady on the Lake hosted her farewell ball on a dreary day that matched everyone's mood perfectly. I looked up into the darkened stands, and I swear I could hear faint cheers echoing to the rafters. As fans milled about, some took pictures. Others knelt to touch the spray-painted turf, as it was here that memorable battles had been fought by players with names like Brown, Kelly, Groza, Matthews and Sipe. And the Pound . . . the 'real' Pound . . . was where real fans poured their emotions into the game and fought almost as hard as the players for the win. My heart still aches when I remember the day I said goodbye to my Sunday home.

Matt Holley wrote: "When the Browns moved, everyone knew that it was coming—but it was still a shock. I was working as an electrician. We listened to the news report on WMMS, and I remember crying like a baby. I joined the Air Force in 1996 and was sitting in the recruiter's office in downtown. His office looked at Municipal Stadium. I remember watching them tear the stadium down while I was answering questions from the recruiter. . . . After the interview and before I went home, I climbed a fence and stole a brick that was from the stadium."

Armand Salvini added: "I went to the Stadium the Monday after the last game. It was 8 in the morning. I wanted to retrieve my seat pad. It had my tickets in the pocket, and I didn't want to lose them. The place was completely open. I could not find a single person in the entire facility. I walked around with a camera, took a picture of myself. I went to where the remains of my old seats were. I had spent the previous several games trying to engineer how to remove my seat from the stanchions that held them down. I had no idea that the answer was tearing them out of the cement, a method made popular by the crowd. I left with three stanchions, and two more seats."

*   *   *

Here is a better stadium memory.

The stadium was a star of a movie, or at least a supporting actor to Jack Lemmon on October 31, 1965. Yes, the defending-champion Browns lost 27-17 to the Minnesota Vikings. But it was the day the stadium was the location for *The Fortune Cookie*, the new film by Oscar-winning writer-director Billy Wilder.

"The hospitality was wonderful, but the weather was murderous," star Jack Lemmon told the Associated Press. "It was frigid, and the temperature in the stadium was 10 degrees lower than outside. I guess California has made me thin-blooded. I was never so cold in all my life."

This was October. The angle of Cleveland Stadium meant arctic winds—love those Alberta Clippers—whipped in off the lake, swirling around. Lemmon played a TV cameraman who is knocked unconscious by one of the Browns as Lemmon was filming a play. Lemmon isn't hurt. His brother-in-law, a lawyer played by Walter Matthau, convinces Lemmon to fake an injury and sue the TV network and the Browns for $1 million. When Lemmon realizes he can extract revenge on his gold-digging ex-wife (an aspiring singer) with the money from the settlement, he agrees. Both the suit and his rekindled romance progress. But the player who ran into Lemmon believes he has paralyzed the photographer—and the player is haunted with guilt. Wilder co-wrote a script that was nominated for an Oscar. The photography and art direction also received nominations. The movie was the first time Lemmon and Matthau had ever worked together. They made a total of 10 movies. *The Fortune Cookie* earned Matthau the Academy Award for Best Supporting Actor for his performance as "Whiplash" Willie Gingrich. Wilder picked Cleveland for the cold-weather location, and he wanted a good team.

Cleveland Stadium is the location of both the first and the last scenes in the movie. Wilder shoots in the press box, under the stands and on the field. The black-and-white film takes advantage of the stadium's poles as ominous shadows in the final scene make it look like the setting of an old murder mystery. The movie even ends with a shot of two characters running down the field, into the end zone in the open end of the stadium.

That's the way to remember the stadium.

CHAPTER 15

The Paul Warfield trade wasn't that bad. Really. It just took eight years.

My favorite Brown other than Jim Brown was Paul Warfield. He was an outstanding track athlete from Warren, Ohio, who held the state high school record for the 180-yard low hurdles. He was also the Big Ten long jump champion. I remember a fake that he put on a Michigan defensive back that caused the Michigan player to fall down. He was Cleveland's first-round choice out of Ohio State. My Dad, who was also a longtime Browns fan, and I were not happy with the selection. But in those days, the Browns seldom made a mistake on their first-round selections. They knew something that we didn't about Warfield. He immediately formed a dynamic receiver tandem with Gary Collins. Warfield was fluid, graceful and made the wide receiver position a thing of beauty. As a boy watching his every move on the field, I tried to emulate his style. He was also a gentleman and a credit to the Browns' organization. He was my favorite and remains so today. I was devastated when the Browns traded him for the rights to Mike Phipps from Miami. I understood why the Browns did it, but they were never better without Warfield.

—**Rich Focht**

My mother was a Browns fan until the day she died in 1990.
She hated the Paul Warfield trade. Every summer, she wrote Art
Modell a letter to tell him what an idiot he was. . . . He never
wrote back.

—William Ewing

Bill Nelsen remembers the night he heard that Paul Warfield
was traded.

It was 1970. The Browns quarterback had appeared on a local
TV show, then met a friend at a bar for a beer.

"Afterwards, I got into the car, turned on the radio," said Nelsen.
"I heard they'd traded Paul to Miami for a guy (Mike Phipps)
who'd take my place. I turned off the radio, shut off the car and
went back into the bar."

Nelsen was in utter shock. In one deal, he'd lost his favorite
receiver, and the Browns had just traded for his replacement.

"For a guy in my spot, it really can't get much worse than that,"
recalled Nelsen, 40 years later.

The Warfield trade was bad, awful, terrible, and even worse
than that—a bit logical.

Just a bit.

But there was something else . . .

It led to Ozzie Newsome.

Really.

In the long run, the Browns traded a Hall of Fame receiver for
a Hall of Fame tight end, although no one knew it would work out
like that—certainly not the Browns.

In 1969, the Browns were 10-3-1. They beat Dallas 38-14 in the
first round of the playoffs, then lost 27-7 to Minnesota in the league
championship game. Nelsen was the quarterback throwing 23
touchdown passes (10 to Warfield), compared to 19 interceptions.
He was a little like Brian Sipe—an undersized quarterback with
a so-so arm who seemed to make others play better when they
were on the field with him.

But there was a problem with Nelsen. Bad knees. Real bad
knees. Aching, throbbing, excruciating knees. Saying "Bill Nelsen

had injury problems" would be like saying that "BP had a leaky well in the Gulf of Mexico." The Pittsburgh Steelers drafted Nelsen in the 10th round (136th overall) in 1963 from Southern Cal. They dumped him after the 1967 season because they believed he would never stay healthy. They had three reasons for that:

1. In 1965, Nelsen injured his knee, missed two games and had surgery after the season.

2. In 1966, he injured the other knee and missed nine games. He had surgery that off-season, too.

3. Guess what happened in 1967? He missed six games and had surgery again.

So why did the Browns trade for him?

Frank Ryan was getting old, and his skills were fading. Nelsen came cheap as he was dealt by the Steelers with defensive back Jim Bradshaw for backup quarterback Dick Shiner and tackle Frank Parker. Pittsburgh had an awful line. The Browns thought Nelsen could stay healthier because they had three Pro Bowl blockers: center Fred Hoaglin, right guard Gene Hickerson and right tackle Dick Schafrath. He also could hand the ball to Pro Bowl running back Leroy Kelly and throw it to terrific receivers Gary Collins and Warfield.

Cleveland sent Nelsen to the surgeon who had treated Joe Namath's knees, hoping better medical care might help. The doctor told them Nelsen's knees were in worse shape than Namath's. He suggested Nelsen should start wearing the same knee braces Namath used, and the Browns shouldn't play him too much. Nelsen indeed wore the braces, made of metal and weighing nearly two pounds each. By the end of his career, Nelsen was getting weekly injections for pain and having fluid drained from both knees before every game.

Consider this is Cleveland, and you know what happens when a Cleveland team usually trades for a player with a history of injuries. Only this time, it didn't happen. Nelsen stayed reasonably healthy. In 1968, he didn't miss a game. He only played 11 games, but he was Ryan's backup for the first three. Coach Blanton Collier benched Ryan after the Browns were 1-2, and Nelsen led the

Browns to a 9-2 record. They ended up losing to the Baltimore Colts in the NFL Championship Game.

In 1969, Nelsen played all 14 games—and the Browns went 10-3-1 and went back to the NFL Championship Game. But he battled pain most of the season. In Game 8 against the Minnesota Vikings, Nelsen suffered a pinched nerve in his throwing shoulder. He played the rest of the season with the injury. The Browns would turn to backup Jerry Rhome when they were far enough ahead or behind. In the NFL Championship Game, Nelsen went only 17-of-33 for 181 yards, with one TD and two interceptions as the Browns lost 27-7 to the Vikings. As he got older, Nelsen's body really began to deteriorate. He had injury issues in both 1970 and 1971 and retired after the 1972 season, when the doctors told him he needed a sixth knee operation.

Their backup quarterback was Jerry Rhome, whose passer rating was a hard-to-imagine 5.7. He played 11 games and was 7-of-19 passing for 35 yards, no touchdowns and two interceptions. Rhome was one of those guys who helped prove that the Heisman Trophy winner wasn't always a good player. The Browns acquired him from Dallas after the 1968 season to replace Frank Ryan.

As 1970 loomed, the Browns knew they had a starting quarterback (Nelsen) who was 28 but had 128-year-old knees. They had Rhome as the backup, and they didn't even trust him to throw a pass in a situation that mattered. They needed a quarterback . . . from somewhere.

Here was the situation:

1. There were two college quarterbacks who were supposed to be can't-miss prospects: Terry Bradshaw of Louisiana Tech and Mike Phipps of Purdue. The Steelers owned the first pick after a 1-13 season. Coach Chuck Noll announced they would pick Bradshaw.

2. Green Bay owned the second pick and had a young quarterback it liked in Don Horn, of San Diego State, who'd been their first-round pick in 1967. But they wanted to use the pick to take defensive tackle Mike McCoy from Notre Dame, so they had no interest in trading with the Browns.

3. The Miami Dolphins were 3-10-1 and owned the third pick. They didn't need Phipps. They had quarterback Bob Griese (who, like Phipps, was from Purdue). What they didn't have were receivers. In 1969, their top wide receiver—a guy named Karl Noonan—had caught 29 passes for 307 yards. Don Shula had just been hired as Miami's new coach. Yes, that's Cleveland native Don Shula. Anyway, he agreed to trade the No. 3 pick to his hometown team. But he wanted Warfield in exchange. No one else, just Warfield.

4. The Browns knew if they traded Warfield, they would weaken their receivers, leaving only Gary Collins and a backup with an unlikely name of Fair Hooker, who wasn't even an OK receiver.

5. The New York Giants had a receiver named Homer Jones, who made the Pro Bowl in both 1967 and 1968. He'd gained more than 1,000 yards and averaged more than 23 yards—clearly a big-play guy. Jones was famous for his signature move after he scored a touchdown. Instead of throwing the ball into the crowd, he hurled it to the ground as hard as he could and let the ball bounce into the crowd. Jones called his trademark "the spike." So far as we can tell, he was the first player to do it. Because he played in New York, it got a lot of attention. Jones had an off-year in 1969, and the Giants were willing to part with him. They also needed running backs. Their leading rusher was 32-year-old fullback Joe Morrison, who'd gained only 387 yards and averaged only 3.6 yards per carry. They would trade Jones to Cleveland in return for Ron Johnson, defensive tackle Jim Kanicki (who'd missed the year with a broken leg and was just about done) and linebacker Wayne Meylan.

6. To get a young quarterback, the Browns made two deals . . . hoping Phipps would be the starter for the next 10 years and Jones would be a reasonable facsimile of Warfield.

My dad grew up in Warren, Ohio. He played little league with Paul Warfield and watched him grow into the fantastic player he would become—with the Browns. At our house, there is an autographed drawing of Paul Warfield, hanging in a place of honor. I remember playing touch football with the guys in the backyard, thinking that I wanted to be a wide receiver when I grew up. I wanted to be like Paul Warfield. My father explained since I was a girl (in the early '70s), I would probably not get to be a football player. I was too small and would get killed if I were tackled. I remember saying, "They can't tackle me if they can't catch me." As a girl, I just wanted to be like Paul, running so fast they couldn't tackle me.

Leanne Was-Thomas

The Browns' plan sounded reasonable, except for one thing—rarely does a deal work when you trade a great player in his prime for an unproven prospect, no matter how talented that player appears to be in college. That is especially true of a quarterback, which is perhaps the most demanding position in all of team sports. At 27, Warfield already had been to three Pro Bowls. The first was in 1964. Then again in 1968 and 1969. The Browns didn't throw the ball all over the field, nor did most NFL teams. The Browns' other receiver was 29-year-old Gary Collins, who was the star of the 1964 championship game. He also caught 11 touchdown pass in 1969, one more than Warfield. While he was healthy in 1969, he missed nine games with injuries in 1968.

Warfield was not only special, he was a pure Cleveland Brown from Warren, about an hour from Municipal Stadium. When the Browns drafted him in 1964, coach Blanton Collier told *The Plain Dealer*'s Hal Lebovitz: "This boy has more potential than any other football player I've ever seen." After watching Warfield as a rookie, Lebovitz quoted a scout saying, "If he had Otto Graham throwing to him, the football field would become a nightmare alley for the guys trying to cover him."

Warfield graduated from Warren G. Harding High School and played at Ohio State, where he was a running back. When the Browns picked him, they thought about Warfield as a defensive back . . . until seeing him work out, whereupon Collier quickly switched him to receiver. Guess how many times the Browns scouted him? Exactly three. Once in each of his three seasons with the Buckeyes. They knew he was a great athlete, a tremendous, disciplined person. He was right in their backyard, and they had lots of information from people who grew up with Warfield in Warren, and who played with and against him in high school. He was good enough as a center fielder to be offered a contract by the Pittsburgh Pirates when he graduated from high school. He was a star long-jumper in college, and also ran hurdles and sprints.

You just don't trade a player such as Warfield.

But the Browns did.

They were desperate for a quarterback . . . and Miami knew it.

When you are desperate, it's easy to lose focus. When you are desperate, it's tempting to tell yourself that you can trade Warfield because you can replace him with Jones. When you are desperate, you sometimes don't do your homework.

That's what happened to the Browns.

They were desperate, so they told themselves that if they traded Warfield, they'd be nearly as strong at receiver with Homer Jones and Collins as they were with Warfield and Collins. On paper, you see the following when comparing Warfield and Jones:

1. Both made two Pro Bowls in the previous three years. Both led the league in touchdown catches once in that same 1967–1969 period.

2. Jones had 12 more catches (136-124) over the three years. He gained more yards (3,010 to 2,655), and had a higher average per catch (22.1 yards to 21.4) than Warfield.

3. Warfield was a year younger and had more touchdown catches (30-21). But Warfield played with weaker quarterbacks (Ryan and Nelsen), compared to Jones who was catching passes from future Hall of Famer Fran Tarkenton.

4. At the time of the trade, an Associated Press story claimed Jones was "one of the fastest and most dangerous receivers in football," adding "his overall performance compares favorably with Warfield's."

But one question no one seemed to ask is why the Giants were so willing to trade Jones. Yes, they needed a running back. Yes, Ron Johnson was a promising running back with the Browns. But he was not an impact starter. Were there warning signs that the

Browns missed, because they were so determined to trade for Phipps?

There were three teams involved in these two deals with the Browns.

Miami was absolutely, positively right about Warfield. He played on their Super Bowl-winning team during their 1972 perfect season.

New York was right about Jones (he was falling apart) and Johnson, the running back from the Browns who indeed was emerging as a 1,000-yard rusher. Johnson gained 1,027 yards in his first season in New York and made the Pro Bowl. The Giants, who finally had a balanced attack to go with Tarkenton's passing, improved to 9-5. An injury limited Johnson to two games in 1971, but he came back in 1972, gaining 1,182 yards and making the Pro Bowl again.

In the big picture, the Browns were a 10-3-1 team in Warfield's final season. They dropped to 7-7 in 1970, and the decline was starting for one of the NFL's great franchises.

Meanwhile, the Giants and Dolphins immediately made dramatic improvements after the trades. To this day, Warfield is not sure why he was traded: "It came as a complete shock. I never wanted to play anywhere but Cleveland. I enjoyed Miami and played in a Super Bowl, but I always loved being with the Browns."

So what went wrong?

Let's start with Phipps, who was 6-foot-3 and 210 pounds. He played for Purdue, which had sent Bob Griese and Len Dawson to stardom as NFL quarterbacks. Academically, he qualified for a Rhodes Scholarship, so he obviously had the brains to play the position. In three years at Purdue, he had a 24-6 record and went 3-0 vs. Notre Dame (who was ranked No. 1, No. 2 and No. 9) all three years.

Phipps passed for 2,527 yards and 23 touchdowns in his senior year—and ran for eight more scores. He finished second in the Heisman Trophy voting.

Sounds great, but there were some areas of concern.

He completed only 51 percent of his passes for his career. He threw nearly as many interceptions (34) as touchdowns (37). You prefer a quarterback to throw twice as many touchdown passes as interceptions and want his completion percentage to be near 60 percent, certainly higher than 55 percent. You can look at tapes and stats of Phipps from college and talk yourself into him being a star (because of his size and athleticism), or out of it because he lacked accuracy and was interception prone.

The Browns decided to believe in Phipps, especially since the plan was for Phipps to sit for several years and watch Nelsen play—while he was being tutored by Blanton Collier. The assumption was Jones would come close to replacing Warfield, that Collins still had some gas in his receiving tank. They also had a Pro Bowl tight end in Milt Morin, who was a very good pass catcher.

If you're a Browns fan, you know what happened next—even if you don't remember it.

Yes, everything that could go wrong, went wrong. And it kept going wrong.

The Giants sure knew when to dump Jones, who played only one season with the Browns and then retired. When he arrived in Cleveland, there were reports that he wasn't happy to leave New York . . . that he didn't want the pressure of replacing Warfield . . . that he wasn't happy with his salary . . . that he didn't want to play in cold weather . . . and that his knees were sore.

> As a youth, I lived by Mike Phipps but wished it was Paul Warfield.
> **—Jeff Chaney**

Who decided to make these trades?

It's very obvious that Art Modell had the final word. He was the one who discussed the deals with *The Plain Dealer*'s Chuck Heaton right after it was announced: "I'm happy. We all are very happy with the trades. I talked this over with the whole staff before either deal was made. Ultimately, the final decision had to be mine."

Modell explained that the "clincher" was obtaining Jones. He added, "Paul (Warfield) played so well for us and is such a high type that I hated like the devil involving him. However, it was the overwhelming consensus of our combined thinking that we had a pressing need for backup protection behind Bill Nelsen. This year's crop of passers is the finest that Paul Bixler has seen in all his years as our head scout. We felt we should try to land one of them even if the price might be high."

Hal Lebovitz had major reservations about the trade and wrote about it. On the editorial page . . . A-8 . . . *The Plain Dealer*'s deep political thinkers ventured into sports and backed the deal in an unsigned editorial, the final paragraph being: "The moral is that fine running backs and even fine receivers can be replaced, but a star quarterback who can make it big among the pros is a rare gem well worth the cost of a game on raw material."

Not sure what "raw material" *The PD* editors meant, since Warfield was clearly a polished gem.

Warfield said he was "stunned" by the deal and never saw it coming.

"I loved the Browns and wanted to spend my entire career with him," Warfield said in 2010.

Warfield said he was so mystified by the trade, that he asked the Dolphins how it happened. Two executives said they knew the Browns had quarterback fever. The No. 3 spot in the draft was like the No. 1 to the Browns—who believed they had to get a quarterback right now, and it had to be Mike Phipps.

"When the talks started, Miami asked for Leroy Kelly," said Warfield. "The Browns turned them down. Then Miami asked for me. They said both of us were 'untouchables.' Miami said if they wanted that pick, then it would cost them one of the untouchable players."

Some in the Miami organization thought the Dolphins should think about other players.

"But (General Manager) Joe Thomas said they should wait, Cleveland would come around," said Warfield. "Joe told me all this. He said he believed Cleveland would trade me if they just stayed patient—and that's what happened."

Once the season started, the deal oozed a distressing odor immediately. It was so bad for Jones, that he lost the starting job to Fair Hooker. He didn't catch a pass until the sixth game of the year and had only 10 receptions all season. He supposedly couldn't grasp the Browns' offense. Looking back, it seems he just didn't want to play in Cleveland. Then there was Gary Collins' sudden decline. After a very good 1969 (54 catches, 11 for scores), Collins caught only 26 balls (four TDs). He caught only 15 passes in 1971 and retired at the end of the year. He was 31.

The Browns were now without any quality receivers, while Phipps was a young quarterback not ready for prime time.

No one should have been expecting Phipps to play well as a rookie, and he didn't. In 1970, he served as Nelsen's relief in all 14 games and had one start. He was 29-of-60 (48 percent) passing with one touchdown and five interceptions. Phipps did take the Browns into the playoffs in 1972—his first season as a starter. But he regressed in 1973. By 1974, fans were screaming for Brian Sipe, who was moving the ball in exhibition games.

While the Browns were 7-7 in 1970, the Dolphins hired Don Shula as coach and had a 10-4 record. Warfield went to his first of five consecutive Pro Bowls with Miami in 1970. The Dolphins went to the next three Super Bowls—losing in 1971, but winning in 1972 and 1973. Trading for Warfield isn't the only reason Miami became an instant power, but it helped. Nor was his departure the only reason the Browns began a slow slide in the mid-1970s, but it looked that way to most fans and media members because Phipps played so poorly.

I moved to Fort Lauderdale, Florida, and found myself among Dolphin Mania the year the fish went undefeated. We drove to the game in a Volkswagen camper with a big "14-1 In Cockroft We Trust" bed sheet stuck into the sliding door on the side of the van. Once in the bleachers, the sign was soon confiscated

by the police. The game was a snoozer until late. The Browns
were trailing in the fourth quarter but driving straight towards
us. The crowd was so quiet, you could hear beer vendors calling
out their wares from on the other side of the stadium. Then
Mike Phipps did what he did best, threw an interception. The
crowd instantly roared to life, as if orchestrated by a great
conductor. We quickly and quietly slunk out of the stadium,
shielding our Browns gear from joyous Dolphin Fans, retreating
to the safety of the VW camper.

—Bruce Miller

Was Phipps a failure, or did the Browns fail to develop him?
We'll never know, but this much is certain—Phipps did not get
the coaching he needed during the critical years. No member
of the Browns' 1970 coaching staff had played quarterback. In a
story from November 1971 under the headline: CAN THE PHIPPS
DEAL BE SAVED?, *The PD*'s Lebovitz wrote, "To date, it's a bad
deal for the Browns, perhaps the worst they ever made."

He had the right to make that assertion, since he didn't like the
trade when it was made.

"OK, so Art had to get a quarterback," wrote Lebovitz. "Every-
body agreed. But to give up a superstar for a kid fresh out of college? That was the risk which so far has backfired."

Lebovitz spent most of the long story on this point: "It's my
distinct impression the Browns are doing little or nothing to make
the deal pay off. Mike Phipps is rusting away. If the deal is to be
turned around, Phipps has to become a first rate quarterback. I
believe he has all the tools. What he needs now is a teacher. My
suggestion is the Browns hire a quarterback coach . . . a personal
tutor."

In 1972, the Browns were 10-4 with Phipps starting. Nelsen
was the backup but had moved into the role of helping Phipps.
Even in this season—Phipps' only good year—he still completed
only 47 percent of his passes, with 13 touchdowns compared to
16 interceptions. The Browns lost in the playoffs to . . . the Miami
Dolphins (on their way to a 17-0 record). The Browns had a 14-

13 lead in the fourth quarter before Miami scored a touchdown. Phipps had a miserable game (9-of-23 for 131 yards, with five interceptions). After that season, Nelsen accepted the position of quarterback coach . . . with the New England Patriots. He coached quarterbacks in Atlanta, Tampa Bay and Detroit over the next 10 seasons. A number of people suggested that the Browns hire Nelsen, but coach Nick Skorich pointed out that John David Crow had been Phipps' coach—and implied that Nelsen might be trying to take credit for someone else's work.

Well, after Nelsen left, Phipps had all kinds of problems.

The Browns drafted a quarterback who was a diamond in the rough, and they didn't hire anyone capable of polishing him. If they'd hired a solid quarterback coach, or had at least given the job to Nelsen, then they would have given Phipps a real shot to succeed. Another indication about how bad things were in the Skorich era is the number of sacks Phipps took. We're talking about a quarterback who finished his career with 254 rushes for 1,278 yards and 13 touchdowns—more than five yards per carry. That's Josh Cribbs territory. But he led the league in getting sacked in 1973, the year after Nelsen left. It didn't help that Phipps was throwing passes to people like Fair Hooker, Steve Holden and Gloster Richardson.

> Draft day means I must be living in a nightmare. When was the last good draft the Browns had? I think the last great draft we had was when we got Ozzie Newsome and Clay Matthews. Since then, we have had a few good picks, but mostly just mediocre players.
> **—Steven Dager**

After the 1976 season, Chicago offered Cleveland its first round pick in 1978 in exchange for Phipps. It was an offer that sane people don't refuse, and the Browns were indeed sane at this point. Phipps had been with the Browns for seven seasons, and the team was 24-25-2 with him as the starting QB. His career passer rating was 51.0, and he had a 40-81 TD-INT ratio. It was a first-round pick—probably not a high one, but still one of the first 28 picks in the draft. Modell and new General Manager Pete Hadhazy asked coach Forrest Gregg for his input, expecting him to say something like "Don't let the Bears off the phone!"

What he said was something like "We can't make that trade—we won't have a veteran backup. If Sipe gets hurt, it'll be the end of our season. We'd be lucky to win one game with backup QB Dave Mays."

Hadhazy and Modell pointed out that this was a chance to add a great young player—in exchange for a guy who was clearly the backup. Gregg pointed out that a team needed to have two reliable quarterbacks if they expected to get through the year. In an October 2009 story by *The Plain Dealer*'s Bill Lubinger, Gregg recalled that Modell had promised Phipps that he'd trade the quarterback if he wasn't going to start—and sent him to the Bears without Gregg's approval.

"As a coach, I never would make a promise like that," Gregg said. "I wouldn't make that kind of promise to anybody."

They made the deal over Gregg's objections, and what a deal!

On draft day of 1978, the Browns traded Chicago's pick (No. 20) to the Rams for their first-rounder (No. 23) and a fourth-round pick.

Then they called the name of Ozzie Newsome from Alabama.

Sam Rutigliano had just been hired as coach.

"I had been working in New Orleans for the Saints, so I was very aware of Ozzie," recalled Rutigliano. "If you live in the South, you pay attention to SEC football. He was a split end for a team that ran the wishbone, so he didn't get that many chances to catch passes. But I also knew Bear Bryant had said Ozzie was the best receiver that he'd ever coached."

The exact quote before the 1978 draft from Bryant was this: "He is the greatest end in Alabama history and that includes Don Hutson. A total team player, fine blocker, outstanding leader, great receiver with concentration, speed, hands."

Newsome caught 102 passes in his college career, but he

started for four years—so that didn't seem like a lot. The Browns and Rutigliano thought he'd be best at tight end.

"I wanted to know if he had a big butt, because I wanted him to weigh between 230-240 pounds," said Rutigliano. "I couldn't tell on film, so I sent (assistant) Rich Kotite to take a look at the size of his rear end. We liked everything else about Newsome."

Kotite came back with these words . . . Newsome's butt was big enough.

At the time, Newsome was listed at 6-foot-3, 206 pounds. Browns scout Mike Nixon raved to *The Plain Dealer*'s Russell Schneider on draft day that Newsome's hands were the best of anyone in the draft, "He's also a tough kid, a smart kid, and a flexible kid. There's no doubt he can play split end, tight end or whatever Sam wants."

On draft day, Rutigliano said, "He can catch a BB in the dark."

Yes he did, setting a team record for career receptions and ending up in the Hall of Fame.

By the way, the Browns drafted someone else that day . . . a guy named Clay Matthews at No. 12. He played from 1978 to 1993, and one day, he should join Newsome in the Hall of Fame.

As for Phipps, he spent five years with the Bears, mostly as a backup. In 1979, Phipps started 12 games for the Bears and had a 9-3 record despite his very modest passing stats—50 percent. He did throw more TDs (nine) than INTs (eight) for the first time in his career. But in 1980, he was pulled after six starts, with a 2-4 record, with only two TDs compared to nine interceptions.

And Phipps made the Hall of Fame, too. In 2006, he was voted into the National College Football Hall of Fame for what he did at Purdue. As for what could have been in the NFL? Who knows? But it seems that from the moment he was part of the Warfield deal, he and the Browns were doomed in that endeavor—until Ozzie Newsome came to town.

Fan Favorites

STEVE EVERITT

A player who played with a blue-collar chip on his shoulder, and played a big, nasty position . . . Steve Everitt.

He was drafted to the Browns after his college career at Michigan. Everitt was what Cleveland Brown football was supposed to be: Long-haired, tattoos, a big man with an unbelievable ability to play his position.

Everitt was not a running back, not a quarterback, nor was he the wide receiver who caught all the touchdown passes. Those positions were too flashy for Steve, anyway. Steve was *proud* to be the man who made the flashy players' jobs as easy as possible. He was a center. That consisted of more pain and more contact, and more bruises. Steve wouldn't have it any other way. Cleveland loved Everitt, and Everitt loved Cleveland. Everitt bought a house in the area, and dedicated his life, his love of art, his love of his family to the love of this city. Cleveland fell in love with this football warrior, who had a love for the arts. The Modern Day Renaissance Man had planted the seeds of his passion in Cleveland.

Then the move. Talk about scars. Everitt was crushed. "I remember David Modell congratulating me about the house that fall," he says. "After the move was announced, I tried to break his hand every time I shook it." Everitt, like all of us, was angry, heartbroken, and quite frankly pissed off. Despite knowing an NFL fine was coming, Everitt wore a Browns bandanna and let the whole world see his heart stood in Cleveland and with the Browns. He knew a fine was imminent, but that bandanna under his Ravens helmet was a big, left-handed middle finger to one organization, and a thankful handshake of thank you to another organization and their barking, bone-eating, loyal, blue-collar fans.

—Jacob Elerick

Johnny Morrow, Mike Baab, Steve Everitt, Hank Fraley. Tough, hardnosed centers who played good, tough Cleveland Browns football. Not your flashy guys but guys who did the dirty work on the O-line and guys who played with heart. Also Ryan Tucker, Doug Dieken and Cody Risien.

—Steve Harris

DOUG DIEKEN

One of the most memorable lines I heard most through those years, "Holding, No. 73." Poor Doug Dieken. He had big shoes to fill, following Hall of Famer Dick Schafrath at left offensive tackle. He did all right for himself.

—Kevin F. Lynch

Doug Dieken often visited my secretary's kid when Doug knew the young boy suffered from brain cancer—no one asked him to visit the boy, he just went.

—Wade Larkin

ERNIE DAVIS

My favorite all-time Browns player is a guy who never played a down for the team. I just got through reading the biography of Ernie Davis. He not only was a great football player but an outstanding human being. If I could somehow acquire half his class, sense of humor and kindness, I'd be a great individual.

—Jeff Biletnikoff

I moved to Los Angeles in 1997 to pursue a career in the film business. I've been fortunate to have had some success over the last decade or so. . . . I had just had the tremendous experience of making a movie about Ernie Davis called *The Express*. I didn't know much about Ernie before making the movie, other than my dad had once said that he and Jim Brown could have been the greatest backfield of all time. After we were finished telling his story on film, we wanted the world to know Ernie's story.

—*Derek Dauchy*

MILT MORIN

When I was a kid growing up in Canton, Milt Morin made an appearance at a local car dealer. My buddy and I were two of only a handful of fans to show up to see Milt. He took to us and spent most of the evening talking to us, drawing out plays (which I still have) and taking pictures with us. If there was a pigskin available, I'm sure he would have run a few routes with us. I think we were there for two hours. That one unforgettable night cemented my passion for Cleveland Browns football. By the next season, I had season tickets, which I kept for years.

—*Bruce Hiller*

My mom took me to a barbershop at the Richmond Mall. While I was getting my haircut, the barber asked if I was a Browns fan. I said yes. He asked me if I knew who was sitting in the chair next to me. I said no. He said it was Milt Morin. Morin got up from his chair and to me looked like a giant. He said hello, but I was too startled to speak. I can't imagine players today would get their hair cut in a regular barbershop.

—*Kevin O'Connell*

For our St. Patrick's (West Park) CYO football banquet, Mike Setta (our coach) and Fr. Yarnavick arranged for Milt Morin to speak. What an inspiration and impression he made on us. He told us that no matter what we did to do our best. Certainly cliché, but at that age when you hear it from No. 89, you were inspired.

—*Dan Campbell*

JERRY SHERK

My favorite player is, without a doubt, Jerry Sherk. I had the honor of meeting Jerry while he was in his prime. He leased a house in Westlake from my father in-law. To actually meet and talk to a Browns player was truly "the ultimate" for a Browns fan. We talked about our dogs. We both had Irish setters, and it was great to have something in common with the best All-Pro lineman in football. I was horrified when Jerry got sick with a staph infection that nearly took his life. He had lost so much weight, I was sure he would never play again. Thanks to some medicine that he was taking for a sinus problem, it cleaned out the staph, and he later returned to finish his career with the Browns. Some 30 years later, when Jerry was inducted into the Browns Legends Club, I wanted to meet up with him and have a jersey signed as a gift to my son. He was very gracious, and he met me and my son at the game for some pictures and a signing of the jersey. I was a little kid all over again.

—*John Gentry*

I remember seeing Jerry Sherk at a grocery store when I was a teenager. I had never seen a man that big up close.

—*Kent Maurer*

ERIC METCALF

As a young Browns fan, I loved Eric Metcalf. I was a small kid, and Eric gave me hope. He made me want to play football (and other sports) and gave me confidence in my athletic ability simply because of his success. I was watching the Browns in my parents' room. My dad and mom were cooking the Sunday meal. Eric Metcalf ran the kickoff back for a touchdown, making several players look very stupid in the process. I jumped up and danced around the room as he sprinted into the end zone. I went dancing out to the kitchen to tell my dad, who immediately joined me in the dancing. He quickly finished his part of lunch, we ate as fast as we could, and we finished watching that game together.

—*Jamie Taylor*

Eric Metcalf's epic TD move on "Monday Night Football" that amazed the broadcasters was awesome. But more so, how he would single-handedly beat the Steelers was great, too.

—*Frank Amato*

My best day at the Browns' stadium was when Eric Metcalf returned two punts for touchdowns to help beat the hated Steelers. That big, old stadium was so loud, it was actually shaking!

—*Kent Maurer*

My hate for the Steelers must have been innate. I was in third grade watching the game between the Browns and Steelers. Metcalf had already taken a punt for a TD, and it was late in the fourth quarter, and Pittsburgh was up. When Pittsburgh lined up for the punt, I went crazy and said Metcalf is going all the way! Sure enough, he did, which won us the game.

—*Brice Westhoven*

GREG PRUITT

My favorite Browns player was No. 34, Greg Pruitt. He ran past, through, between and around bewildered defenders. His T-shirts at the time said it all, "HELLO-GOODBYE." He was the most exciting player that I ever saw. He displayed speed, agility, balance, vision, elusiveness and, of course, the beloved tear-away jersey. He could run, catch, return and even pass. My most memorable Greg Pruitt moment was his stop-and-go 57-yard TD run against the Los Angeles Rams at Municipal Stadium in 1978.

He was mobbed by his teammates in the end zone, and I will never forget that day, as well as him getting a Super Bowl ring with the Raiders.

—*Steve Dolinsky*

It's something about the big plays you see as a kid or the tear-away jersey that still makes him my all-time favorite Brownie as I didn't get to see Jimmy Brown play.

—*David K. Rehard*

BRIAN BRENNAN

Number 86 would always bring a relief to my eyes on any third-down play. Brian Brennan was the quintessential "Glue Guy." Need a first down . . . look for No. 86. Need to get a pass over the middle . . . here comes No. 86. Brian Brennan was what true DAWGS hope to see Sundays in Orange and Brown. He was not the heralded high draft pick. He was the relentless and tireless over-achiever whom no one else gave a flip about on draft day.

—*Allen J. Webb*

I have been in the financial industry in Cleveland and have had the honor of meeting Brian Brennan while at work. One time he was in my office when I made a guest appearance on TV. After I was done, he congratulated me on a good job. That was just cool!

—*Chris Staneluis*

Brian Brennan was never the fastest guy, but he always seemed to get open and make a catch. How he did that when some of the faster receivers couldn't get open is beyond me.

—*Ron Sup*

BILL NELSEN

Bill Nelsen was the toughest, grittiest, most courageous man to ever play for the Browns. He had his shoulder knocked out of its socket and returned to a game. He was the last quarterback to lead the Browns to back-to-back NFL Championship Games, and he beat "Broadway" Joe Namath in the first-ever "Monday Night Football" game.

—Gene Stratton

I became a Browns fan in 1968 at the age of 10. I recall Bill Nelsen with his bad knees. He signed a picture of himself that I still have buried in the attic.

—Dale McCombs

ERNIE GREEN

In 1964, Lou Groza was still kicking field goals, even after busting his nose in the Washington game, with blood smeared all over that mill-worker's face of his. I met a new hero that year, too. My dad took me to a local meeting because Ernie Green was appearing as a speaker. Ernie was a handsome kid who spoke with softness and sincerity about commitment and doing the right thing. I ate up every word. At the end, when we all gathered around to get an autograph, he shook my hand and winked at me and smiled. I always wondered if he knew what an impact that wink would have on the rest of my life.

During the championship game, I remember we screamed and yelled and danced around that TV set. For one day, my dad and uncle and me were all 11-year-old boys. *We* won—all of us! The team made us proud to be Clevelanders, guys who went to work every day, tried to treat others with decency and respect, and came home, bone-tired, each night to their families. *We* were all winners. I remember going outside by myself with my football after that game. It's what we did back then. I'd throw that ball as high and long as I could and run like hell to get under it ... touchdown, Collins. Sliding into a pile of snow ... Jim Brown for 6 tough yards. But I became Ernie Green quite a bit after I had met him. Kind of my quiet hero. Running full throttle, head first into that same snowbank.

I feel blessed to have come from a place where people don't ever learn to quit. And so it is, I could never quit either, especially when it comes to my Browns. I don't live in Cleveland anymore, so people naturally ask me, "How can you root for those losers?" Or, "Why don't you get yourself a new team?" They just don't get it, I'm afraid. They weren't with me and my dad and Rich that day. They never threw that football and skidded across the snow. They never met Ernie Green and shook his hand.

—Jack Tapleshay

DICK AMBROSE

Dick Ambrose spoke at my seventh-grade football banquet. What an engaging and articulate man. Totally changed my perception of NFL players.

—Gregg Bollinger

WEBSTER SLAUGHTER

He had the enthusiasm of a kid. When he ran, he was all elbows and knees. I loved that.

—Barry Grey

As a kid, how could you not have that poster of him in front of an F-16 . . . with lightning in the background, of course. Not to mention, his name is *Slaughter*. Way cool in the '80s.

—Chris Kost

TIM COUCH

My favorite player of the new Browns era is Tim Couch. Did you know Tim ranks fifth in all-time Browns passing yards? Right behind the likes of Brian Sipe, Bernie Kosar, Otto Graham and Frank Ryan. I took Tim Couch for granted until he was beaten out by journeyman Kelly Holcomb before the 2003 season. That was the big wakeup call about the direction of the organization. At the time, I said to anyone willing to listen, "this move will set back the progress of the Cleveland Browns five years." Tim Couch's career is the poster child for the failures of the Browns organization over the past decade. I still believe he could have been a solid starter in the NFL, but the lack of a team identity, poor organizational planning, structure, regime instability and a complete inability to develop draft picks were all present in the career of Tim Couch in Cleveland.

—*Chris Hocevar*

SETH MCKINNEY

In 2007, I went to the famous Browns-Bengals shootout. After the game, my wife and I attended a church service in North Ridgeville. We were sitting in the pew, and about one minute before the service started, in walked Seth McKinney, his wife and their three children. They sat in the pew right in front of us. Seth was sweaty and still had visible depressions in his head from wearing a helmet. Seth and his wife are two of the nicest people I've ever met. He went from playing NFL football to attending a church service, all within about an hour-and-a-half. It impressed me that instead of heading home and icing up, his faith was important enough to him to attend a service that night.

—*Daniel Jenkins*

BEN DAVIS

My favorite would be Ben Davis. He was drafted in 1967 in the 17th round out of little Defiance College in Defiance, Ohio. He ran back punts and kickoffs his rookie season and was among the league leaders in both categories. In his second season, he became a starter and a standout cornerback. He was key in the Browns' run to the playoffs in 1968 by intercepting at least one pass in seven consecutive games. He intercepted Don Meredith in the 1968 playoff game in Cleveland. Ben ended his pro career with the Lions but came back to Cleveland to live and pursue his business interests.

—*Gerry Prokupek*

ERNIE KELLERMANN

Ernie Kellermann was a substitute gym teacher at Beachwood High. He was fresh out of Miami and just a little older than his students, but he was on the Browns' taxi squad. We thought he was God. Over the years, it has been something special for local kids to play for the Browns.

—Andy Janovsky

THOM DARDEN

Thom Darden always seemed to be in the right place at the right time, and he would take your head off if you wandered into his area. Just ask Bob Trumpy.

—Mark Di Vincenzo

GARY DANIELSON

He was and is my favorite player. He epitomized professionalism and was the first veteran player to cross the picket line in 1987. He was a great mentor to Bernie Kosar and came across to young, male Browns fans as a sort of father figure.

—Brian Gold

LEROY KELLY

When I was a little shaver, I think it was my dad that took me to Uncle Bill's, and Leroy Kelly was there for autographs or hand-shaking. He was *huge!* I was so small, I never even got to shake his hand. I just remember looking up and seeing this "mass of humanity" standing there.

—Dan Rubinski

I admired Leroy Kelly for following in the footsteps of the greatest play ever and being great in his own right.

—Jeff Joseph

CHAPTER 16

The Browns' best draft pick since 1999 wasn't drafted.

Why Josh Cribbs is easily my favorite player since 1999: He was an underdog. Whether he goes 10 yards on a play or 100 is fun to watch. He has a rare combination of speed, power, instincts and bravery. . . . Whether the game is tied or the Browns are down by 21 in the forth quarter, Josh plays with the same constant intensity. When fans are shelling out big bucks to see a sub-par product, we love to see a guy play hard to the end. He flies in the face of the perception of the spoiled athlete who is just out for himself.

—Greg Huzicka

Opening day 2008 against Dallas. For the entire off-season, we thought we had a team that could compete for the AFC championship. Those thoughts went out the door when Donté Stallworth hurt his groin warming up, Braylon Edwards dropped five balls and we were down 21-7 at the half. My heart sank.

—Justin L. Wagner

While away at college, my Dad would call every Sunday, and the Browns would be the first thing we'd talk about. I now have an 11-year-old son who was born in Pennsylvania, but he knows what's good for him . . . so he is also a Browns fan. I feel so bad for what he has to endure at school in his Kellen Winslow/ Charlie Frye/Braylon Edwards/Brady Quinn jerseys. It shows how

much he respects his dad. Thank goodness for Josh Cribbs! The
kids tend to be quiet when he's wearing that one.
  —David K. Rehard

And with the Number 3 pick in the National Football League
Draft, the Cleveland Browns select . . . Joshua Cribbs.

Actually, it was Braylon Edwards.

And Joshua Cribbs? His name wasn't called. By anyone. Not
after seven rounds. Not after a career in which, for three seasons,
he passed for at least 1,000 yards. And also rushed for 1,000 yards.
And clearly was the most gifted athlete in the Mid-American
Conference. But Cribbs played at Kent State, where he was quarterback for a losing team. If any scouts thought Cribbs had a pro
future, he would have to do it as a receiver or defensive back—
meaning a change of positions.

And that often doesn't work.

So no one drafted Cribbs. No one ever dreamed Cribbs would
become the best rookie to join the Browns in 2005, especially
after they threw a $17 million signing bonus at Edwards—who
had been a star receiver at Michigan. In that same draft class, the
Browns picked Brodney Pool and Charlie Frye.

They signed Cribbs for $2,500 and a promise that he'd be given
a fair chance to make a bad team.

Edwards showed up for his draft news conference in Cleveland already having bought a Bentley—even before he signed his
contract. He showed up with agents and family members, who
billed themselves as Team Braylon.

Edwards was All-Big Ten for three years. As a senior, he caught
91 passes (15 touchdowns). That came after 86 catches (14 touchdowns) as a junior.

Here's part of the *Sports Illustrated* scouting report heading
into the 2005 NFL Draft: "Big, physical receiver who breaks games
wide open or controls them from the get-go. Quick releasing off
the line, boxes out opponents with his frame and easily makes receptions in traffic. Fast down the field, gets vertical then contorts
in mid-air for the acrobatic grab. Displays good eye/hand coor-

dination, looks the pass in and extends to offer the quarterback a nice target. Easily beats jams at the line of scrimmage or physically pounds opponents to come away with the ball. Displays open-field running skills after the reception and blocks with solid technique. . . . Not always mentally on top of his game, loses focus or takes his eye off the ball. . . . A superior athlete who plays bigger and faster than his computer numbers, Edwards makes truly amazing plays on the football field with regularity. A terrific red-zone target who creates mismatches, he has an unusually high ratio of touchdown receptions. Worthy of an early first round selection and should have a long and productive NFL career once he learns to focus and give attention to detail."

That's about what former General Manager Phil Savage said about Edwards on draft day, a pick that was not seriously second-guessed anywhere. But Edwards wanted no part of Cleveland. He hoped to go No. 2 to Miami, a city that was more to his taste. He also ripped then-Dolphins coach Nick Saban for not selecting him, claiming Saban indicated Miami would draft Edwards.

It's odd how Edwards, who was a Midwestern guy from Detroit, had such disdain for Cleveland. But Edwards had a sense of entitlement that never seemed to end. Being the No. 3 pick in the draft on a bad team where he immediately became the highest-paid player just fueled his ego and also alienated him from his teammates. He acted as if he were a Pro Bowl selection before his first pro game.

He also is a product of the crazy NFL system, where the salary cap applies to everyone but rookies. It's also why some coaches such as Bill Belichick hate having high draft picks, often trading them for multiple selections in lower rounds. They know the rookie with big bucks can cause resentment in the dressing room among veterans, especially if the rookie doesn't immediately produce.

Edwards is representative of so much that went so wrong with the Browns after their return in 1999. They had the top pick that first season, and Tim Couch was not ready for prime time in his first season with an expansion team. Looking back, former Browns

President Carmen Policy and General Manager Dwight Clark had one thing right—veteran Ty Detmer should have started most, if not all, of that first season. Instead, he was pulled in the first game by coach Chris Palmer. He believed if you have a young quarterback on a bad team who is considered the future starter, then start him now. The theory was, the fastest way to learn was in the heat of battle. In Couch's case, it also was the fastest way to take a physical pounding, as he never played after the 2003 season because of various injuries. Some with the Browns also believed Couch didn't have a lot of drive, that he wasn't the first in the building, the last to leave. They believe it was because he was paid so much, so soon as the NFL's top pick in 1999. There may be some truth to that, but the real problem was injuries—and perhaps playing too much, too soon.

I never could feel much animosity for Couch or Courtney Brown. Back-to-back top picks in the drafts, back-to-back decent guys who sustained significant injuries. In the end, they were draft busts because they failed to produce. But did they underachieve? Did they act as if Cleveland were the NFL's version of Devil's Island and couldn't wait to get out? Not at all. Both seemed to like it here and want to make it work for the team and the fans. But Brown had one injury after another, micro-fracture knee surgery being the worst. Couch had major shoulder and elbow injuries.

Brown played his last NFL game at the age of 27; Couch was done at 26.

The Browns passed on LaDainian Tomlinson and Richard Seymour to draft defensive tackle Gerard Warren, who had a reputation as an underachiever. So was it a surprise that Warren drew criticism for his lack of work in practice and the off-season? It's what the Browns and coach Butch Davis bargained for when they made him the No. 3 pick in the 2001 draft.

I have no plans to buy another Browns jersey, especially since my 3-year-old son Ben's first Browns jersey was a No. 17 Braylon Edwards, which is now a relic.
—**Andy Nichols**

Edwards is the one player who annoys me the most.

At least Gerard Warren was smart enough not to rent a helicopter to attend the Ohio State-Michigan game in Columbus. That was in 2006, and Edwards arrived late for a Saturday team meeting as the Browns were preparing for their next game. Making it worse, he appeared surprised that anyone would be upset by his actions. Why not rent a helicopter to see your alma mater play? It's part of being Braylon, of having the $17 million bonus and a sense of entitlement that wiped out any sensitivity to what his coaches, teammates or fans may think of the incident.

Edwards consistently has been near the league lead in passes dropped, but his mother said that stat was "created because of him," according to a story by Greg Bishop in *The New York Times*— as if no one would have noticed all the passes being dropped. And Mrs. Edwards, they were counting dropped passes long before your son arrived in the NFL. But that is his mentality and the enabling approach by the people around him.

After being traded to the Jets in 2009, Edwards caught 35 passes in 12 games, four for touchdowns and four drops.

In the playoffs, he caught six passes in three games, one for a touchdown. Those Jet numbers were no better than what he did with the Browns in 2008, when he had 55 catches (and 16 drops) in 16 games. In 2008-09, he averaged about three catches per game and had a total of seven touchdowns. You can argue the Jets were a run-first team (true), but is there any reason to consider Edwards a star other than his insistence that that's how he should be treated? Remember that Edwards ripped the play-calling after the Jets lost to Indianapolis in the AFC Championship Game: "I don't call the plays, I just run them."

In the same *New York Times* story, Edwards said: "There's nothing going on in Cleveland. There's no real estate. There's no social life, no social networking. All the people who have something going on leave Cleveland. So Cleveland has nothing, and I came in there with a New York-type of essence. So what? That was the attitude I came in with. Like, this is who I am. They didn't like the flash."

Can you imagine Paul Warfield, Reggie Langhorne or even Keenan McCardell saying something like that? Hey, Braylon, that $17 million bonus was paid so you can go to work! Catch some passes! As for the "New York essence," Edwards is from Detroit! No one was complaining about Edwards in 2007 when he caught 16 touchdown passes and the Browns were 10-6. Instead, he was cheered by Browns fans.

The New York Times story almost sounds like a parody of a spoiled athlete. My goodness, his mother said, "No one would understand what he's been through unless you've been drowning." His mother also said that Edwards told her that his "career was over" after the Browns lost to Cincinnati last season and he didn't catch a pass.

If Edwards happened to be a guy who was simply drafted too high but at least tried hard—think of Tommy Vardell, Antonio Langham or Kamerion Wimbley—there would be very few complaints. But Edwards is far more physically gifted. He also loves to rip coaches and, sometimes, quarterbacks. Hardcore Browns fans remember him on the sidelines during a game, grabbing Charlie Frye by the shirt, screaming at his quarterback and other teammates. After the game, he accused the team of "flat-out not playing."

There are so many other problems. He was ticketed for speeding . . . at 2 a.m. . . . while driving 120 miles per hour. He was drinking with Donté Stallworth the night the former Browns receiver left a hotel and hit a pedestrian, killing him. Edwards was wise enough that night not to get into his car. The bill for that night was $3,443—much of it spent on champagne and other hard liquor. He punched a friend of LeBron James outside a bar; that final act triggered the trade to the Jets. It also was the kind of story that has made it very hard for some fans to remain attached to the Browns.

I wish the Browns would bring back the same blue-collar attitude they had before they left. Cleveland didn't have any divas like Dallas or criminals like Cincinnati. They had hard-working, tough players who loved the game and didn't get caught up in all the glamour like Braylon Edwards or Kellen Winslow. I miss those days. It's cool to look back and know how hard players would play on a Sunday afternoon, where they were treated like kings, and return to their normal lives afterward and seem like normal, ordinary men.

—Ryan Glasener

Josh Cribbs plays meritoriously, not merely well. Cribbs plays with honor. Cribbs plays hurt. Cribbs also attended Kent State and professed his love for Cleveland, the loyalty that inspires a Clevelander's love. Cribbs looks nearly superhuman when he does his thing, like Jim Brown did doing his thing two generations earlier. Cribbs is transcendent, and he loves us back. It does not get any better than that.

—Bill Beck

Number 16, Joshua Cribbs. Now there's a jersey that Browns fans can wear proudly. Cribbs could have played for Paul Brown, for Blanton Collier, for Sam Rutigliano or any other Browns coach. They all would have loved the guy. He runs back kicks. He runs back punts. He runs out of the wildcat formation, taking a long snap from the center, then sprinting and daring the defense to stop him. He also covers kicks. And punts. And he would play safety, if they'd let him.

Best of all, he hates the Pittsburgh Steelers. And the undrafted free agent from Kent State plays like it.

In the expansion era, fans needed a player such as Cribbs, a player who said after the Browns beat Pittsburgh 13-6 in 2009: "For our fans, [beating Pittsburgh] would be the season for us. They would be like, 'OK, we forgive you.' We were the team that imposed our will on this game. I am so happy for the fans."

There's a player who gets it, when it comes to bleeding orange and brown.

Jim Brown called Cribbs: "A spiritual force. What he does is so pure. It's running the ball, then going down to make a tackle.

It's playing the game with the right attitude, giving himself all the way."

Cribbs entered the 2010 season with an NFL-record eight kick-offs returned for touchdowns. He was named the top return man on the NFL's all-decade team for the 2000s.

Eric Mangini has gushed about Cribbs: "It's not just how he plays, but it's his preparation. He has no ego, he just wants to help us win. He is a great guy, a great teammate, a guy who makes you excited as a coach."

But the fans can say it even better than any coach or sports-writer:

Cribbs is everything a football player should be. Good teammate. Leader. Many times, the first to make a tackle on special teams as well. Possibly the most exciting player to watch in football when returning kicks.
— **Samuel Hafner**

I'm a professional writer, but when I try to describe the thrill of watching him return a kick . . . or cover one . . . or take the direct snap from center . . . words fail me. He's the most exciting Brown in 45 years, since the retirement of Jim Brown.
— **Barry Grey**

Josh Cribbs is one of the best all-around football players I've ever seen. He is a breath of fresh air and plays exactly like the old Browns I love so much.
— **Al Kelly**

The best Brown since they returned to the league, and not just because he's good on the field. He's loyal to the fans and the city—despite his bluff during his contract negotiations. He knows and appreciates the fact that the Browns were the only NFL team to give him a shot out of college. His loyalty is not unlike Bernie Kosar's, so it's no wonder the fans love him.
— **Bob Blandeburgo**

My wife and I have a 10-year-old son who has CP (cerebral palsy). He just became a fan in the last year. This is something that I can share with him like my father did with me. We listen to games outside in the fall and play catch with his football. He'll pretend he's Josh Cribbs.

— **Kevin O'Connell**

Look at who we drafted and who we could have had! Who is STILL here? First-round picks of a team were designed to build your franchise around, to be the FRANCHISE player? Since 1999, I don't think it has worked yet! We have only one true Pro Bowler—Joe Thomas! And the BEST pick-up over the past 11 years? An undrafted quarterback from Kent State in 2005, JOSH CRIBBS, the Cleveland Browns' ONLY "FRANCHISE" player and history maker!

— **Steve Pavlik**

My four kids, ages 6 to 16, have never really experienced a winning team. I've bought jerseys of players for them who keep getting cut or traded. They've stopped wanting them because they can't compete with the neighbor kids who wear Peyton Manning, Carson Palmer and Brett Favre jerseys. Now I can confidently buy them a Cribbs jersey that they can wear proudly as the best return man in football, and know that in two years I don't have to trade it in for another one.

— **Michael Tarrant**

CHAPTER 17

Loving the Browns doesn't make sense. But we just can't help ourselves.

Growing up in Northeast Ohio, I know fans loved the Browns. I know that the love is often irrational and unrequited. For many too many, the Browns Backers have felt like the Lonely Hearts Club.

You know the litany: The Drive . . . The Fumble . . . The Move.

How much are the fans expected to take?

After reading and sorting through more than 1,000 e-mails from fans about the team, I underestimated everything that I thought about the Browns.

The love for the team is greater, the passion is deeper than even the hardest core fan can imagine.

The connection to family is real; many of the fans do bleed orange and brown. Winning or losing is not the ultimate, it's how the team is tied to certain points in the lives of families. A father was around for Red Right 88 but not for The Fumble. Mom always loved Bernie Kosar, and thank God she wasn't alive when he was cut. That would have stopped her heart a second time. Those emotions are real.

The reverence and knowledge of the team's past is remarkable. Too bad most of us don't know the history of our own country—or even our own families—as well as we know the Browns. A big part of this book was to bring out even more history of the team, telling stories behind the biggest stories. How many of us ever knew (or remembered) that the dreaded Paul Warfield trade eventually turned into Ozzie Newsome . . . or that in the same draft where they picked Newsome, they were all set to pass on Clay Matthews?

This book about a storied franchise that hasn't won a title since 1964 and has never appeared in the Super Bowl is really about stories.

Browns stories and your stories.

They are stories that may only be special to your family and close friends. They certainly are stories that only Browns fans can understand.

They are stories like this, from Les Levine.

Full disclosure: I've done a weekly television talk show with Les Levine since 2000. He pays me. He also is a good friend, a man who knows his Browns history more than I do. His father was friends with Morrie Kono, the Browns' equipment manager under Paul Brown. Levine and his brother, Bill, would be in the dressing room during practices. They were just kids, but they were able to meet the players—close up. Les and/or his family have been Browns season-ticket holders since 1956. Unlike most media members, when he criticizes the team, he also does it as a paying customer. And no one will ever accuse him of being soft on the Browns.

But when I asked him for his favorite Browns story, he e-mailed this: "Browns receiver Ray Renfro was my favorite player in the 1950s. I went trick-or-treating in my South Euclid neighborhood, and he came to the door loaded with candy. I had no idea he lived two streets from me. . . . Frank Ryan lived in Lyndhurst, and it was not unusual for him to show up at Brush High football games on Friday nights."

Levine has met and interviewed all of the Browns stars and coaches for more than 30 years, but he comes up with this Hallmark card of a story about Renfro and Ryan.

Which brings up this e-mail from Frank Rupnik: "After Frank Ryan retired from playing, he became a professor at Case Western Reserve University. I took Calculus II and didn't know who my professor was going to be until he walked into class the first morning in late August 1970. I nearly fainted. What a thrill it was to see an NFL player *up close*, let alone knowing that I would be seeing him three times a week for the next four months. When he first started to lecture, he put his foot up on one of the desks. I was amazed at the size of his thighs. He had a photographic memory. He never brought a book to class, nor did he bring a lot of notes. He would be working through a problem one day, get half finished and class would be over. When he came in the next class, he would say, 'I think we were about here, is that right?' He always seemed to be dead on. If anyone knows what calculus problems are like, they can be quite lengthy at times. But the best part was that we were in the fall semester. Once the season began, if the Browns were on TV, we would spend the first part of Monday's class with a critique or analysis of the game. He would state what the play they scored on was . . . and give the name. Then he would proceed to diagram the play as to who was doing what."

Yes, that is the same Frank Ryan who quarterbacked the Browns to the 1964 title. It also was the same Frank Ryan who was studying for his Ph.D. that championship season. And the same Frank Ryan who was "throwing a football around with some kids in the street," according to his wife, when Hal Lebovitz called Ryan's home for an interview.

So much of the Browns' history revolves around missed opportunities: Trades that shouldn't have been made and the wrong players who were picked. There were championships that could have been won and games that never should have been lost. It's rotten weather in a lousy stadium with a team that you love but don't quite trust.

The weather is in the middle of so many stories from fans. Once upon a time, a nice day for a Browns game in late fall was called "Modell Weather." You never hear that mentioned these days. Some people can't say the name of the man who moved the Browns. As Debra Harwood e-mailed: "I can't see the Modell Sporting Goods sign behind the batter at Yankee Stadium without my jaw locking. I cried for days when the Browns moved and memorized the fax number to the NFL headquarters so I could provide others with a 'protest number.' You'd think it was time to get over it . . . and a 56-year-old woman would have better things to focus on, don't you?"

Then Hardwood added: "Most women when they turn 50 get a nice pair of diamond earrings from their family. I got a personalized Browns jersey. My number is 53, the year was I born. My player name is DEBBIE!"

Don't even try to explain this stuff rationally.

As Dave Klinect e-mailed: "Brian Sipe is still my favorite player, a fact that stems from reaching adulthood around the same time the Kardiac Kids were at their best. I still have 'The 12 Days of Cleveland Browns Christmas' and play it every year in December."

Know what happened after the upbeat tune "The 12 Days of a Cleveland Browns Christmas" in 1980? That's right, Red Right 88. And Bob Frey wrote a song about that. Actually, it is more like an opera: "I am a teacher and musician. The song is pretty long, 18½ minutes. But it tells the story of my father and me riding the train, as we often did, to watch that game. It's about the Kardiac Kids, the 1980 season, a father, a son and being a kid growing up in Cleveland in the 1970s and 1980s."

Frey said he mailed a CD to Sipe, who responded with a kind, handwritten letter.

A friend of mine recently told me, "It's been 40 years since I started paying attention to the Browns. How many hours have I spent on this? Not just watching the games, but reading the papers and magazines and websites, listening to Pete Franklin and the other guys talk. Or all the time arguing with people about the team and what they needed. There's all the time I've spent reading books and looking at statistics and crunching numbers. . . . Has it all been worth it? . . . Jeez, I don't know. . . . They haven't won a championship. When they've been bad, they've been painful to watch. When they've been good, they've been excruciating."

Putting an exclamation point on that, James Bankhurst

e-mailed: "I am 52 years old. Since I first became a Browns fan when I was 8, my misery can best be expressed in terms of time. Assuming 44 years times 16 games per year times 5 hours per game (conservative!), it's been a staggering 3,520 hours, or 146 days, that I've spent watching this mess. It's been said that one cigarette cuts 11 minutes off your life. While I don't smoke, I may as well have, since 19,200 cigarettes would have reduced my life by an equivalent amount. At least smoking cigarettes would be a vice that I could one day quit."

Marshall Siegel expressed the same thoughts in this e-mail: "In 1973 I was 7 years old, and we happened to be in Los Angeles, where my dad took us to see a Browns-Rams exhibition game. Greg Pruitt was a rookie and ran a kickoff back for a touchdown. Of course it was called back because of a holding penalty. Unfortunately, I had no clue that it essentially symbolized my next 37 years as a fan."

Then Siegel added: "You heard it here first! The Browns will win the Super Bowl in 2012. Since I was very young, my friends and I have always said that if the Browns ever get to the Super Bowl, we are definitely going. In 2012 it happens to be in Indianapolis, which would be an easy drive. . . . Also, 2012 is supposedly the year of the Apocalypse. I can't think of anything more likely to cause the end of the world as we know it other than the Browns actually winning a championship."

How about this from Janean Nagorski: "If you always do what you've always done, you'll always get what you've always gotten . . . . as in Metcalf up the middle."

Most sports fans would hear that and have no clue what Nagorski was writing about. But Browns fans would remember when former coach Bill Belichick would run his fleet Eric Metcalf into the middle of the line as if Metcalf were a bruising fullback. The idea was to surprise the defense, which supposedly would think, "They'll never run Metcalf up the middle."

But no one was surprised when the play was stuffed, least of all, Browns fans. They knew it was coming, and they knew it would never work.

I have a friend named Mike Jozic, and every time a Browns player has a significant injury, he spouts off: "It's just a teeny-tiny fracture of a non-weight-bearing bone."

Hearing this, most Browns fans would laugh, remembering how former coach Butch Davis tried to shrug off the broken leg suffered by quarterback Kelly Holcomb.

Then there is this phrase: "Diminishing skills."

That's how Belichick explained his reason for cutting Bernie Kosar in 1993.

Or "Null and void."

That's what Art Modell said, breaking his promise (and a stadium lease) by saying the team would move after the 1995 season.

I did like this e-mail from William Van Stolk: "As you may, (or may not) know, Elvis was a Browns fan. As a lifelong Browns fan I find that ironic, because their histories mirror each other. Both Elvis and the Browns were great in the '50s, lousy in the '70s, showed signs of life in the '80s and were proven dead in the '90s."

Then he added: "Go Browns! They're still my team no matter what."

Mary Kelly would agree with that: "My addiction started back in my grade school years . . . going to the very first 'Monday Night Football' game, Browns verses N.Y. Jets and Joe Namath. It was such a thrill, a game won by the Browns. Being at training camp in Hiram, getting autographs. . . . .A special thrill the last 14 years has been being the 'Browns Poet.' After each game, win or lose, I wrote a poem about the game and read it to the people at my workplace on Fridays."

OK, I also know Mary, and she wears all this Browns jewelry. She met another friend, Sue Klein. They immediately talked about poems and Browns outfits and memories. Understand this about Sue Klein. One day, Franco Harris visited her office. He was retired and in the Hall of Fame. Sue said he was a "very nice guy, especially for a Steeler." She enjoyed listening to him talk. Sue is the people-person who immediately likes to make strangers feel like friends. But when Harris offered to shake her hand, Sue refused.

"He's a Steeler. I just couldn't do it," she said.

Only Browns fans would understand any of this.

Kelly also mentioned, "watching the man in the brown suit catch those balls after field goals."

Fred and Carol Matthews e-mailed this: "There was a man in a brown suit who came to every game and tried to catch footballs in the end zone. His name was Abe Abrahams. I first met Mr. Abrahams at a restaurant he owned at Chatfield and West 150th Street called The Caboose. The restaurant had a great collection of Browns memorabilia. I still remember Abe leaning on the coffee urn handle, moving a cup up and down, telling Browns stories. The progress of the Rapid Transit tore down the Caboose restaurant and its Cleveland Browns memories of old. . . . Gone were the days of 50-cent games."

I remember an aging Abe in a brown business suit catching most of those footballs kicked through the uprights. So does almost any Browns fans with a few gray hairs. Don't ask us why the team had this guy in a brown suit catching footballs during games, but they did. And fans loved to cheer when Abe made a nice grab.

Matt Michaels sent me this 1981 story about his grandmother, Anne Michaels. It was written by Hal Lebovitz:

"I received a letter, 'a desperate one,' said the writer, Keith Allie. It told about his auntie, Anne Michaels. She had worked for the Yellow Cab Co. for years, starting there when it was owned by Mickey McBride. Mickey owned the Browns, too, and Auntie Anne, according to her family, became the Browns' No. 1 booster.

"This year, it was discovered she had cancer. She refused to complain, serving as an inspiration to everyone who knew her. Each day, against doctor's orders, she continued to go to work. But by late October, it became impossible. She was bedridden. Auntie Anne was dying. Yet, she eagerly continued to follow the Browns. According to the letter, 'She eats, sleeps and talks football. And while every Browns game is in progress, she forgets completely about the cancer and how it is killing her.'

"The letter mentioned that her favorite players were Lyle

Alzado, Brian Sipe and Dave Logan, and her nephew wondered if one of them might visit Auntie Anne. It would be the most glorious gift she could receive. Would I tell them about Auntie Anne and tell them to come? This was a busy time for the players. . . . From all sides, people beg for their time. Instead, I made three copies of the letter, put them in the lockers of Alzado, Sipe, and Logan, and that was the last I thought of it.

"A few days ago, I received another letter from Keith Allie. The morning the players found the copies, 'Mr. Lyle Alzado called,' wrote Keith. 'He said he was going to visit Auntie Anne that evening, and Brian Sipe and Dave Logan were coming with him.' There was one problem. Her funeral services were being held in a few hours. 'Our beloved Auntie Anne had died two days before.' Although Auntie Anne never got to see her three favorites, the phone call from Alzado never will be forgotten by those she left behind."

Twenty-nine years later, this story is still being told.

That's what makes this team . . . and this book . . . unique.

It's your stories.

It's Tom Brennan writing that he met former Browns tackle Tony Jones on a beach in the Bahamas. "I was with my friend, Steve. We showed Tony our Browns helmet tattoos on our legs. He rolled up his sleeve and showed us the Dawg Pound tattoo on his arm. His wife took a picture of the three of us showing our tattoos. He made our day."

It's an e-mail from Alessandro Sacilotto: "I left Ohio when I was commissioned in the U.S. Navy and spent nearly all of my adulthood from 1972 to 2008 overseas, a 36-year period with only three short tours of duty back in the U.S. . . . During the playoff game against the Raiders in January 1981, I was visiting my Mom at home in northern Italy. I borrowed a short wave radio from a neighbor, managed to pull in the broadcast from an Armed Forces Network transponder atop a mountain overlooking Aviano Air Base, listened to the game all the way to the heartbreaking end, sharing the agony of 'Red Right 88' with all Browns fans everywhere. 'The Drive' was viewed in Heidelberg, Germany, in the annoying company of a football-ignorant Turkish friend who asked the dumbest questions at the tensest times."

He then compared following the 1980s Browns to, "the Greek classics from high school, particularly the myth of Sisyphus . . . fated to come ever so close only to see the prize roll away at the end."

So what is the bottom line of all this?

As Todd Alexander e-mailed: "I continue to watch this mess for two reasons—character and deferred gratification. I think it says something about who you are when you identify the team you root for. Character is what will take you far in life. It shows character to choose a favorite team, to stick with that team no matter what and not run off to a new team every time your team slides. Our union with the Browns is a marriage, for better or worse."

And in Browns Town, there are some temporary separations, but divorces just don't happen.

ACKNOWLEDGMENTS

A lot of people helped with this book, starting with the more than 1,000 fans who e-mailed with their thoughts and stories about the Browns. They made this project come alive, because they bring a perspective on the team that I never could as a career sportswriter. They spent the Sundays in the parking lots, in the Dawg Pound, in their favorite seats—not in the press box. They paid for tickets then froze in the wind and snow off Lake Erie, I did not. Their attachment to the team is deeper than any member of the media's, because just like Bernie Kosar—they chose the Browns.

After the fans, I was blessed with a tremendous researcher.

Geoff Beckman supplied amazing background material on everything from the early days of the Steelers, Municipal Stadium and Paul Brown, to going through play-by-play . . . and almost frame by frame . . . the key games in team history. His contribution was as powerful and productive as the best of Jim Brown's sweeps. Beckman has worked on my two books (written with Brian Windhorst) on LeBron James, along with *False Start,* about the Browns, and *Dealing,* about the Indians.

If there are any mistakes in the book, it's on me—not the researcher.

Publisher David Gray was a huge supporter of the project, which was very vague in the beginning but developed thanks to all the e-mails from fans. Rob Lucas dealt with all the details. I have been blessed for years to be backed by the rest of the team at Gray and Company: Jane Lassar, Chris Andrikanich, Jane Wipper and Frank Lavallo. Also, thanks to Butch Maier for his copyediting work.

The Plain Dealer also was a huge supporter of this and my

other books, so special thanks go to Terry Egger, Susan Goldberg, Debra Adams Simmons and Roy Hewitt.

Several former Browns were interviewed, often for newspaper stories that later turned into chapters for the book. Special thanks go to Bernie Kosar, Sam Rutigliano, Clay Matthews, Brian Sipe, Frank Minnifield, Eric Mangini, Paul Warfield and Earnest Byner.

SOURCES

GENERAL SOURCES

Three sets of annual publications were used to check different facts at different points: *The Sporting News Pro Football Guide, The NFL Record and Fact Book, Pro Football Weekly Football Almanac.*
Team media guides were of course valuable references.
It is impossible to list the number of different things that can be learned from reading the publications of the Pro Football Researchers Association. While not as well-known as the Society for American Baseball Research, their members do excellent work, in much tougher circumstances.

BOOKS

PB: The Paul Brown Story, by Paul Brown and Jack Clary.
Out of Bounds, by Jim Brown and Steve Delsohn.
Pressure, by Sam Rutigliano.
The Toe, by Lou Groza and Mark Hodermarsky.
Last Team Standing: How the Steelers and the Eagles—"The Steagles"—Saved Pro Football During World War II, by Matthew Algeo.
Paul Brown: The Man Who Invented Modern Football, by George Cantor.
Municipal Stadium: Memories on the Lakefront, A 50 year Pictorial History 1931 to 1981, edited by George Cormack.
Pittsburgh Steelers: The Complete Illustrated History, by Lew Freedman and Dick Hoak.
Cleveland Browns History, by Frank M. Henkel.
Opening Day: Cleveland, the Indians, and a New Beginning, by Jonathan Knight.
Return to Glory: the Story of the Cleveland Browns, by Bill Levy.
Glory for Sale: Inside the Browns' Move to Baltimore & the New NFL, by Jon Morgan.
NCAA Football Award Winners, by the National Collegiate Athletic Association (e-book).
Paul Brown: The Rise and Fall and Rise Again of Football's Most Innovative Coach, by Andrew O'Toole.
The Official Ohio State Football Encyclopedia, by Jack Park.
Dan Rooney: My 75 Years With the Pittsburgh Steelers and the NFL, by Dan Rooney, with Andrew E. Masich and David F. Halaas.
The New Thinking Man's Guide to Pro Football, by Paul Zimmerman.

KEY ARTICLES

The Coffin Corner, the newsletter of the Pro Football Researchers Association:
   Bonus Picks, by Donald Kosakowski (Volume 6, Issues 9 and 10).
   Bill Nelsen: The Quarterback as Commander, by Ed Grover (Volume 22, Issue 3).
   Milt Plum, by Jim Sargent (Volume 22, Issue 6).
   D.Card-Pitt: The Carpits, by James Forr (Volume 25, Issue 3).
Cleveland Municipal Stadium (from ballparks.com).
The Crowning Jewel to the Mistake on the Lake: The Story of the Construction of Cleveland Municipal Stadium, by Dryck Bennett (from ballparks.com).
Steelers Shared Resources With 2 Teams During World War II, by Joshua Robinson (from NYTimes.com).
Don Coryell Belongs in Hall of Fame (from voiceofsandiego.org).
Homer Jones, a Football Retrospective (from Giantsfans.net).
Homer Jones, a True Texan Legend (from juddspressbox.blogspot.com).

WEBSITES

Wikipedia.com: Geoff Beckman is a contributor to the site, so he knows its strengths and weaknesses very well. The information on the site is often not entirely correct—but a compromise between interest groups involved in the creation. So it was a starting point, but not even close to the final authority.

Google.com: It helps to find special-interest sites. Google News contains scans of many newspapers and is the source of most of the contemporary articles and news stories.

Amazon.com: If you're trying to find available books on a person or a topic, it's better than any card catalogue and much faster. The "Look inside" option and full-text search tells you to what extent the author deals with a topic.

Pro Football Reference.com: A good place for the statistics, draft listings, Pro Bowls, All-Pros and Hall of Fame awards and (to a limited degree) the position information.

Cleveland.com: It has a page that lets you look up the game story for every single game played (except for those games played during the newspaper strike). Very helpful for detail.

Youtube.com: Great place to find the original broadcasts of games, as well as NFL Films and ESPN specials.

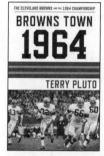

ALSO BY **TERRY PLUTO**...

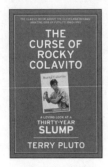

The Curse of Rocky Colavito
A Loving Look at a Thirty-Year Slump

Terry Pluto

A baseball classic. No sports fans suffered more miserable teams for more seasons than Indians fans of the 1960s, '70s, and '80s. Here's a fond and often humorous look back at "the bad old days" of the Tribe. The definitive book about the Indians of that generation, and a great piece of sports history writing.

"The year's funniest and most insightful baseball book." – Chicago Tribune

Our Tribe
A Baseball Memoir

Terry Pluto

A son, a father, a baseball team. Sportswriter Terry Pluto's memoir tells about growing up and learning to understand a difficult father through their shared love of an often awful baseball team. Baseball can be an important bridge across generations, sometimes the only common ground. This story celebrates the connection.

"A beautiful, absolutely unforgettable memoir." – Booklist

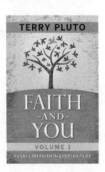

Faith and You Vol. 1
Essays on Faith in Everyday Life

Terry Pluto

Thoughtful essays on faith in everyday life from award-winning sportswriter Terry Pluto, who has also earned a reputation—and a growing audience—for his down-to-earth musings on spiritual subjects. Topics include choosing a church, lending money to friends, dealing with jerks, sharing your faith, visiting the sick, even planning a funeral.

To find out about Terry Pluto's latest book, visit:
www.TerryPluto.com

Read samples at **www.grayco.com**